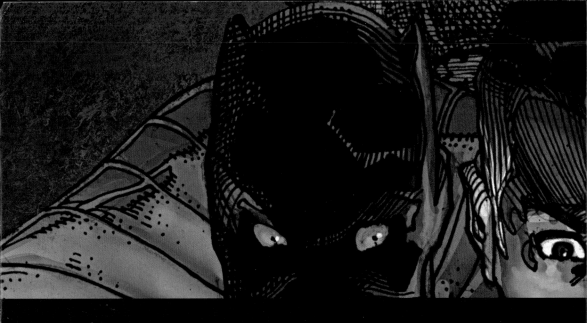

COLLECTION EDITOR: **JENNIFER GRÜNWALD**
ASSISTANT EDITOR: **SARAH BRUNSTAD**
ASSOCIATE MANAGING EDITOR: **ALEX STARBUCK**
EDITOR, SPECIAL PROJECTS: **MARK D. BEAZLEY**
SENIOR EDITOR, SPECIAL PROJECTS: **JEFF YOUNGQUIST**
SVP PRINT, SALES & MARKETING: **DAVID GABRIEL**
BOOK DESIGN: **JEFF POWELL**

EDITOR IN CHIEF: **AXEL ALONSO**
CHIEF CREATIVE OFFICER: **JOE QUESADA**
PUBLISHER: **DAN BUCKLEY**
EXECUTIVE PRODUCER: **ALAN FINE**

NEW AVENGERS VOL. 3: OTHER WORLDS. Contains material originally published in magazine form as NEW AVENGERS #13-17. First printing 2015. ISBN# 978-0-7851-8959-6. Published by MARVEL WORLDWIDE,
a subsidiary of MARVEL ENTERTAINMENT, LLC. OFFICE OF PUBLICATION: 135 West 50th Street, New York, NY 10020. Copyright © 2013, 2014 and 2015 Marvel Characters, Inc. All rights reserved. All characters fea
in this issue and the distinctive names and likenesses thereof, and all related indicia are trademarks of Marvel Characters, Inc. No similarity between any of the names, characters, persons, and/or institutions i
magazine with those of any living or dead person or institution is intended, and any such similarity which may exist is purely coincidental. **Printed in the U.S.A.** ALAN FINE, EVP - Office of the President, Marvel Worl
Inc. and EVP & CMO Marvel Characters B.V.; DAN BUCKLEY, Publisher & President - Print, Animation & Digital Divisions; JOE QUESADA, Chief Creative Officer; TOM BREVOORT, SVP of Publishing; DAVID BOGART, S
Operations & Procurement, Publishing; C.B. CEBULSKI, SVP of Creator & Content Development; DAVID GABRIEL, SVP Print, Sales & Marketing; JIM O'KEEFE, VP of Operations & Logistics; DAN CARR, Executive Di
of Publishing Technology; SUSAN CRESPI, Editorial Operations Manager; ALEX MORALES, Publishing Operations Manager; STAN LEE, Chairman Emeritus. For information regarding advertising in Marvel Comics
Marvel.com, please contact Niza Disla, Director of Marvel Partnerships, at ndisla@marvel.com. For Marvel subscription inquiries, please call 800-217-9158. **Manufactured between 1/2/2015 and 2/9/2015 b**
DONNELLEY, INC., SALEM, VA, USA.

10 9 8 7 6 5 4 3 2 1

WRITER: **JONATHAN HICKMAN**

ISSUES #13-15

ARTIST: **SIMONE BIANCHI**

INK & INKWASH: SIMONE BIANCHI & RICCARDO PIERUCCINI

COLOR ARTIST: ADRIANO DALL'ALPI

COVER ART: SIMONE BIANCHI

ISSUES #16-17

ARTIST: **RAGS MORALES**

COLOR ARTIST: FRANK MARTIN

COVER ART: MIKE DEODATO & FRANK MARTIN (#16) AND
LEINIL FRANCIS YU & DAVID CURIEL (#17)

LETTERER: VC'S JOE CARAMAGNA

ASSISTANT EDITOR: JAKE THOMAS

EDITORS: TOM BREVOORT with LAUREN SANKOVITCH & WIL MOSS

AVENGERS CREATED BY STAN LEE & JACK KIRBY

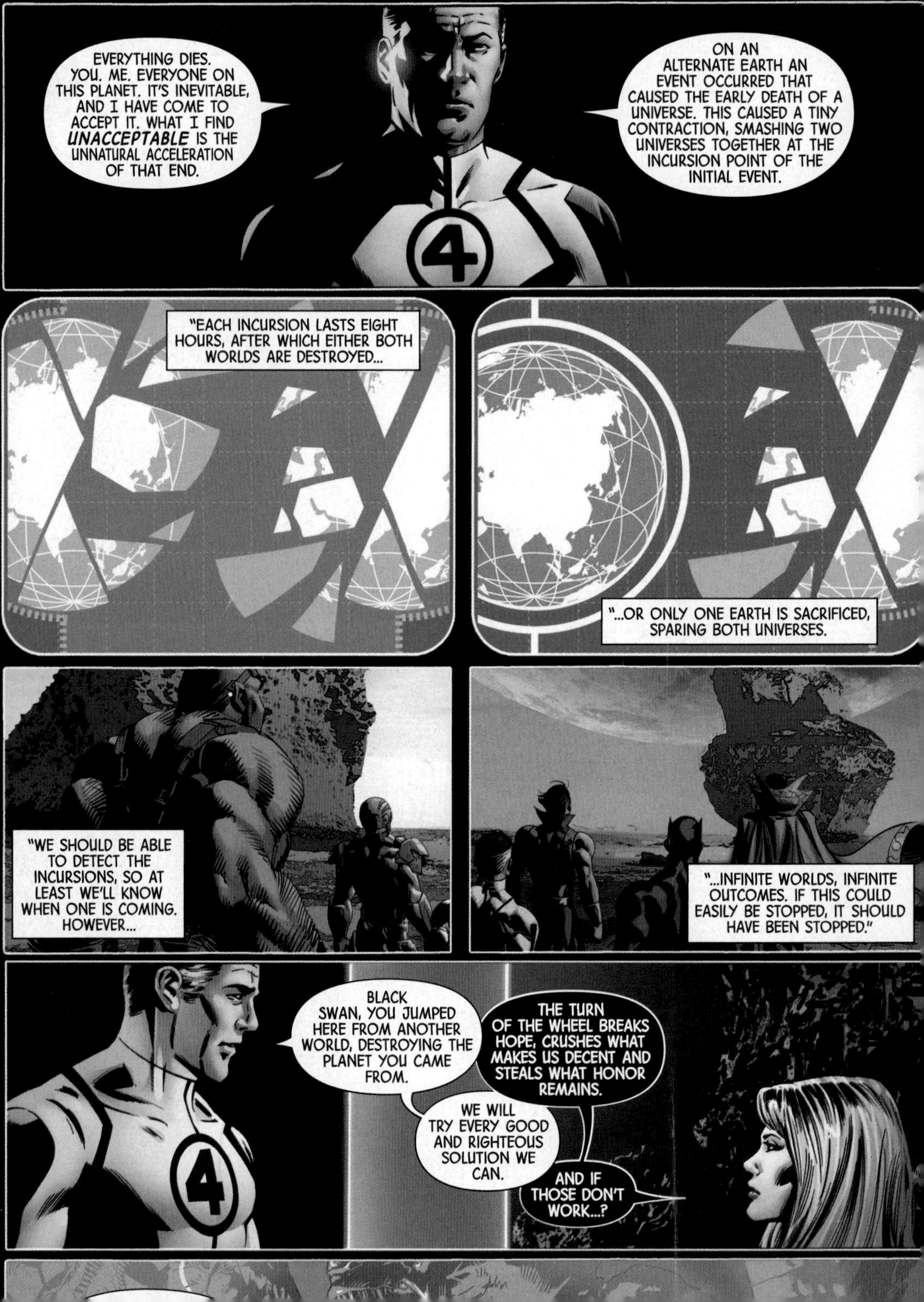
EVERYTHING DIES. YOU. ME. EVERYONE ON THIS PLANET. IT'S INEVITABLE, AND I HAVE COME TO ACCEPT IT. WHAT I FIND UNACCEPTABLE IS THE UNNATURAL ACCELERATION OF THAT END.
ON AN ALTERNATE EARTH AN EVENT OCCURRED THAT CAUSED THE EARLY DEATH OF A UNIVERSE. THIS CAUSED A TINY CONTRACTION, SMASHING TWO UNIVERSES TOGETHER AT THE INCURSION POINT OF THE INITIAL EVENT.
"EACH INCURSION LASTS EIGHT HOURS, AFTER WHICH EITHER BOTH WORLDS ARE DESTROYED...
"...OR ONLY ONE EARTH IS SACRIFICED, SPARING BOTH UNIVERSES.
"WE SHOULD BE ABLE TO DETECT THE INCURSIONS, SO AT LEAST WE'LL KNOW WHEN ONE IS COMING. HOWEVER...
"...INFINITE WORLDS, INFINITE OUTCOMES. IF THIS COULD EASILY BE STOPPED, IT SHOULD HAVE BEEN STOPPED."
BLACK SWAN, YOU JUMPED HERE FROM ANOTHER WORLD, DESTROYING THE PLANET YOU CAME FROM.
THE TURN OF THE WHEEL BREAKS HOPE, CRUSHES WHAT MAKES US DECENT AND STEALS WHAT HONOR REMAINS.
WE WILL TRY EVERY GOOD AND RIGHTEOUS SOLUTION WE CAN.
AND IF THOSE DON'T WORK...?

THE ILLUMINATI

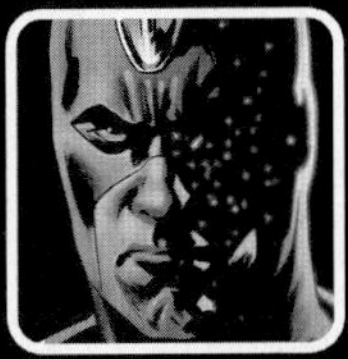

BLACK BOLT
Celestial Messiah

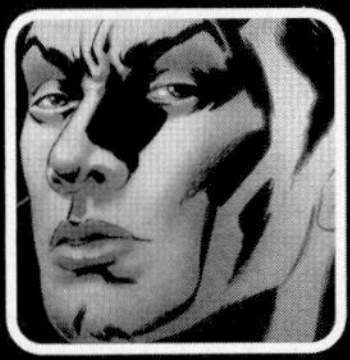

NAMOR
Imperius Rex

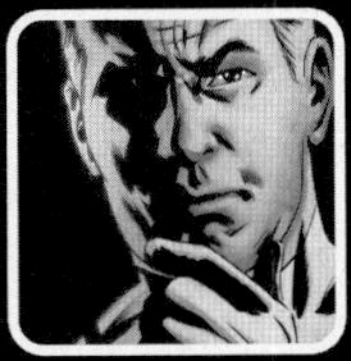

REED RICHARDS
Universal Builder

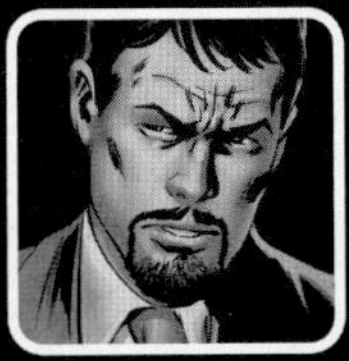

IRON MAN
Master of Machines

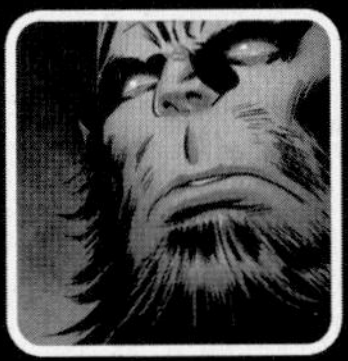

BEAST
Hero of Legend

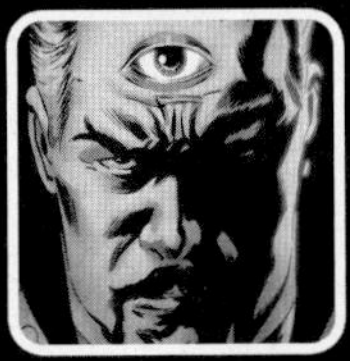

DOCTOR STRANGE
Sorcerer Supreme

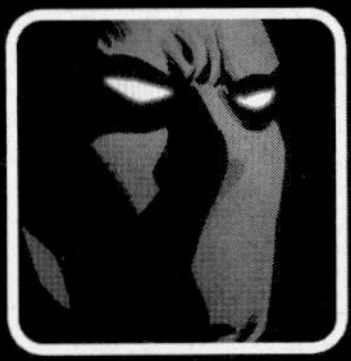

BLACK PANTHER
King of the Dead

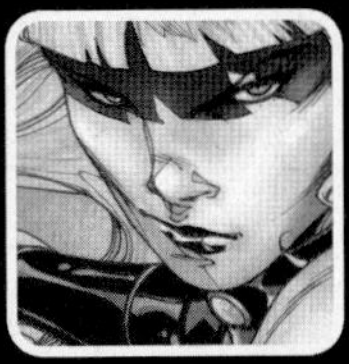

BLACK SWAN
Incursion Survivor

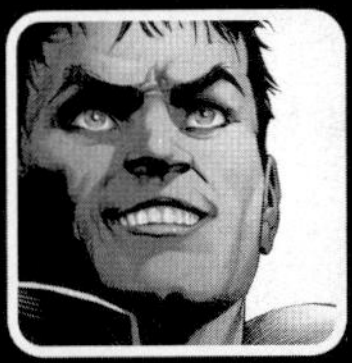

MAXIMUS
Inhuman Madman

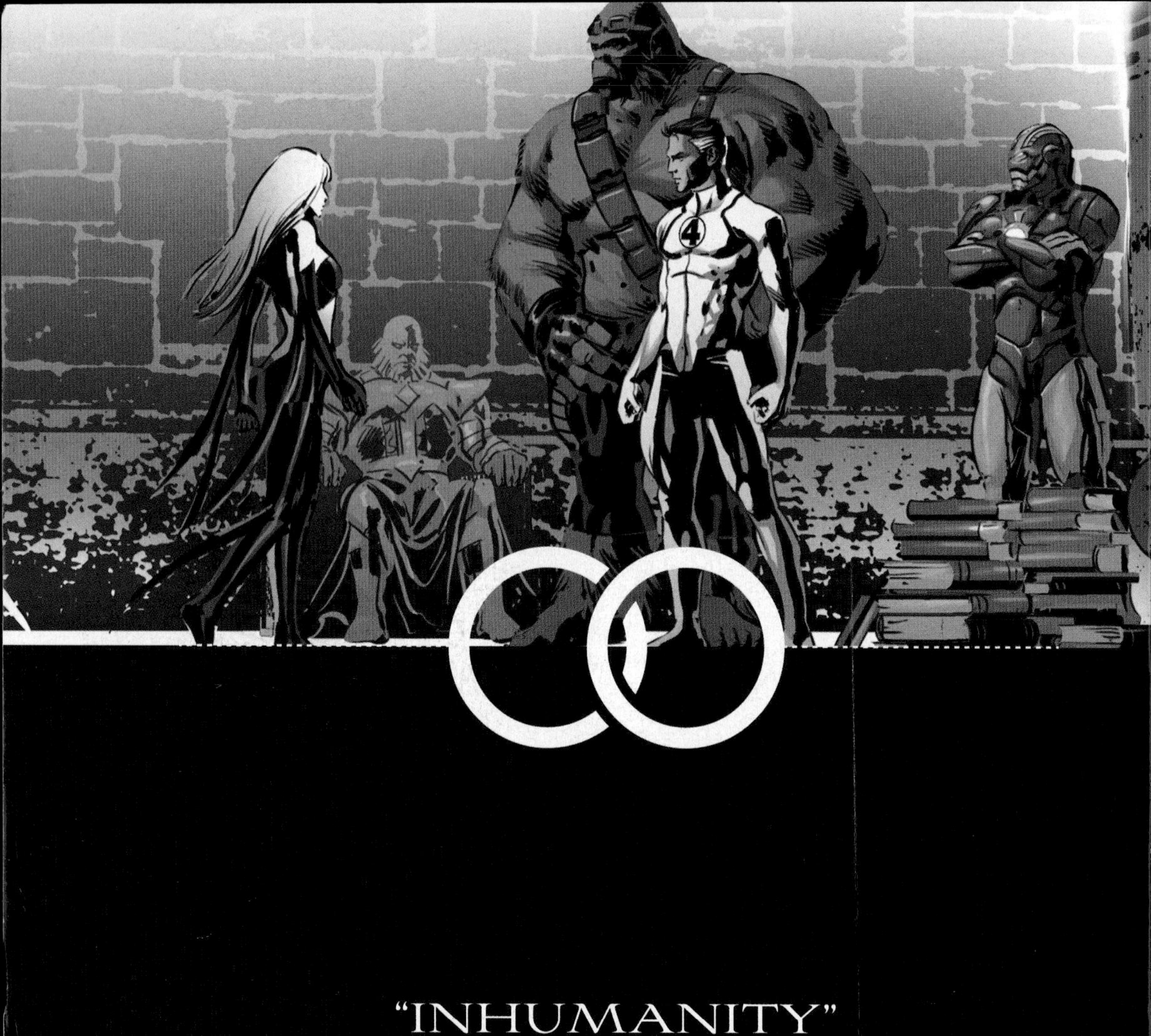

"INHUMANITY"

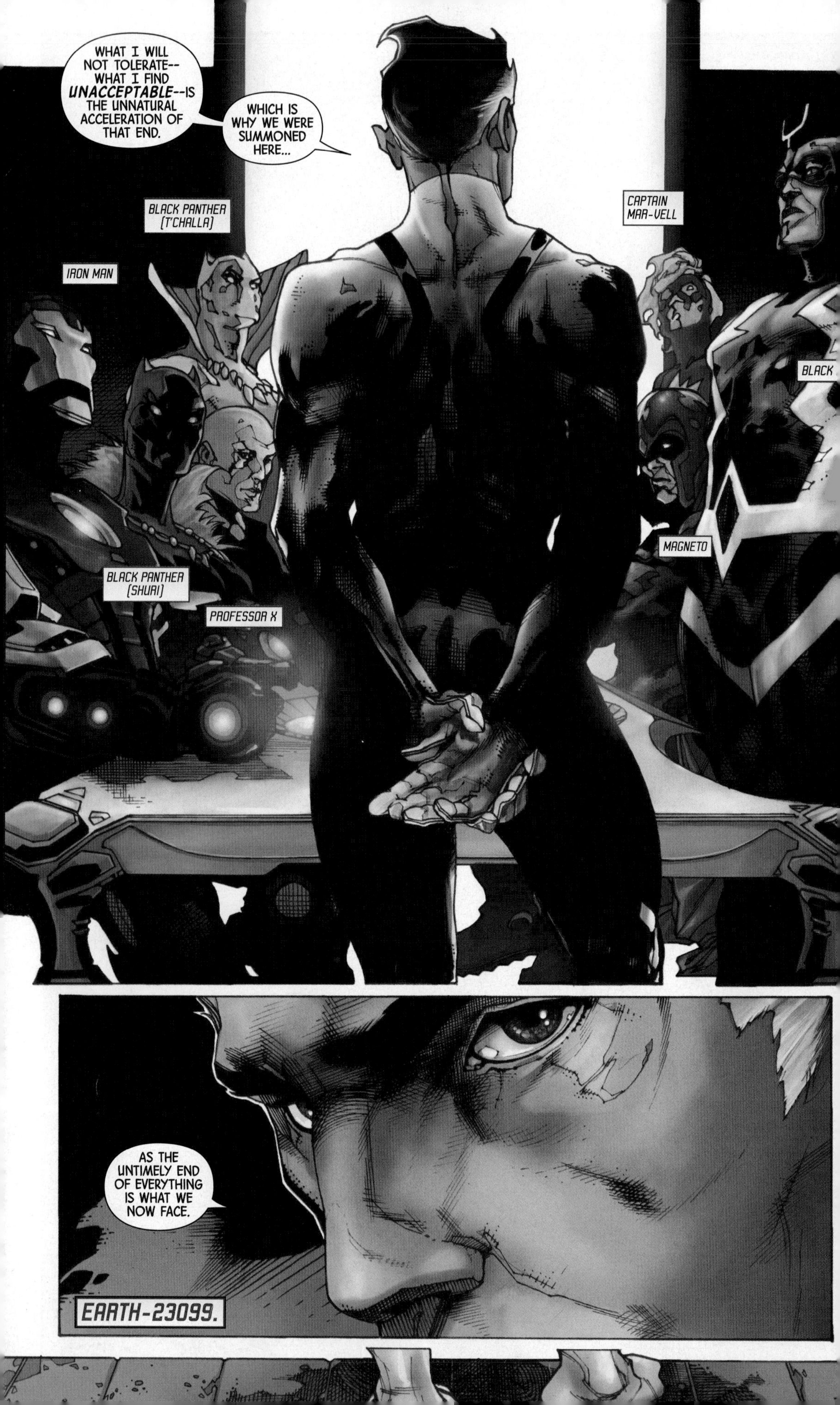
WHAT I WILL NOT TOLERATE-- WHAT I FIND UNACCEPTABLE--IS THE UNNATURAL ACCELERATION OF THAT END.
WHICH IS WHY WE WERE SUMMONED HERE...
BLACK PANTHER (T'CHALLA)
CAPTAIN MAR-VELL
IRON MAN
BLACK
MAGNETO
BLACK PANTHER (SHURI)
PROFESSOR X
AS THE UNTIMELY END OF EVERYTHING IS WHAT WE NOW FACE.
EARTH-23099.

THE WORLD CHANGED OVERNIGHT AS THE GREAT MACHINE CAUSED CASCADING GLOBAL TERRIGENESIS.

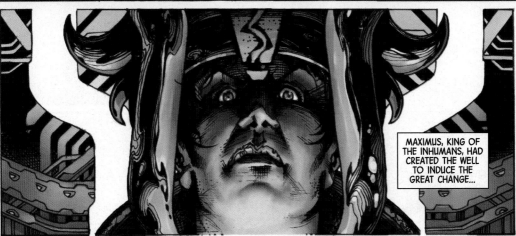

MAXIMUS, KING OF THE INHUMANS, HAD CREATED THE WELL TO INDUCE THE GREAT CHANGE...

AND TO USHER IN A NEW DAY FOR HIS EXPANDING KINGDOM.

THE ROYAL FAMILY WATCHED AS ALL THE UNCHANGED-- THE LOST TRIBES AND THE HIDDEN ONES--BEGAN TO METAMORPHOSE AS THE MIST--THE TRANSFORMATIVE FALLOUT--SPREAD ACROSS THE GLOBE.

IT SHOULD HAVE BEEN THE START OF A NEW INHUMAN AGE.

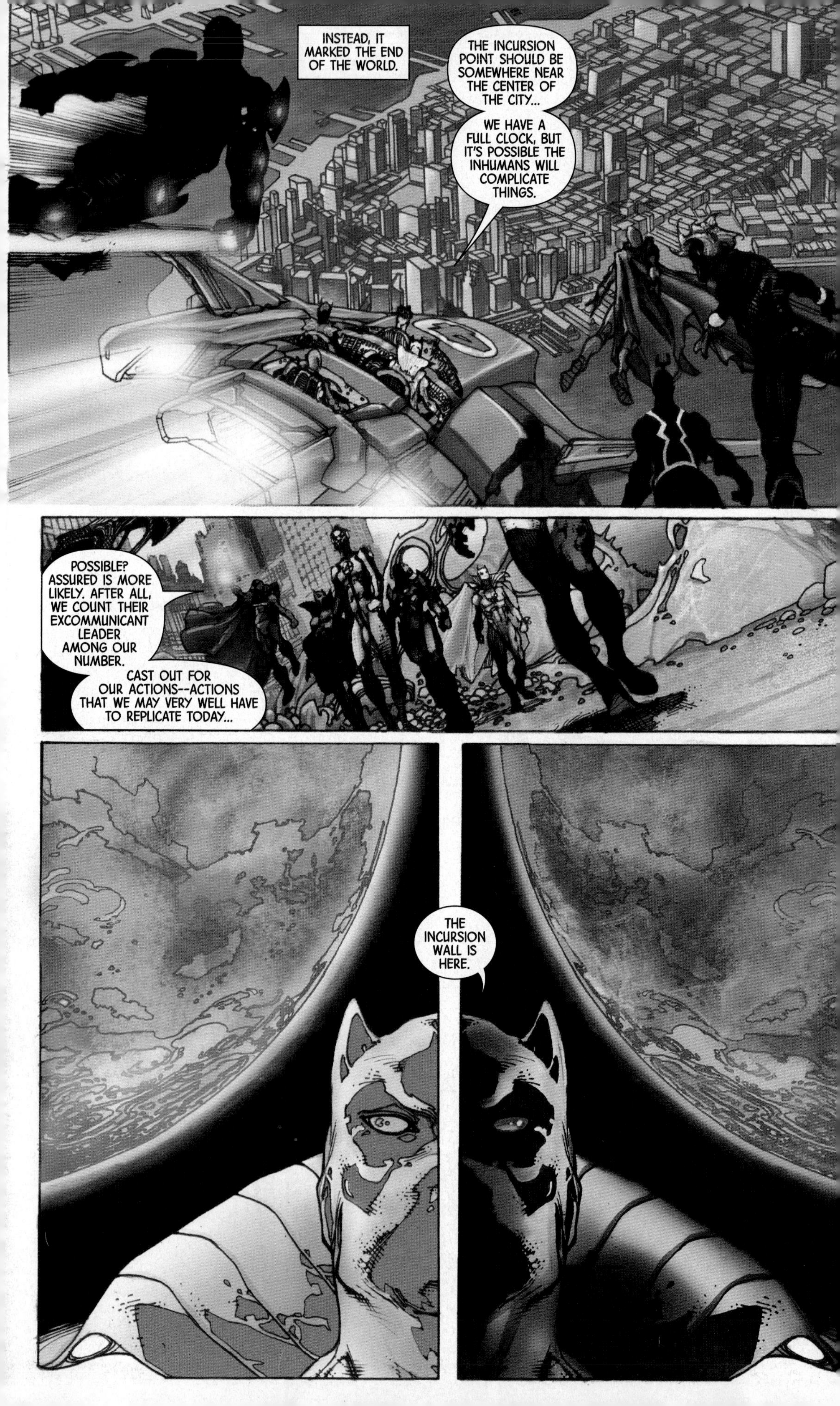
INSTEAD, IT MARKED THE END OF THE WORLD.
THE INCURSION POINT SHOULD BE SOMEWHERE NEAR THE CENTER OF THE CITY...
WE HAVE A FULL CLOCK, BUT IT'S POSSIBLE THE INHUMANS WILL COMPLICATE THINGS.
POSSIBLE? ASSURED IS MORE LIKELY. AFTER ALL, WE COUNT THEIR EXCOMMUNICANT LEADER AMONG OUR NUMBER.
CAST OUT FOR OUR ACTIONS--ACTIONS THAT WE MAY VERY WELL HAVE TO REPLICATE TODAY...
THE INCURSION WALL IS HERE.

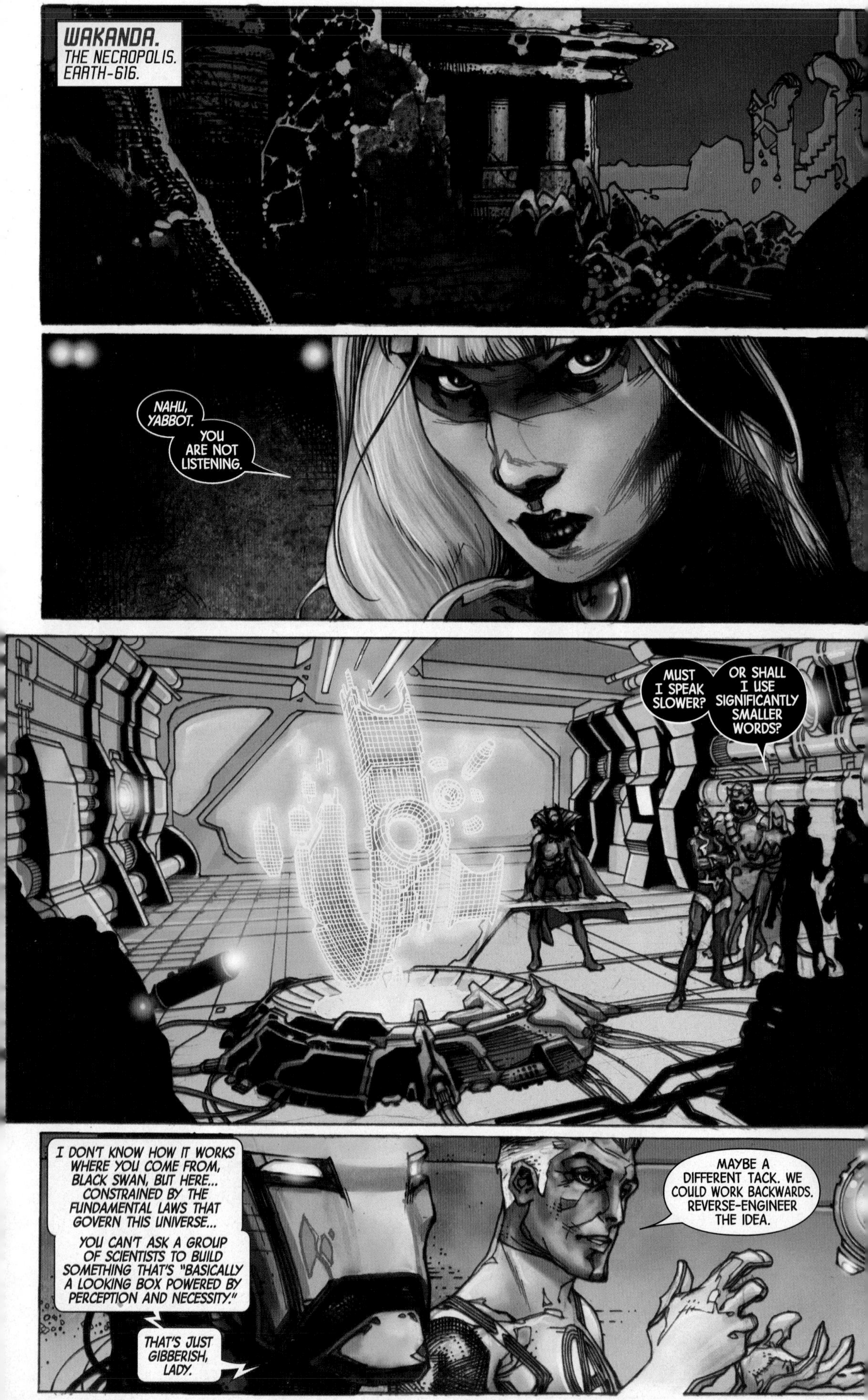
WAKANDA.
THE NECROPOLIS.
EARTH-616.
NAHU, YABBOT.
YOU ARE NOT LISTENING.
MUST I SPEAK SLOWER?
OR SHALL I USE SIGNIFICANTLY SMALLER WORDS?
I DON'T KNOW HOW IT WORKS WHERE YOU COME FROM, BLACK SWAN, BUT HERE... CONSTRAINED BY THE FUNDAMENTAL LAWS THAT GOVERN THIS UNIVERSE...
YOU CAN'T ASK A GROUP OF SCIENTISTS TO BUILD SOMETHING THAT'S "BASICALLY A LOOKING BOX POWERED BY PERCEPTION AND NECESSITY."
THAT'S JUST GIBBERISH, LADY.
MAYBE A DIFFERENT TACK. WE COULD WORK BACKWARDS. REVERSE-ENGINEER THE IDEA.

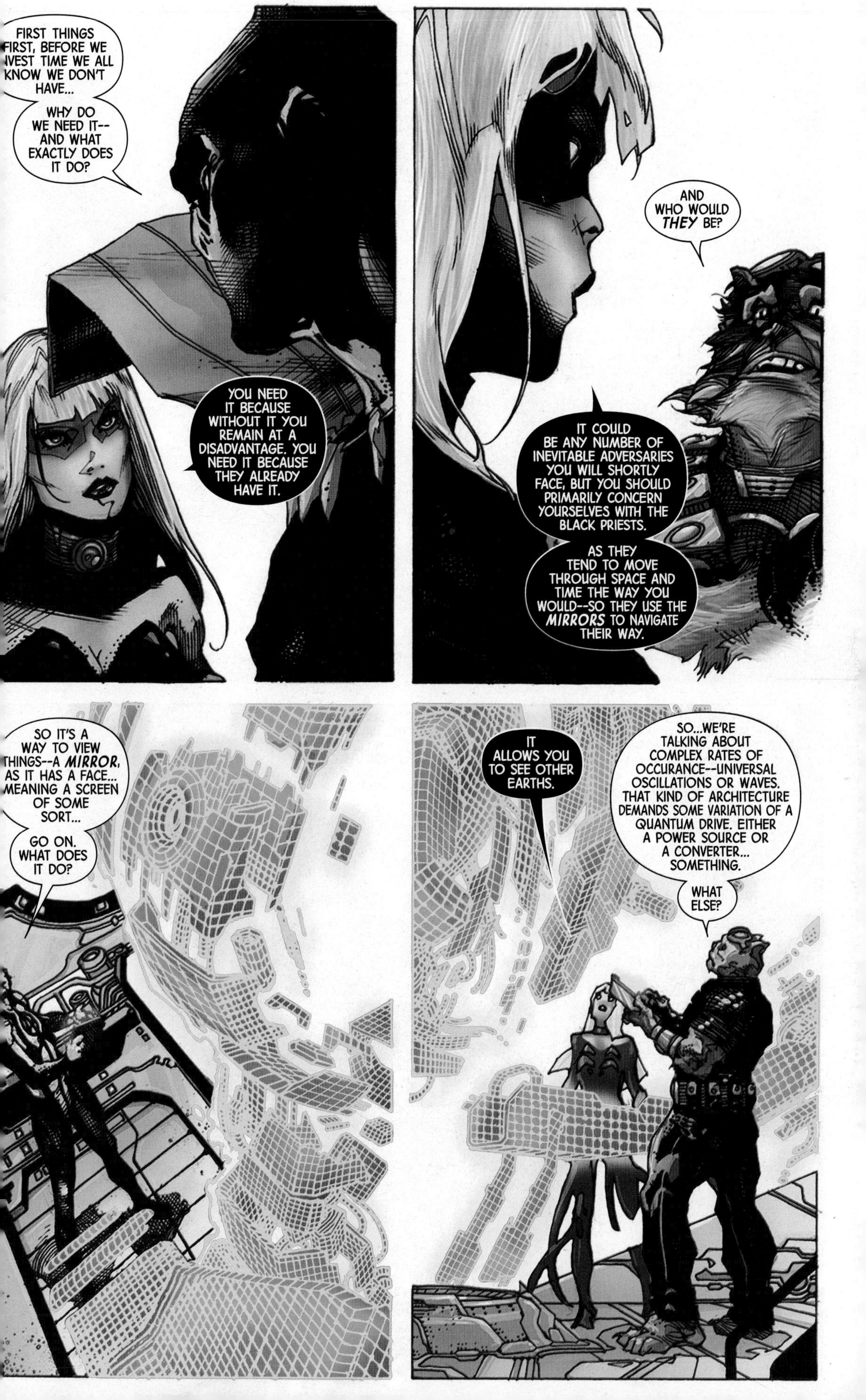
FIRST THINGS FIRST, BEFORE WE NVEST TIME WE ALL KNOW WE DON'T HAVE...
WHY DO WE NEED IT-- AND WHAT EXACTLY DOES IT DO?
YOU NEED IT BECAUSE WITHOUT IT YOU REMAIN AT A DISADVANTAGE. YOU NEED IT BECAUSE THEY ALREADY HAVE IT.
AND WHO WOULD *THEY* BE?
IT COULD BE ANY NUMBER OF INEVITABLE ADVERSARIES YOU WILL SHORTLY FACE, BUT YOU SHOULD PRIMARILY CONCERN YOURSELVES WITH THE BLACK PRIESTS.
AS THEY TEND TO MOVE THROUGH SPACE AND TIME THE WAY YOU WOULD--SO THEY USE THE *MIRRORS* TO NAVIGATE THEIR WAY.
SO IT'S A WAY TO VIEW HINGS--A *MIRROR*, AS IT HAS A FACE... EANING A SCREEN OF SOME SORT...
GO ON. WHAT DOES IT DO?
IT ALLOWS YOU TO SEE OTHER EARTHS.
SO...WE'RE TALKING ABOUT COMPLEX RATES OF OCCURANCE--UNIVERSAL OSCILLATIONS OR WAVES. THAT KIND OF ARCHITECTURE DEMANDS SOME VARIATION OF A QUANTUM DRIVE. EITHER A POWER SOURCE OR A CONVERTER... SOMETHING.
WHAT ELSE?

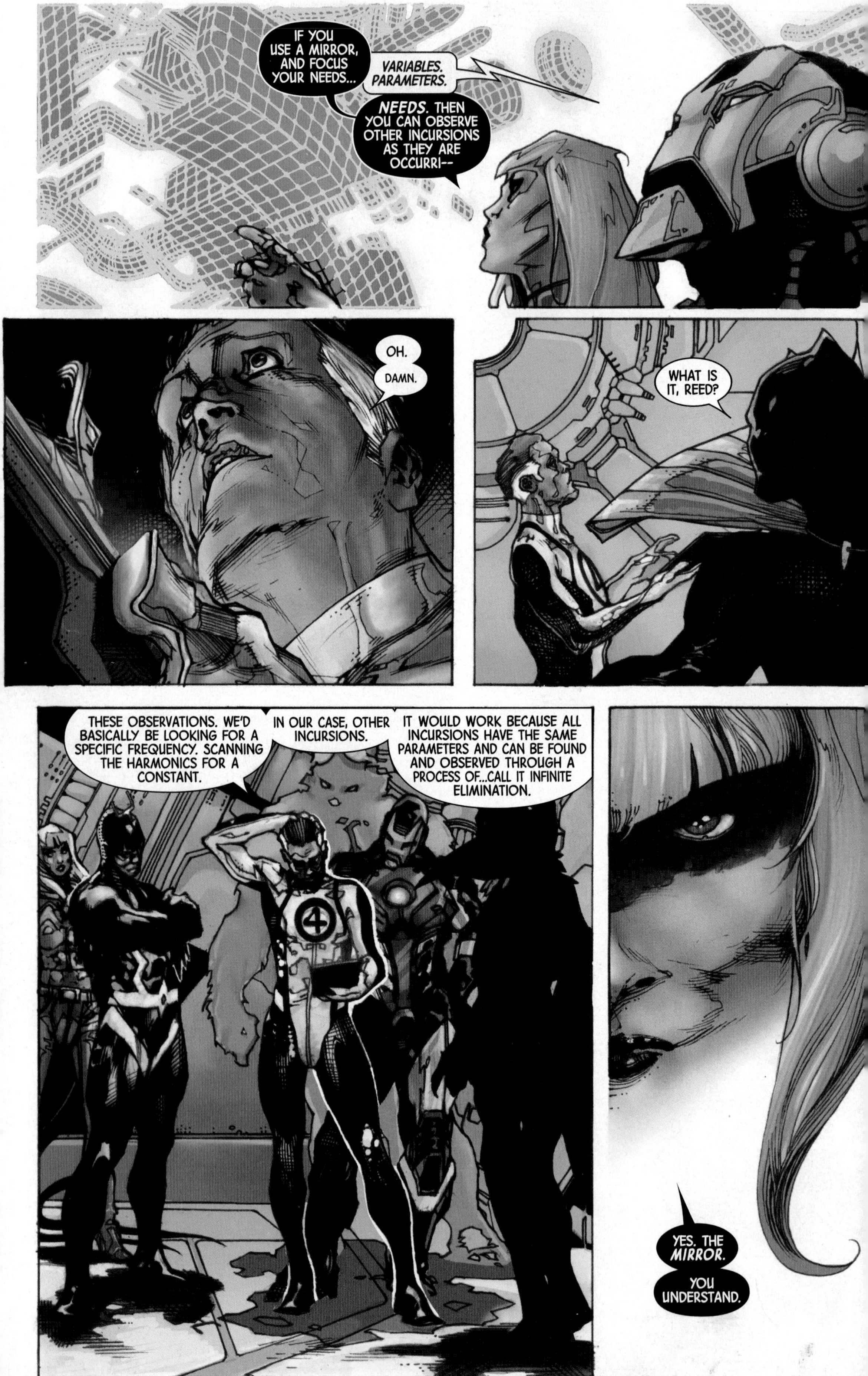
IF YOU USE A MIRROR, AND FOCUS YOUR NEEDS...
VARIABLES. PARAMETERS.
NEEDS. THEN YOU CAN OBSERVE OTHER INCURSIONS AS THEY ARE OCCURRI--
OH.
DAMN.
WHAT IS IT, REED?
THESE OBSERVATIONS. WE'D BASICALLY BE LOOKING FOR A SPECIFIC FREQUENCY. SCANNING THE HARMONICS FOR A CONSTANT.
IN OUR CASE, OTHER INCURSIONS.
IT WOULD WORK BECAUSE ALL INCURSIONS HAVE THE SAME PARAMETERS AND CAN BE FOUND AND OBSERVED THROUGH A PROCESS OF...CALL IT INFINITE ELIMINATION.
YES. THE MIRROR.
YOU UNDERSTAND.

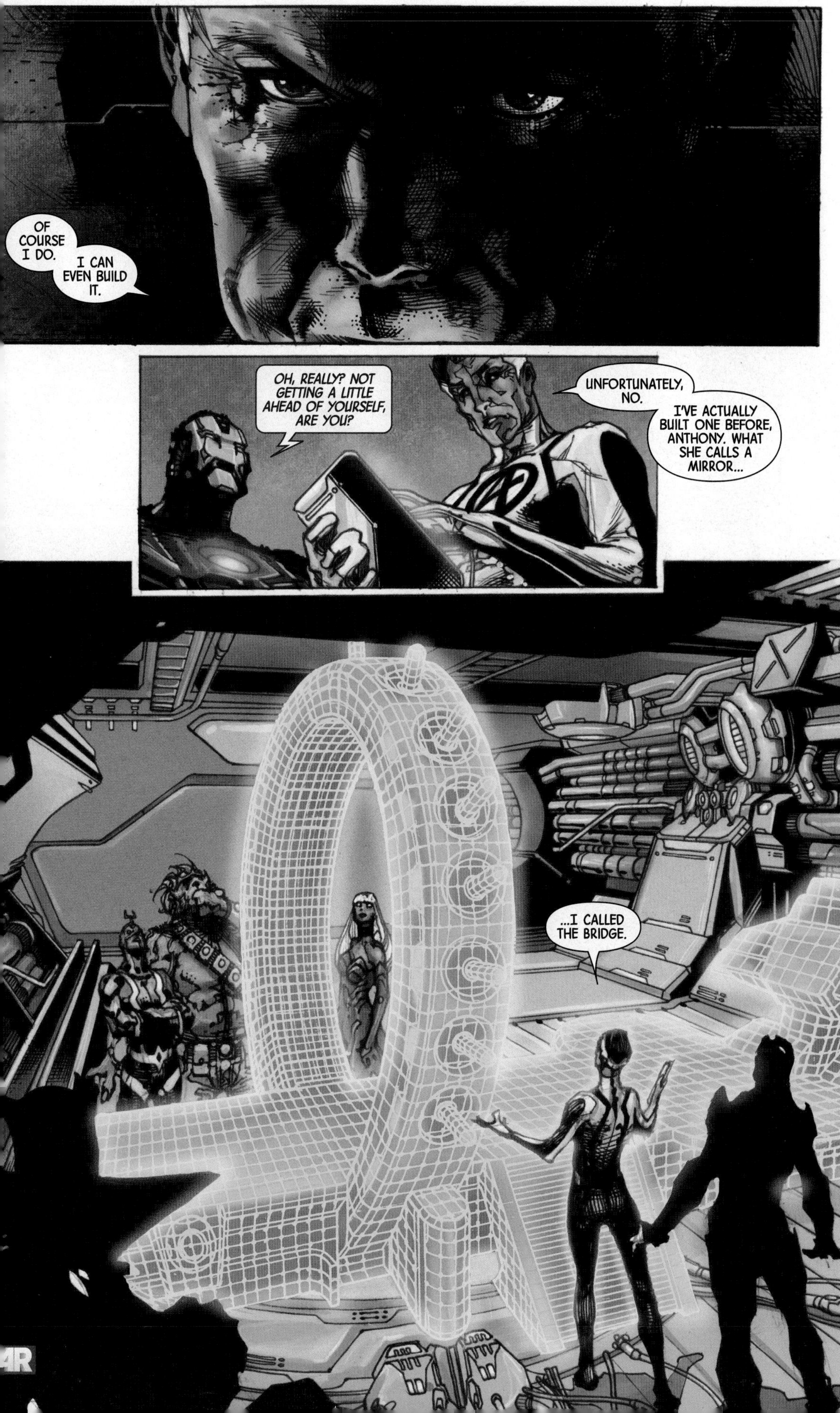
OF COURSE I DO.
I CAN EVEN BUILD IT.
OH, REALLY? NOT GETTING A LITTLE AHEAD OF YOURSELF, ARE YOU?
UNFORTUNATELY, NO.
I'VE ACTUALLY BUILT ONE BEFORE, ANTHONY. WHAT SHE CALLS A MIRROR...
...I CALLED THE BRIDGE.

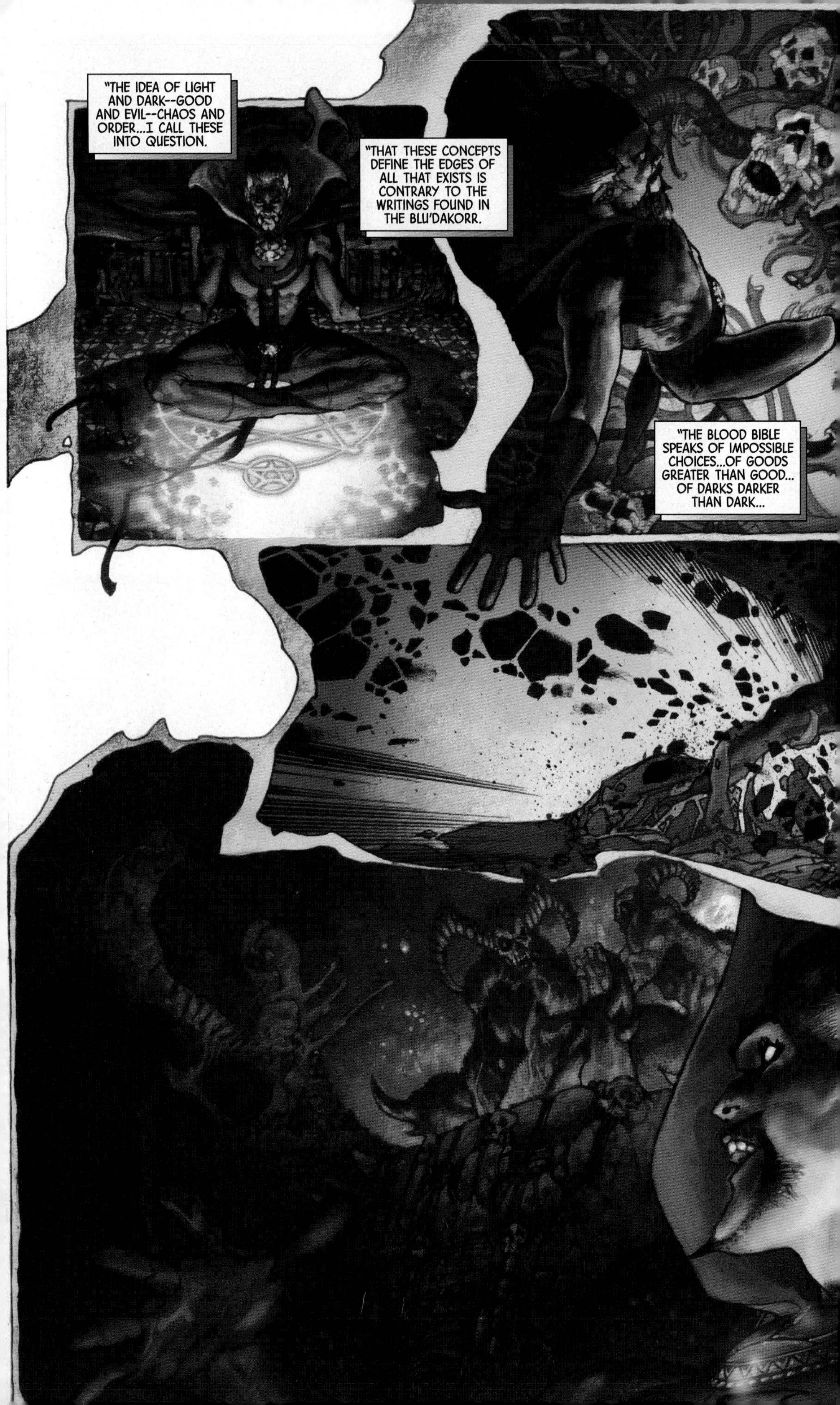
"THE IDEA OF LIGHT AND DARK--GOOD AND EVIL--CHAOS AND ORDER...I CALL THESE INTO QUESTION.
"THAT THESE CONCEPTS DEFINE THE EDGES OF ALL THAT EXISTS IS CONTRARY TO THE WRITINGS FOUND IN THE BLU'DAKORR.
"THE BLOOD BIBLE SPEAKS OF IMPOSSIBLE CHOICES...OF GOODS GREATER THAN GOOD... OF DARKS DARKER THAN DARK...

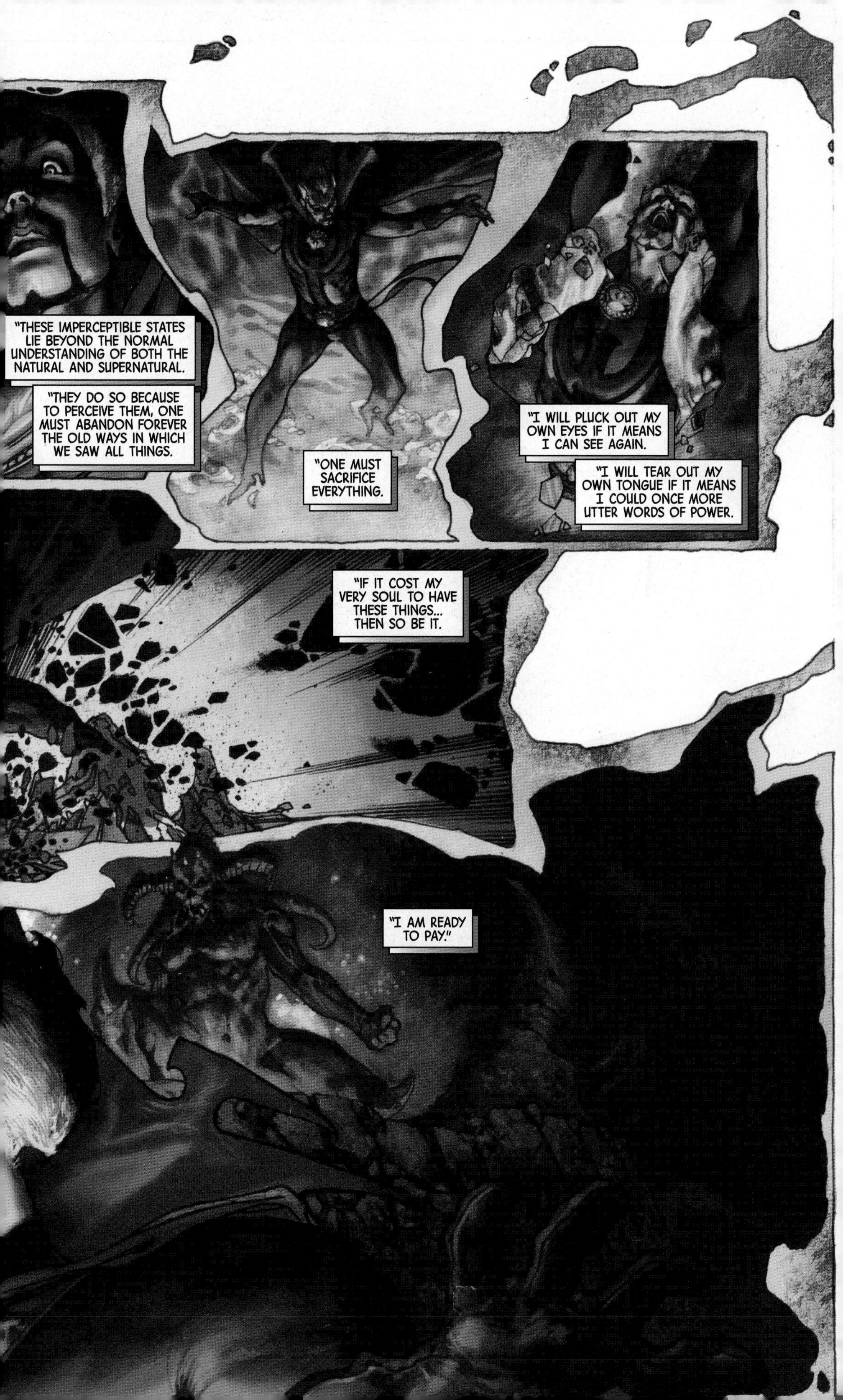
"THESE IMPERCEPTIBLE STATES LIE BEYOND THE NORMAL UNDERSTANDING OF BOTH THE NATURAL AND SUPERNATURAL.
"THEY DO SO BECAUSE TO PERCEIVE THEM, ONE MUST ABANDON FOREVER THE OLD WAYS IN WHICH WE SAW ALL THINGS.
"ONE MUST SACRIFICE EVERYTHING.
"I WILL PLUCK OUT MY OWN EYES IF IT MEANS I CAN SEE AGAIN.
"I WILL TEAR OUT MY OWN TONGUE IF IT MEANS I COULD ONCE MORE UTTER WORDS OF POWER.
"IF IT COST MY VERY SOUL TO HAVE THESE THINGS... THEN SO BE IT.
"I AM READY TO PAY."

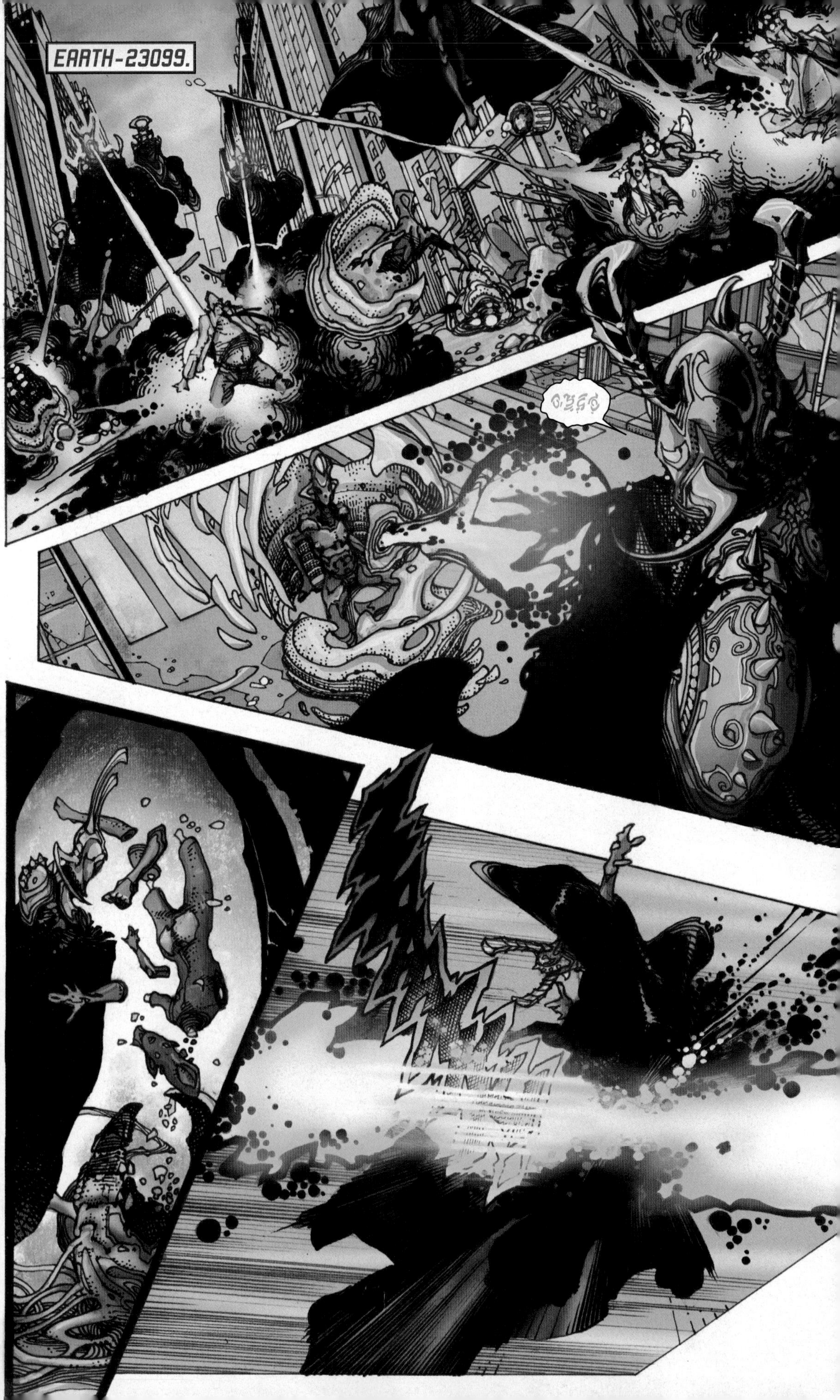
EARTH-23099.

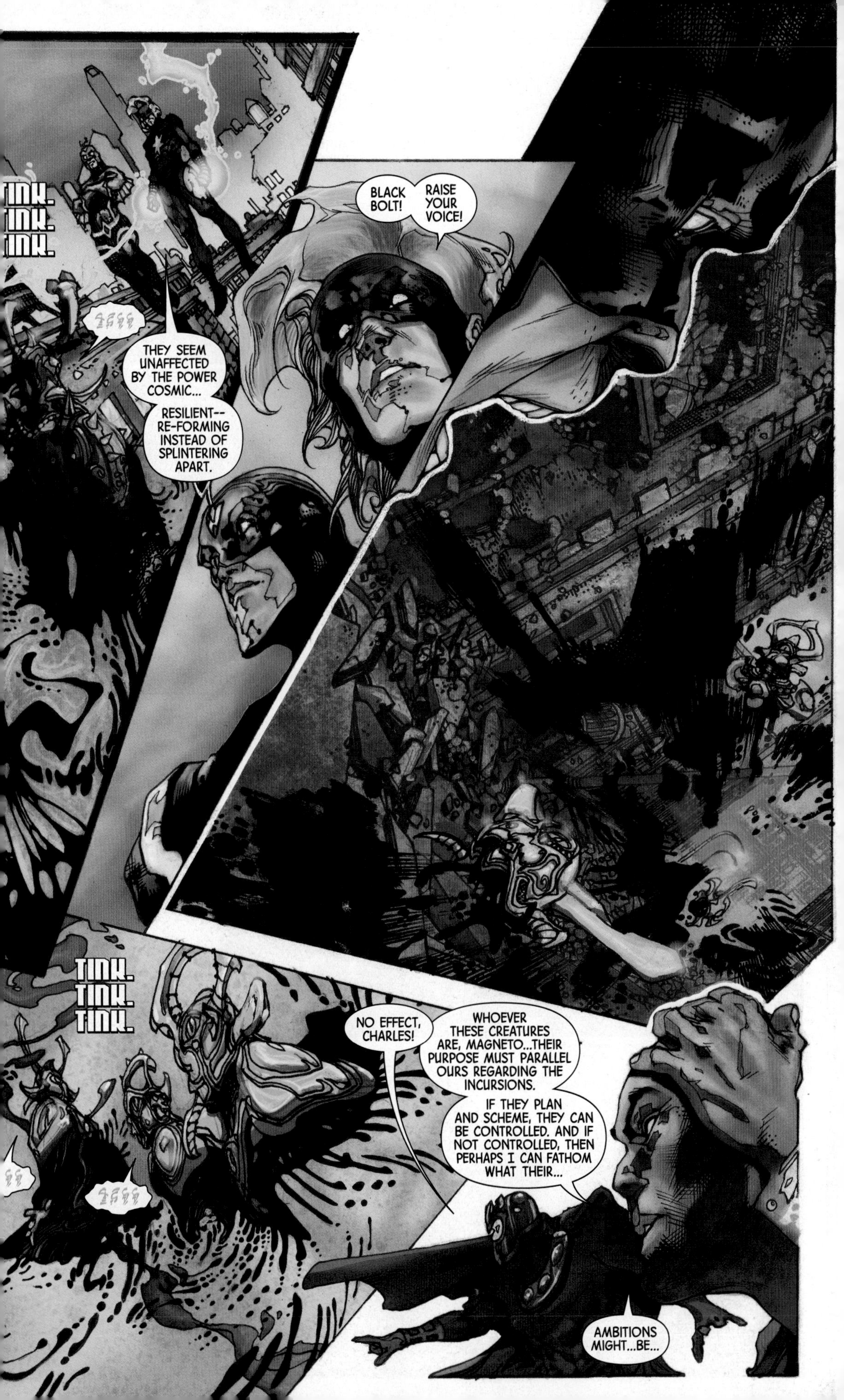
TINK.
TINK.
TINK.
BLACK BOLT!
RAISE YOUR VOICE!
THEY SEEM UNAFFECTED BY THE POWER COSMIC...
RESILIENT-- RE-FORMING INSTEAD OF SPLINTERING APART.
TINK.
TINK.
TINK.
NO EFFECT, CHARLES!
WHOEVER THESE CREATURES ARE, MAGNETO...THEIR PURPOSE MUST PARALLEL OURS REGARDING THE INCURSIONS.
IF THEY PLAN AND SCHEME, THEY CAN BE CONTROLLED. AND IF NOT CONTROLLED, THEN PERHAPS I CAN FATHOM WHAT THEIR...
AMBITIONS MIGHT...BE...

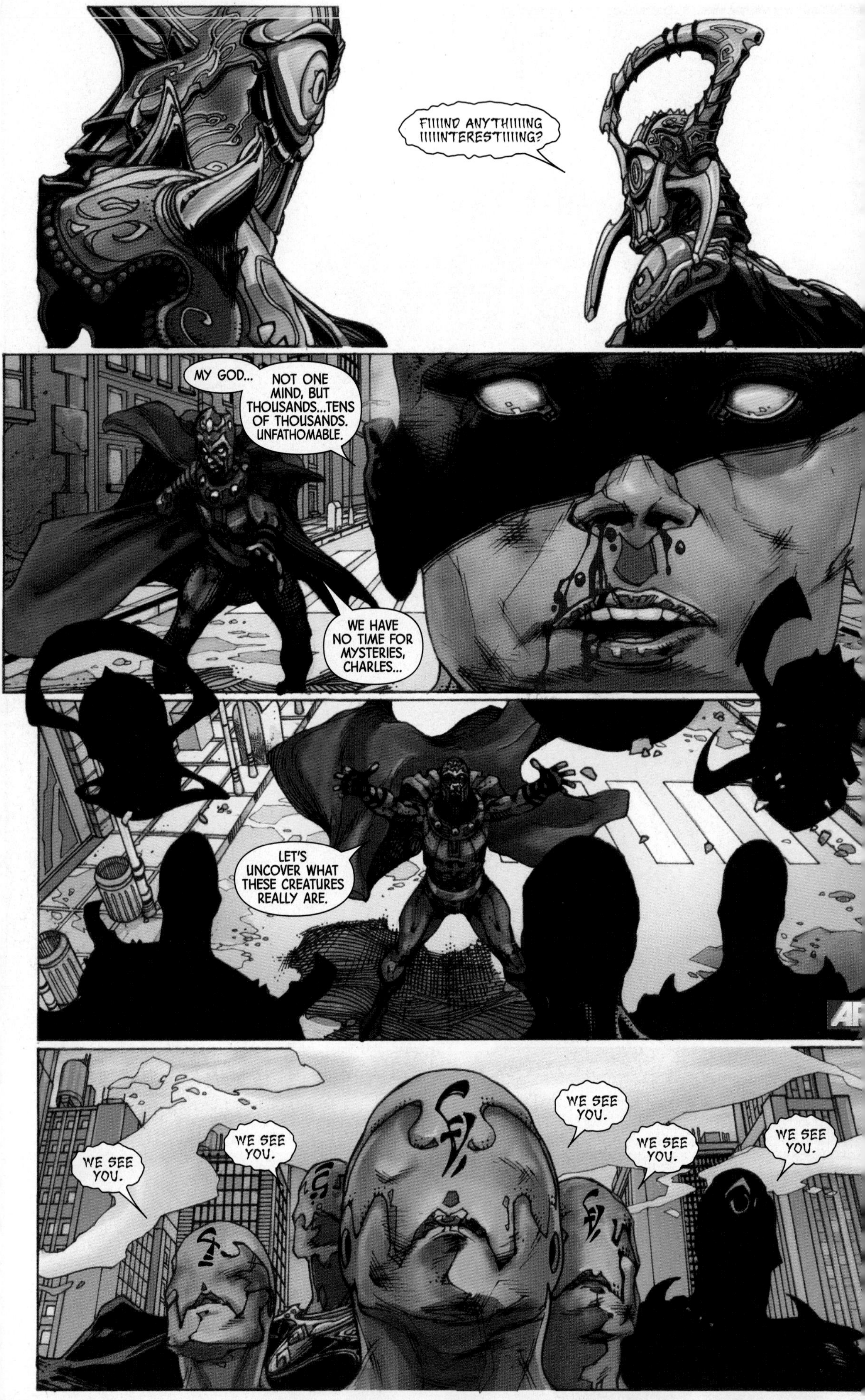
FIIIIND ANYTHIIIING IIIIINTERESTIIIING?
MY GOD...
NOT ONE MIND, BUT THOUSANDS...TENS OF THOUSANDS. UNFATHOMABLE.
WE HAVE NO TIME FOR MYSTERIES, CHARLES...
LET'S UNCOVER WHAT THESE CREATURES REALLY ARE.
WE SEE YOU.
WE SEE YOU.
WE SEE YOU.
WE SEE YOU.
WE SEE YOU.

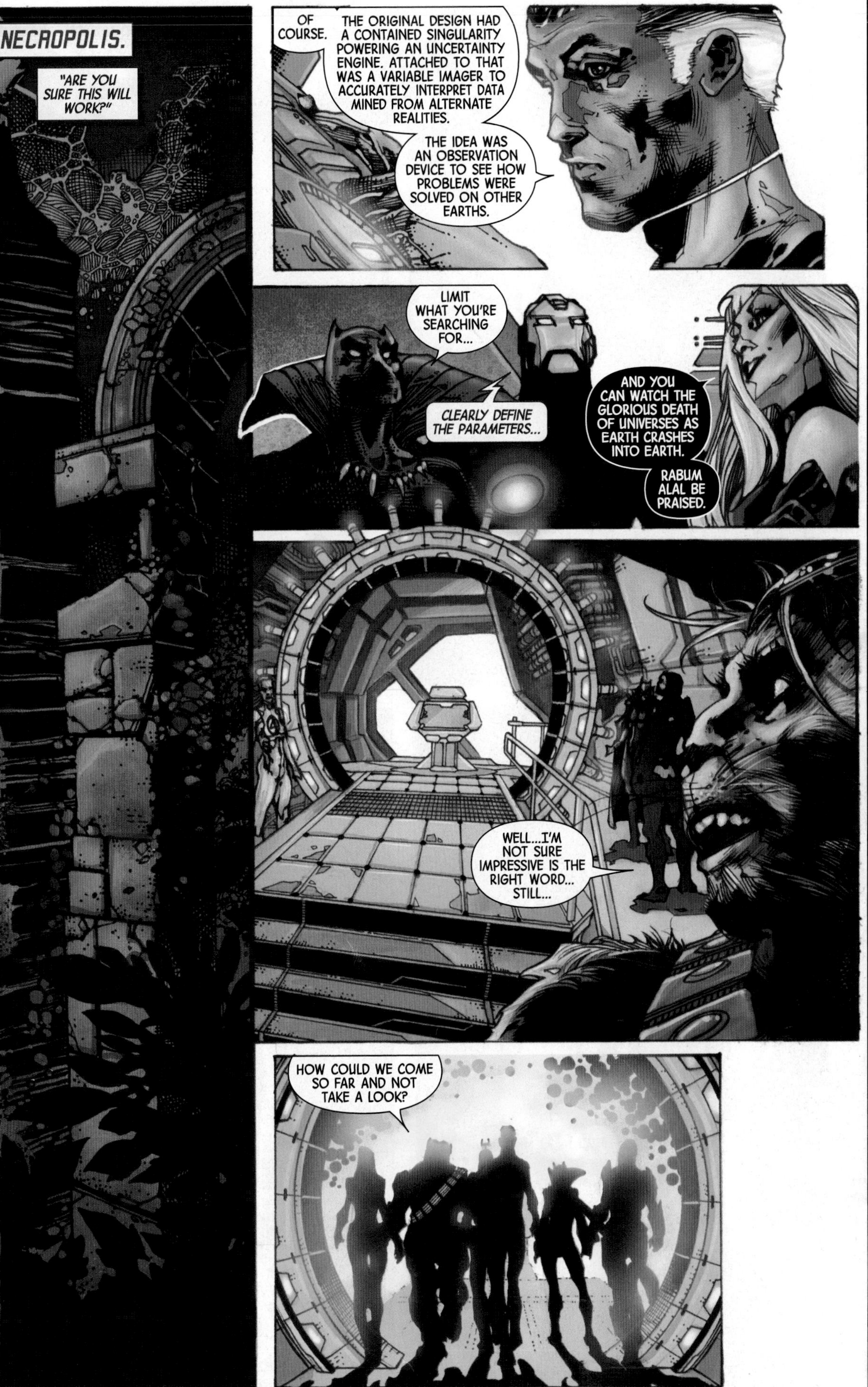
NECROPOLIS.
"ARE YOU SURE THIS WILL WORK?"
OF COURSE.
THE ORIGINAL DESIGN HAD A CONTAINED SINGULARITY POWERING AN UNCERTAINTY ENGINE. ATTACHED TO THAT WAS A VARIABLE IMAGER TO ACCURATELY INTERPRET DATA MINED FROM ALTERNATE REALITIES.
THE IDEA WAS AN OBSERVATION DEVICE TO SEE HOW PROBLEMS WERE SOLVED ON OTHER EARTHS.
LIMIT WHAT YOU'RE SEARCHING FOR...
CLEARLY DEFINE THE PARAMETERS...
AND YOU CAN WATCH THE GLORIOUS DEATH OF UNIVERSES AS EARTH CRASHES INTO EARTH.
RABUM ALAL BE PRAISED.
WELL...I'M NOT SURE IMPRESSIVE IS THE RIGHT WORD... STILL...
HOW COULD WE COME SO FAR AND NOT TAKE A LOOK?

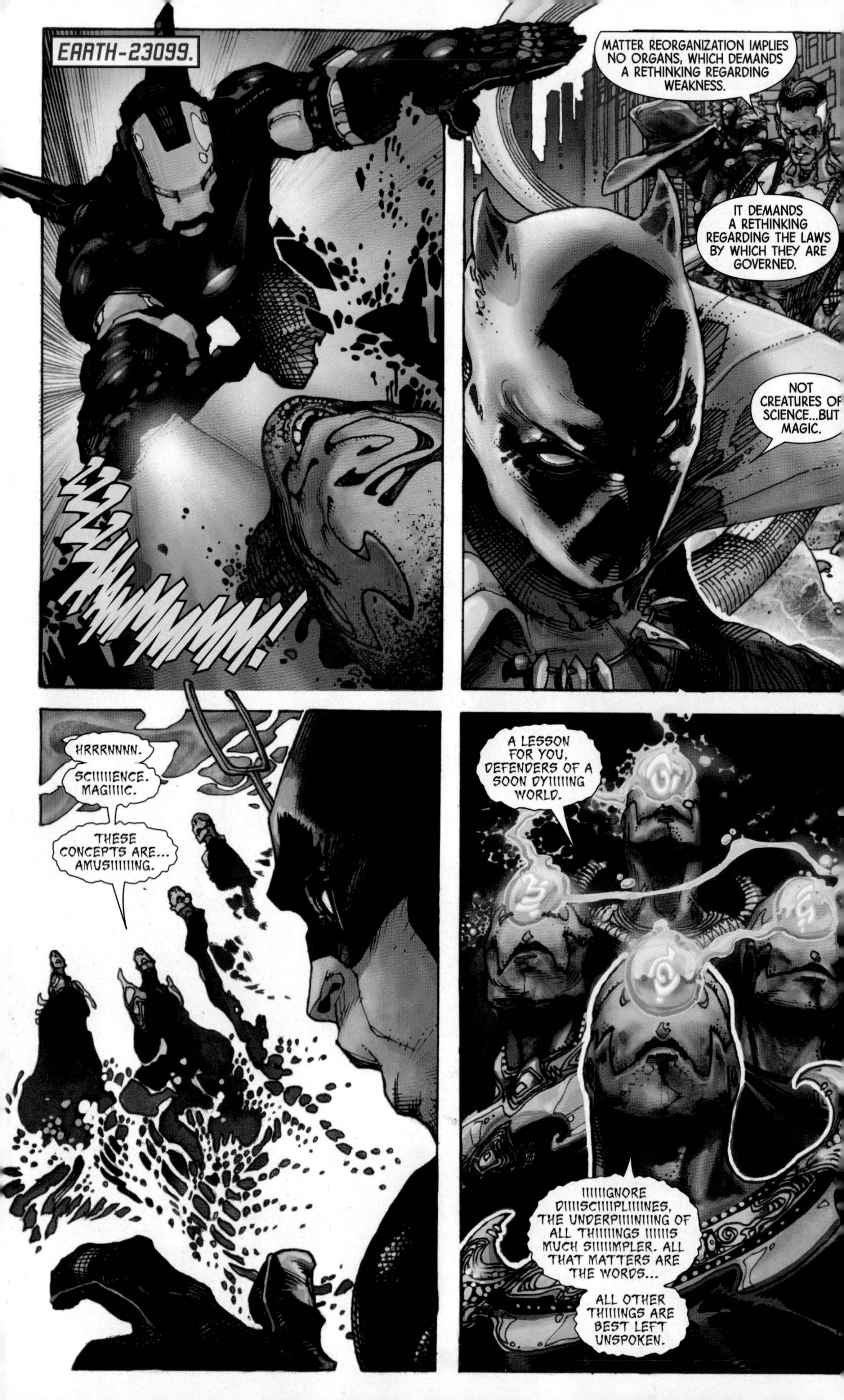
EARTH-23099.
MATTER REORGANIZATION IMPLIES NO ORGANS, WHICH DEMANDS A RETHINKING REGARDING WEAKNESS.
IT DEMANDS A RETHINKING REGARDING THE LAWS BY WHICH THEY ARE GOVERNED.
NOT CREATURES OF SCIENCE...BUT MAGIC.
ZZZZHWMMMM!
HRRRNNNN.
SCIIIIENCE. MAGIIIIC.
THESE CONCEPTS ARE... AMUSIIIIIING.
A LESSON FOR YOU, DEFENDERS OF A SOON DYIIIIING WORLD.
IIIIIIGNORE DIIIISCIIIPLIIIINES, THE UNDERPIIIINIIING OF ALL THIIIINGS IIIIIIS MUCH SIIIIIMPLER. ALL THAT MATTERS ARE THE WORDS...
ALL OTHER THIIIINGS ARE BEST LEFT UNSPOKEN.

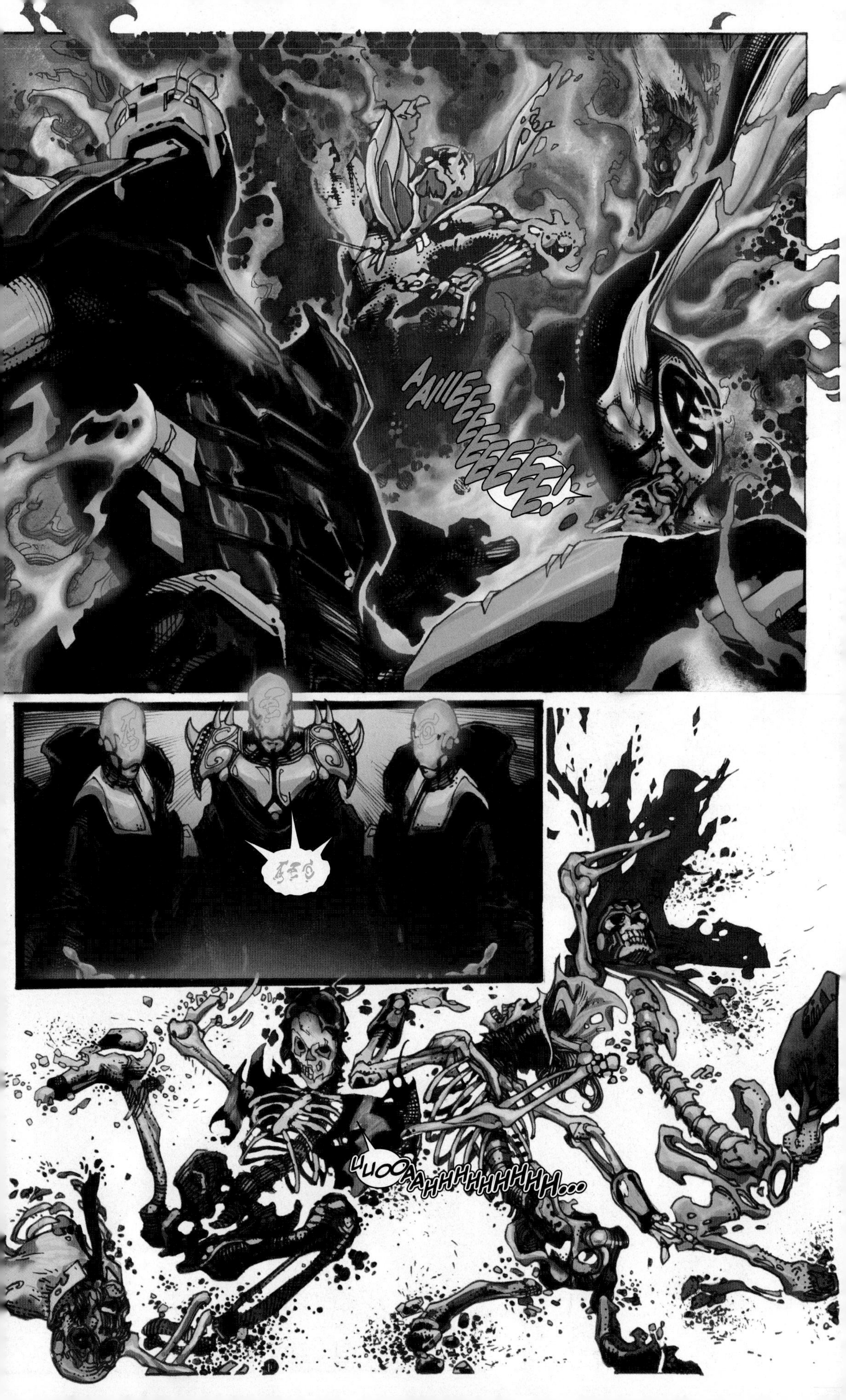
AAIIIEEEEEEEEE!
UUOOAAHHHHHHHHH...

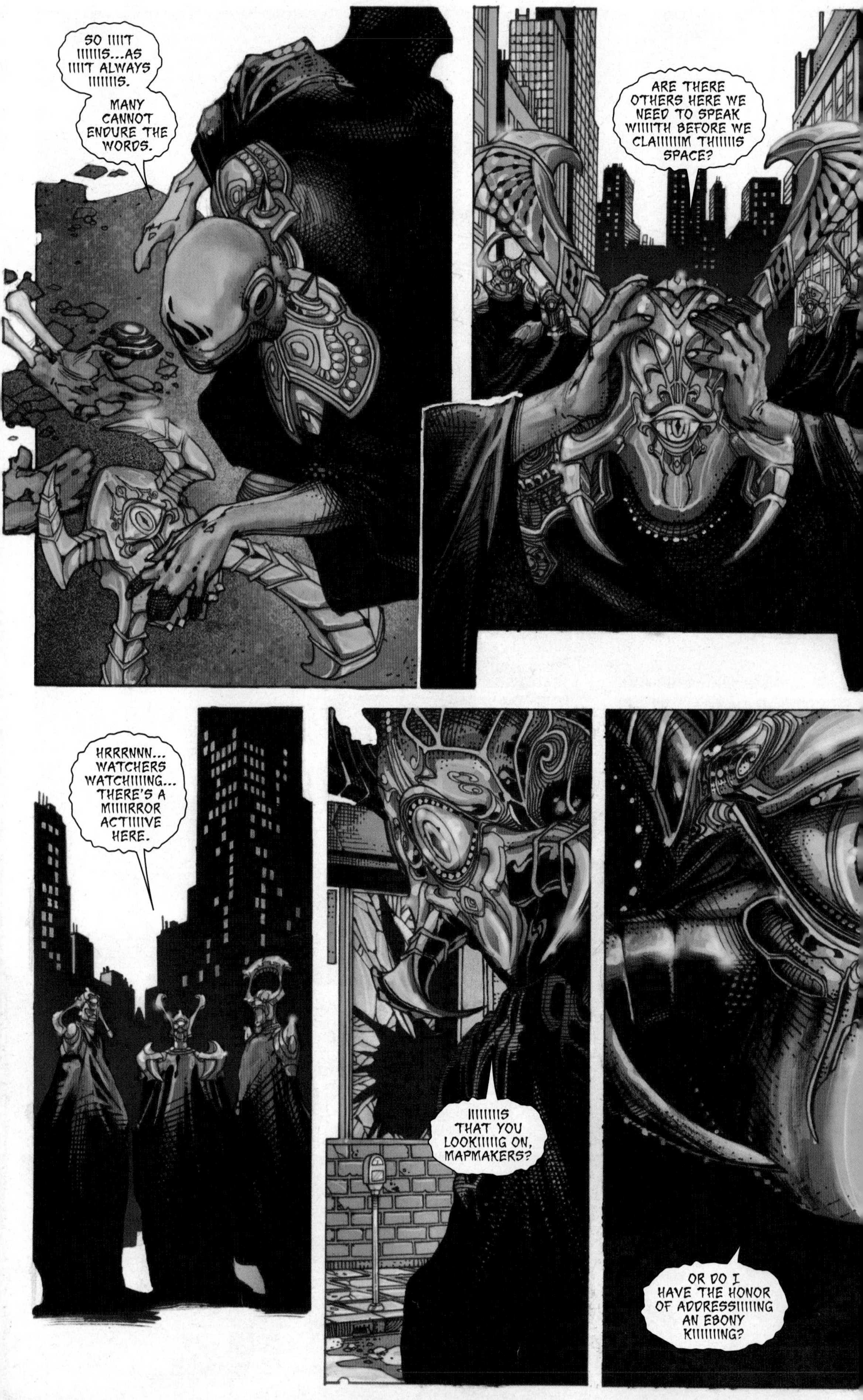
SO IIIIT IIIIIIS...AS IIIIT ALWAYS IIIIIIIS.
MANY CANNOT ENDURE THE WORDS.
ARE THERE OTHERS HERE WE NEED TO SPEAK WIIIITH BEFORE WE CLAIIIIIIM THIIIIIS SPACE?
HRRRNNN... WATCHERS WATCHIIIIING... THERE'S A MIIIIRROR ACTIIIIVE HERE.
IIIIIIIS THAT YOU LOOKIIIIIG ON, MAPMAKERS?
OR DO I HAVE THE HONOR OF ADDRESSIIIIIING AN EBONY KIIIIIIING?

A DAY IIIIS COMIIIING-- CONVERGENCE.

AND ON THAT DAY, THE FIIIIINAL WORD WIIIIILL BE SPOKEN.

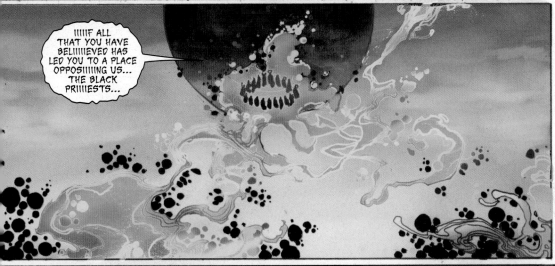

IIIIIF ALL THAT YOU HAVE BELIIIIIEVED HAS LED YOU TO A PLACE OPPOSIIIIING US... THE BLACK PRIIIIESTS...

"THEN YOU HAVE TO ASK YOURSELVES...

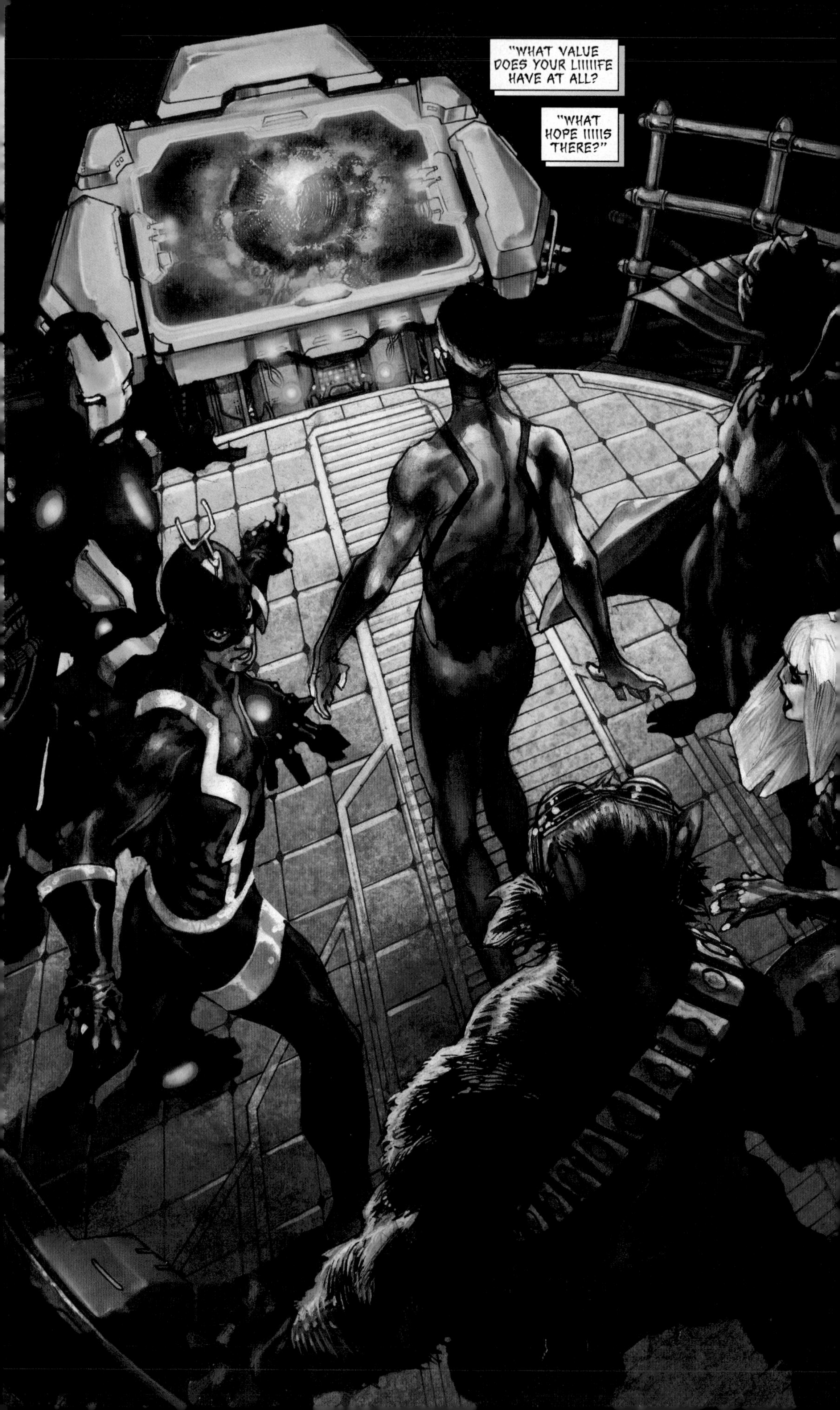
"WHAT VALUE DOES YOUR LIIIIIFE HAVE AT ALL?
"WHAT HOPE IIIIIS THERE?"

"THE AGAMOTTO GAMBIT"

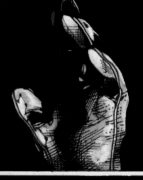

EVERYTHING DIES.

YOU. ME. EVERYONE ON THIS PLANET.

OUR SUN, OUR GALAXY AND, EVENTUALLY, THE UNIVERSE ITSELF.

THIS IS SIMPLY HOW THINGS ARE.

IT'S INEVITABLE.

AND I ACCEPT IT.

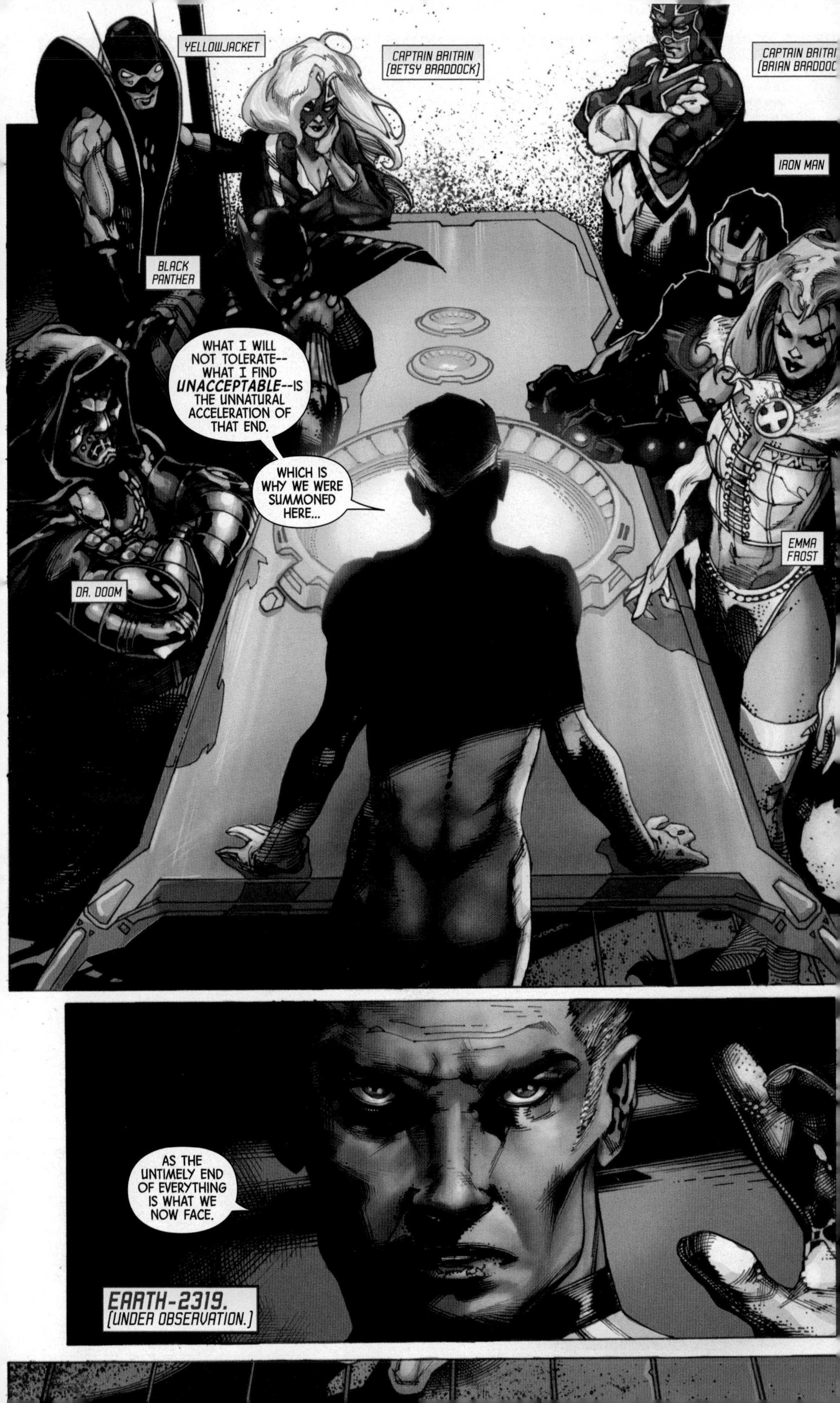

YELLOWJACKET
CAPTAIN BRITAIN [BETSY BRADDOCK]
CAPTAIN BRITAI [BRIAN BRADDOC
IRON MAN
BLACK PANTHER
WHAT I WILL NOT TOLERATE-- WHAT I FIND UNACCEPTABLE--IS THE UNNATURAL ACCELERATION OF THAT END.
WHICH IS WHY WE WERE SUMMONED HERE...
EMMA FROST
DR. DOOM
AS THE UNTIMELY END OF EVERYTHING IS WHAT WE NOW FACE.
EARTH-2319. [UNDER OBSERVATION.]

THE FOURTH AGE OF
[A]CALYPSE ENDED WITH
[TH]E FOUNDING OF THE
[CIT]Y-NATION OF TIAN
[AN]D THE COLLAPSE OF
[TH]E PHOENIX EGGS.

MAGNETO, SAVIOR OF ALL
MUTANTS, HAD GATHERED THE
SURVIVORS OF THE WORLD'S
SECOND HOLOCAUST AND
BROUGHT THEM TO HIS
NEW KINGDOM.

A PLACE CALLED
HEAVEN, WHERE
ALL HIS ANGELS
WOULD BE SAFE...

SAFE FROM ALL THE DEVILS
THAT STILL HUNTED THEM.

IT SHOULD HAVE BEEN
A BETTER WORLD.

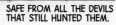

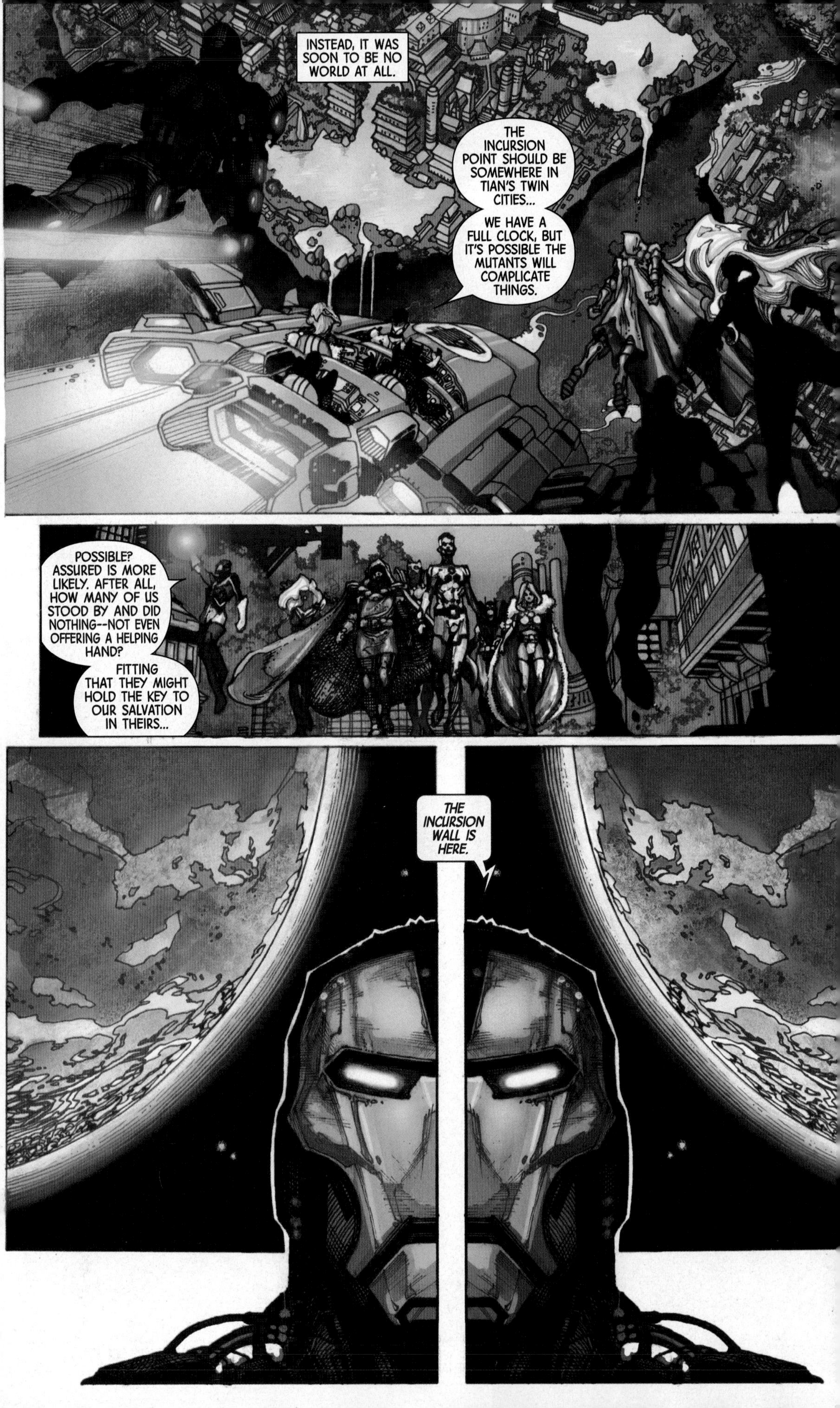

INSTEAD, IT WAS SOON TO BE NO WORLD AT ALL.
THE INCURSION POINT SHOULD BE SOMEWHERE IN TIAN'S TWIN CITIES...
WE HAVE A FULL CLOCK, BUT IT'S POSSIBLE THE MUTANTS WILL COMPLICATE THINGS.
POSSIBLE? ASSURED IS MORE LIKELY. AFTER ALL, HOW MANY OF US STOOD BY AND DID NOTHING--NOT EVEN OFFERING A HELPING HAND?
FITTING THAT THEY MIGHT HOLD THE KEY TO OUR SALVATION IN THEIRS...
THE INCURSION WALL IS HERE.

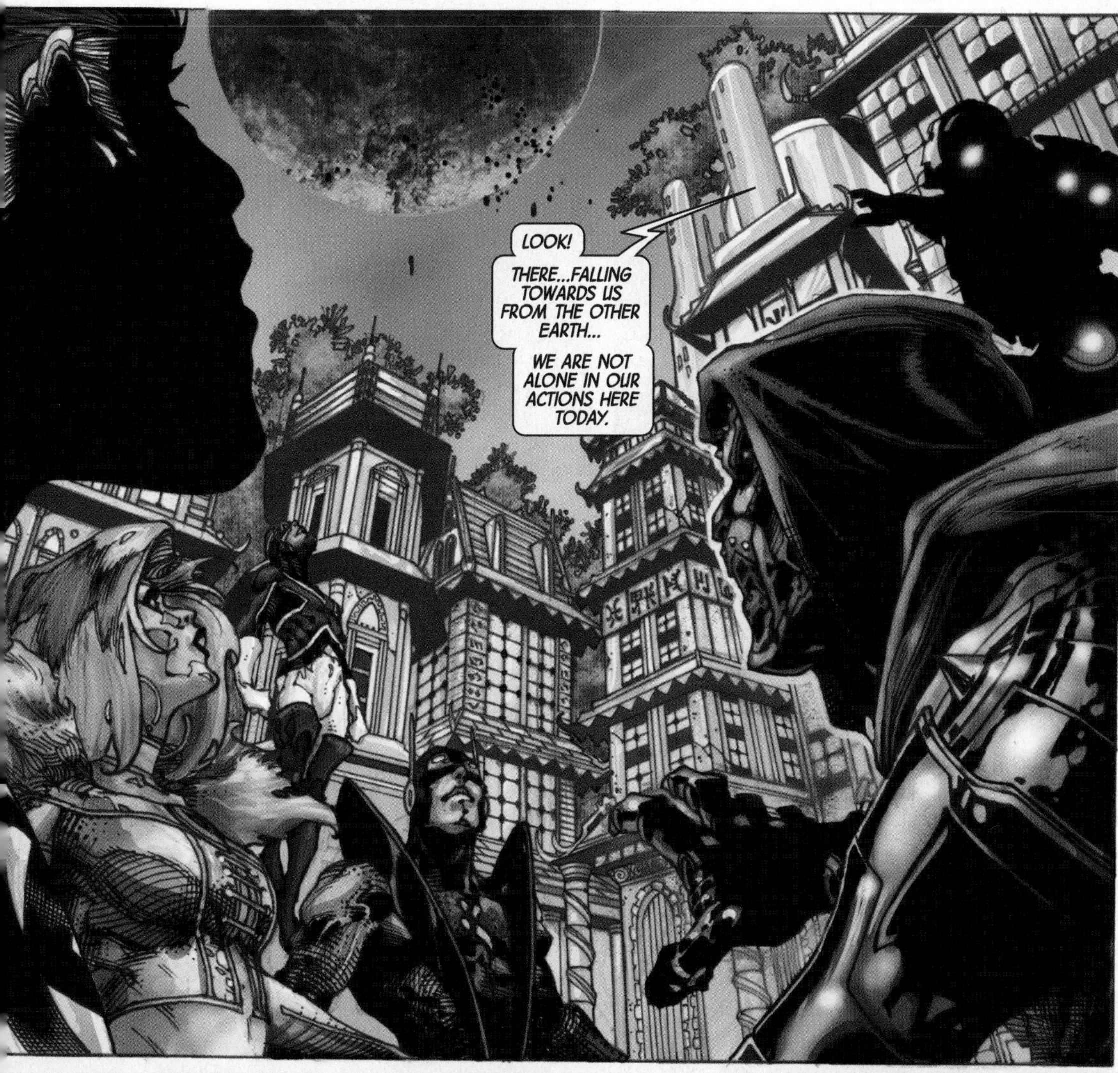
LOOK!
THERE...FALLING TOWARDS US FROM THE OTHER EARTH...
WE ARE NOT ALONE IN OUR ACTIONS HERE TODAY.

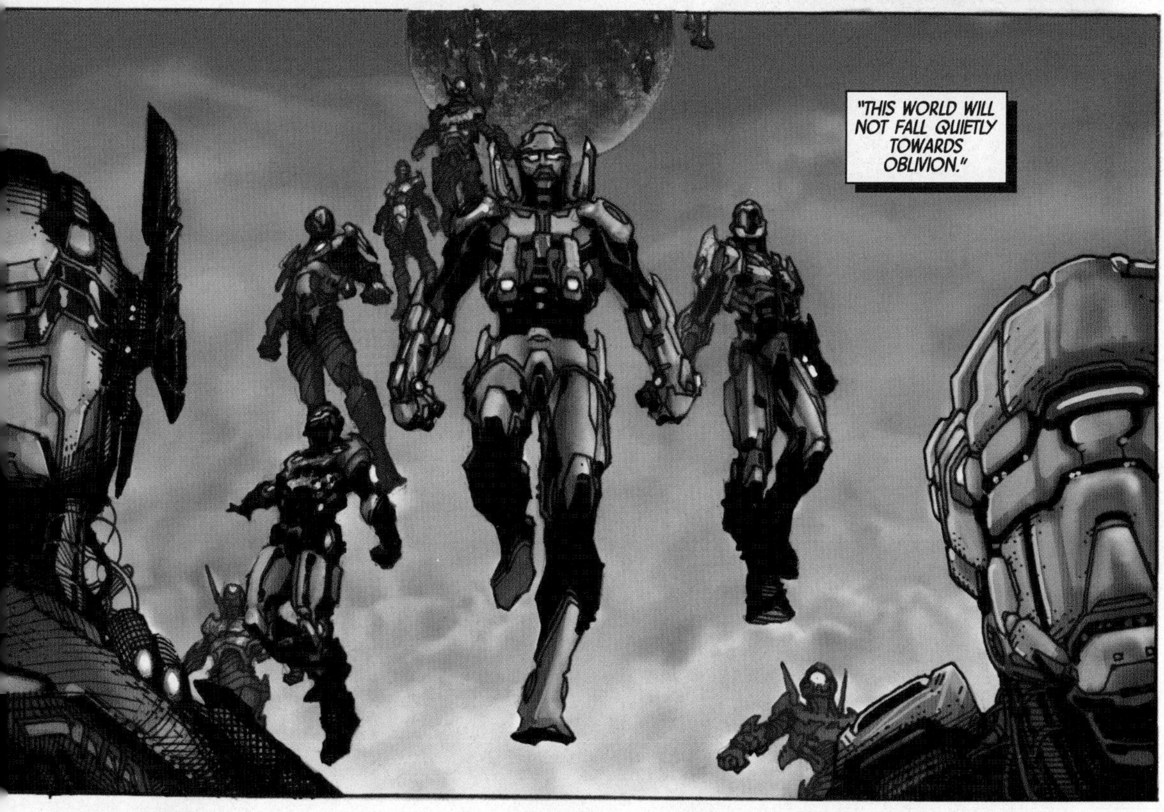
"THIS WORLD WILL NOT FALL QUIETLY TOWARDS OBLIVION."

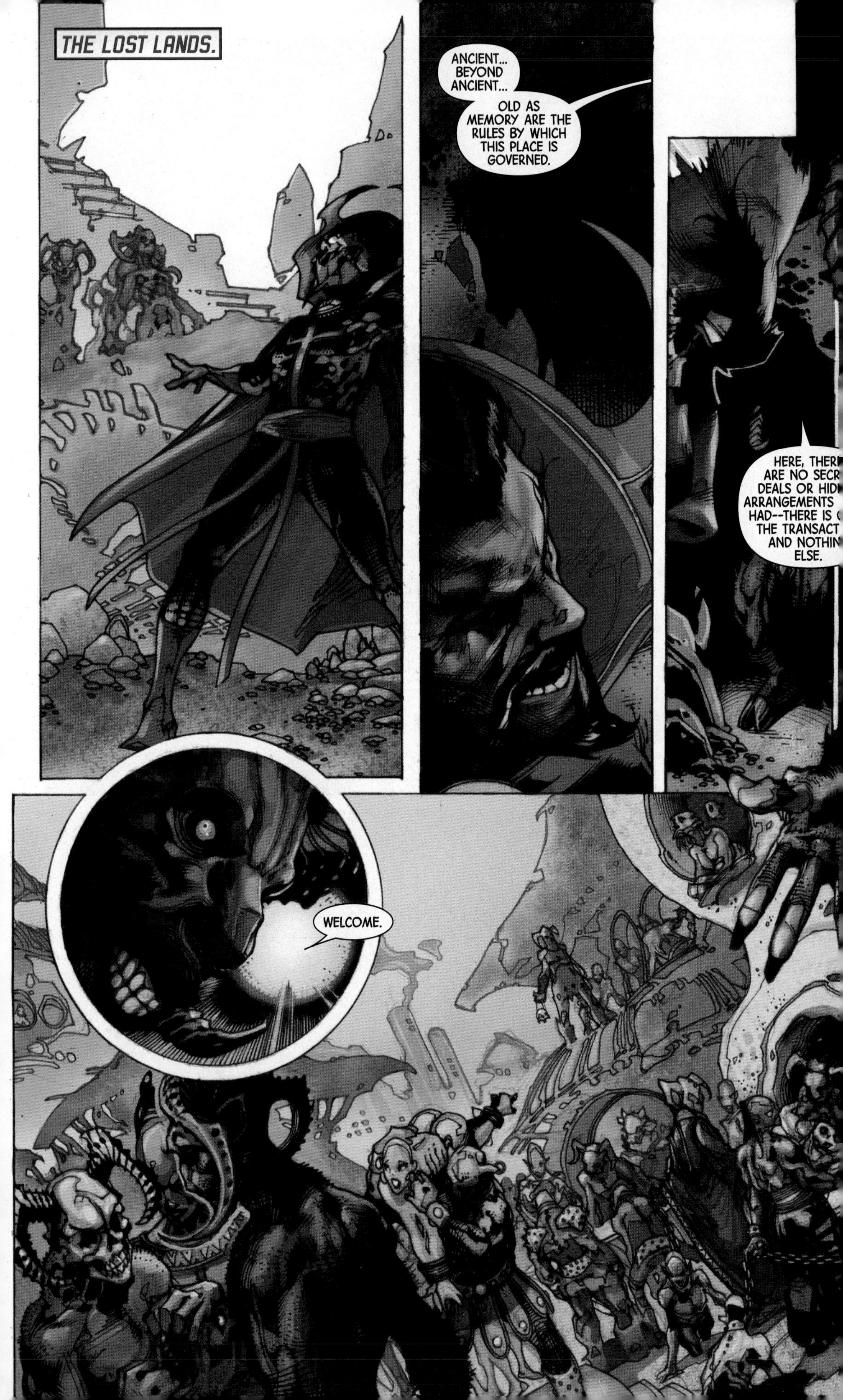
THE LOST LANDS.
ANCIENT... BEYOND ANCIENT...
OLD AS MEMORY ARE THE RULES BY WHICH THIS PLACE IS GOVERNED.
HERE, THER ARE NO SECR DEALS OR HID ARRANGEMENTS HAD--THERE IS THE TRANSACT AND NOTHIN ELSE.
WELCOME.

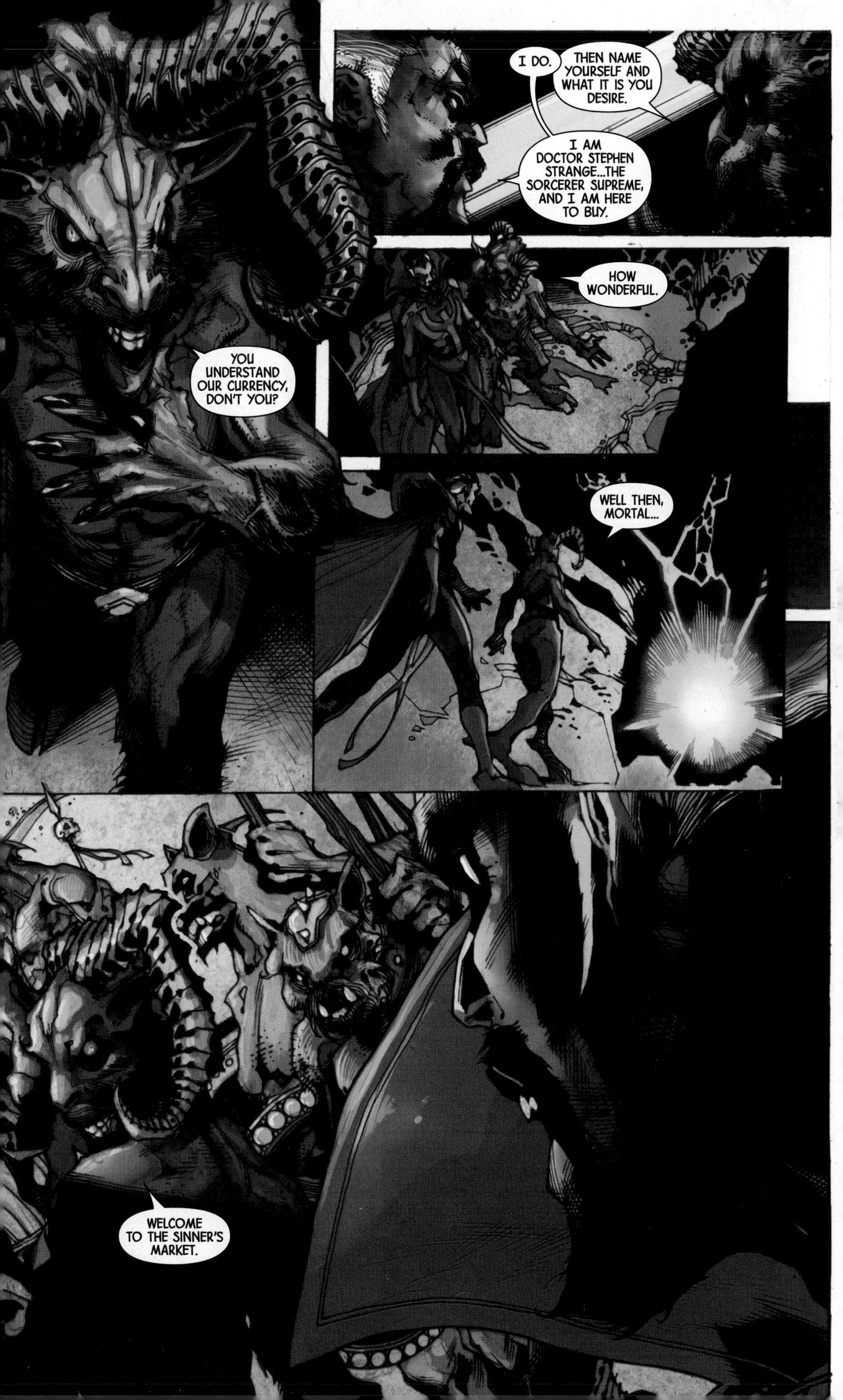
YOU UNDERSTAND OUR CURRENCY, DON'T YOU?
I DO.
THEN NAME YOURSELF AND WHAT IT IS YOU DESIRE.
I AM DOCTOR STEPHEN STRANGE...THE SORCERER SUPREME, AND I AM HERE TO BUY.
HOW WONDERFUL.
WELL THEN, MORTAL...
WELCOME TO THE SINNER'S MARKET.

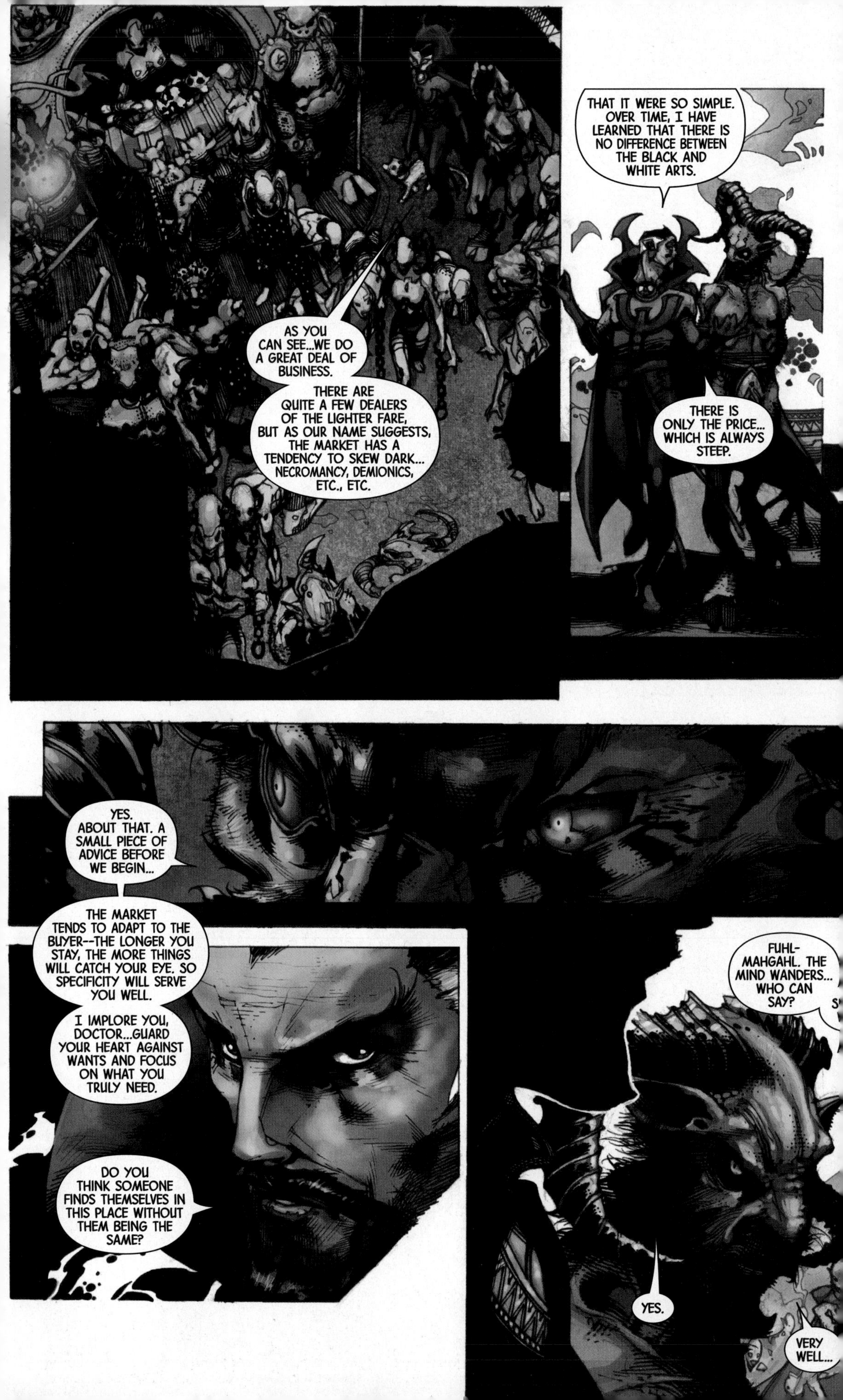
AS YOU CAN SEE...WE DO A GREAT DEAL OF BUSINESS.
THERE ARE QUITE A FEW DEALERS OF THE LIGHTER FARE, BUT AS OUR NAME SUGGESTS, THE MARKET HAS A TENDENCY TO SKEW DARK... NECROMANCY, DEMIONICS, ETC., ETC.
THAT IT WERE SO SIMPLE. OVER TIME, I HAVE LEARNED THAT THERE IS NO DIFFERENCE BETWEEN THE BLACK AND WHITE ARTS.
THERE IS ONLY THE PRICE... WHICH IS ALWAYS STEEP.
YES. ABOUT THAT. A SMALL PIECE OF ADVICE BEFORE WE BEGIN...
THE MARKET TENDS TO ADAPT TO THE BUYER--THE LONGER YOU STAY, THE MORE THINGS WILL CATCH YOUR EYE. SO SPECIFICITY WILL SERVE YOU WELL.
I IMPLORE YOU, DOCTOR...GUARD YOUR HEART AGAINST WANTS AND FOCUS ON WHAT YOU TRULY NEED.
DO YOU THINK SOMEONE FINDS THEMSELVES IN THIS PLACE WITHOUT THEM BEING THE SAME?
FUHL-MAHGAHL. THE MIND WANDERS... WHO CAN SAY?
YES.
VERY WELL...

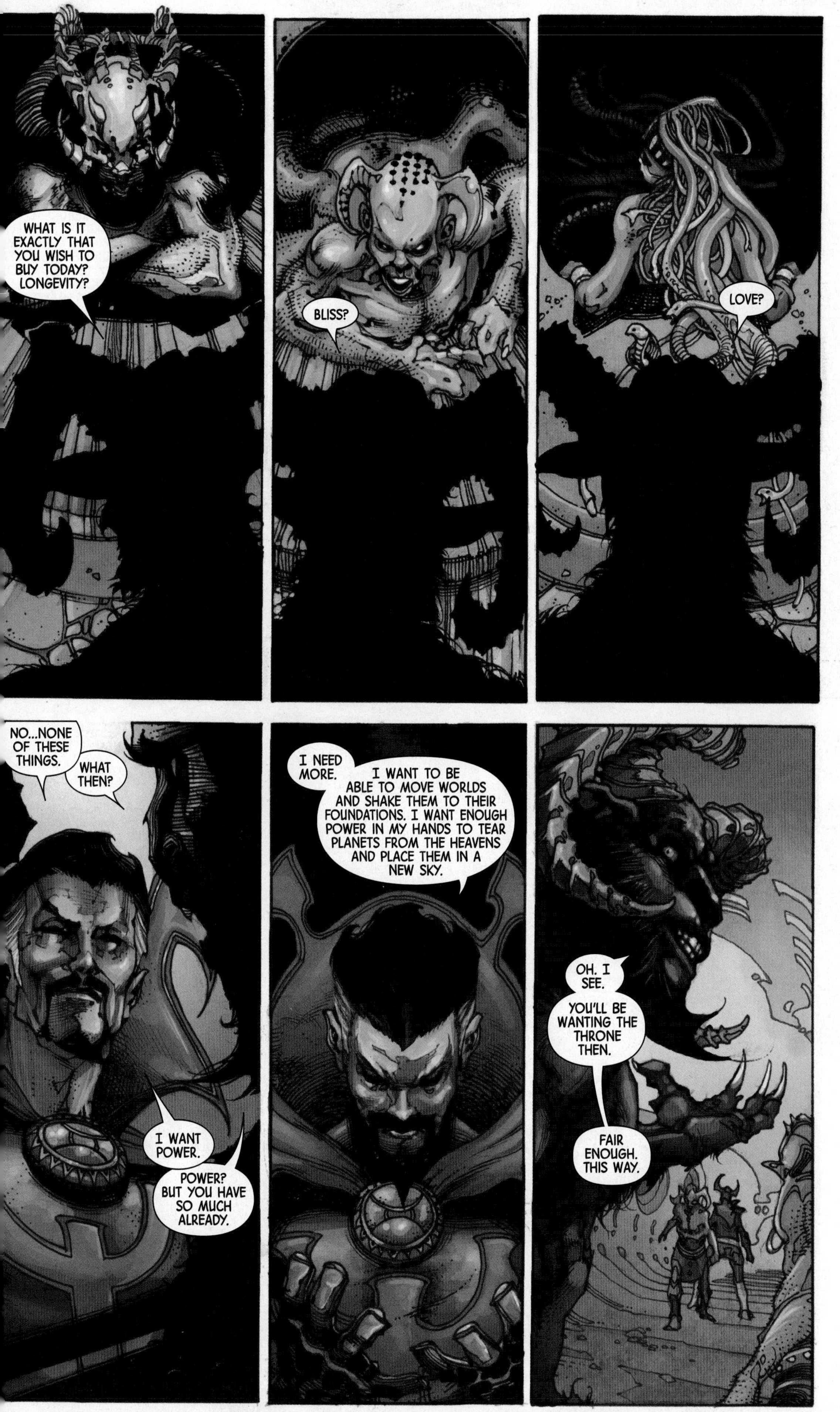
WHAT IS IT EXACTLY THAT YOU WISH TO BUY TODAY? LONGEVITY?
BLISS?
LOVE?
NO...NONE OF THESE THINGS.
WHAT THEN?
I WANT POWER.
POWER? BUT YOU HAVE SO MUCH ALREADY.
I NEED MORE.
I WANT TO BE ABLE TO MOVE WORLDS AND SHAKE THEM TO THEIR FOUNDATIONS. I WANT ENOUGH POWER IN MY HANDS TO TEAR PLANETS FROM THE HEAVENS AND PLACE THEM IN A NEW SKY.
OH. I SEE.
YOU'LL BE WANTING THE THRONE THEN.
FAIR ENOUGH. THIS WAY.

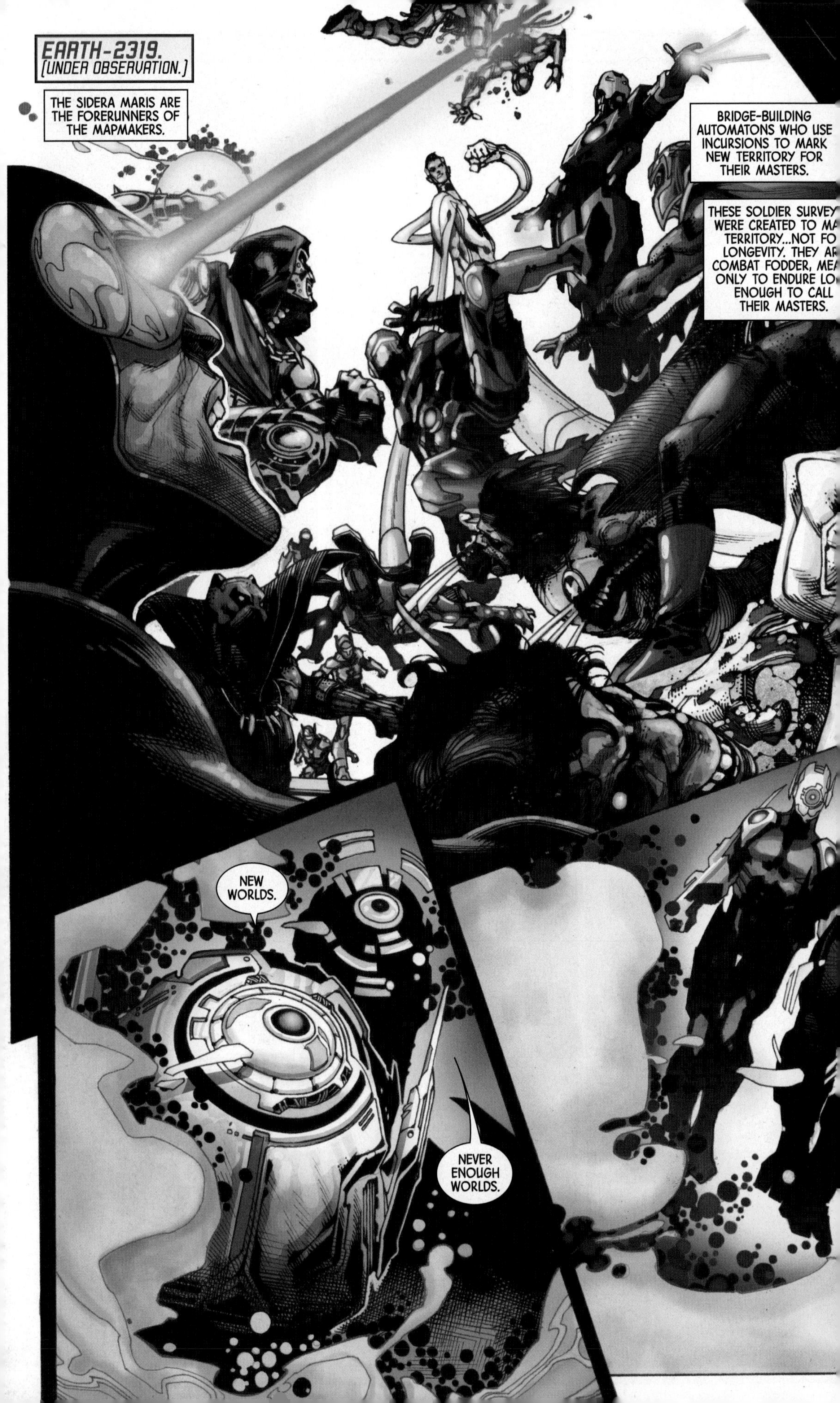
EARTH-2319.
(UNDER OBSERVATION.)
THE SIDERA MARIS ARE THE FORERUNNERS OF THE MAPMAKERS.
BRIDGE-BUILDING AUTOMATONS WHO USE INCURSIONS TO MARK NEW TERRITORY FOR THEIR MASTERS.
THESE SOLDIER SURVEY WERE CREATED TO MA TERRITORY...NOT FO LONGEVITY. THEY AR COMBAT FODDER, MEA ONLY TO ENDURE LO ENOUGH TO CALL THEIR MASTERS.
NEW WORLDS.
NEVER ENOUGH WORLDS.

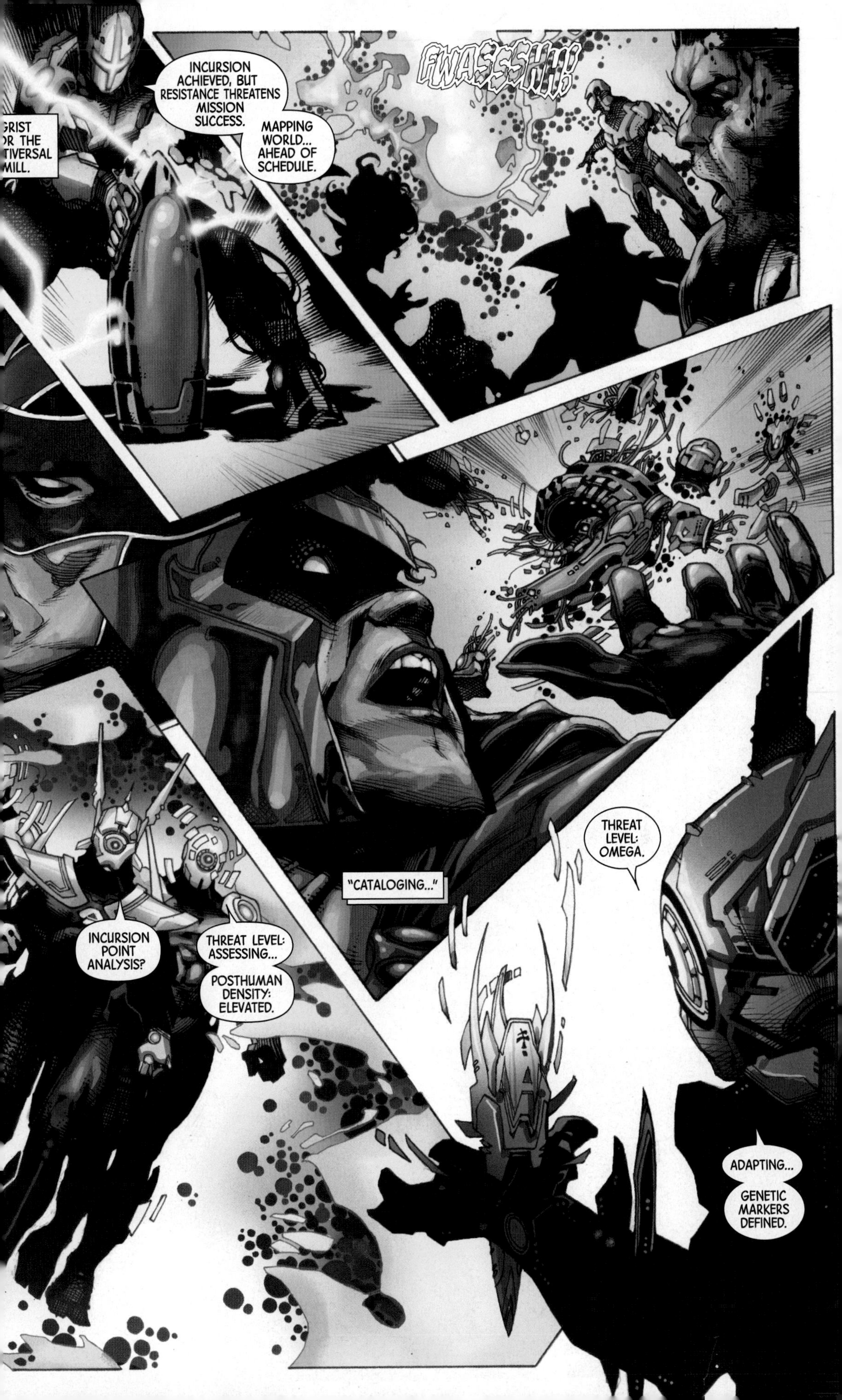

GRIST
OR THE
TIVERSAL
MILL.
INCURSION ACHIEVED, BUT RESISTANCE THREATENS MISSION SUCCESS.
MAPPING WORLD... AHEAD OF SCHEDULE.
FWASSSHH!
"CATALOGING..."
THREAT LEVEL: OMEGA.
INCURSION POINT ANALYSIS?
THREAT LEVEL: ASSESSING...
POSTHUMAN DENSITY: ELEVATED.
ADAPTING...
GENETIC MARKERS DEFINED.

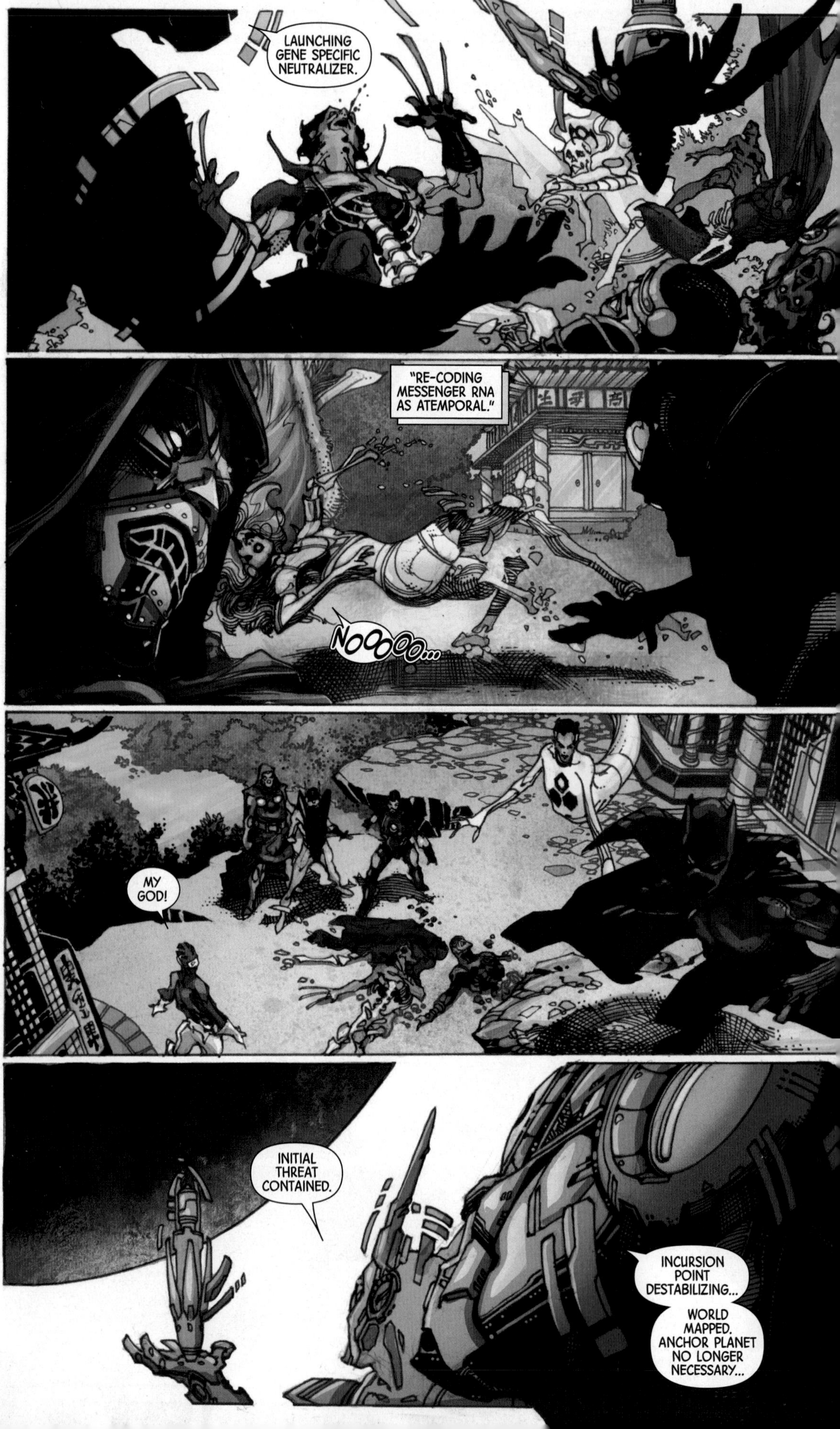
LAUNCHING GENE SPECIFIC NEUTRALIZER.
"RE-CODING MESSENGER RNA AS ATEMPORAL."
NOOOOO...
MY GOD!
INITIAL THREAT CONTAINED.
INCURSION POINT DESTABILIZING...
WORLD MAPPED. ANCHOR PLANET NO LONGER NECESSARY...

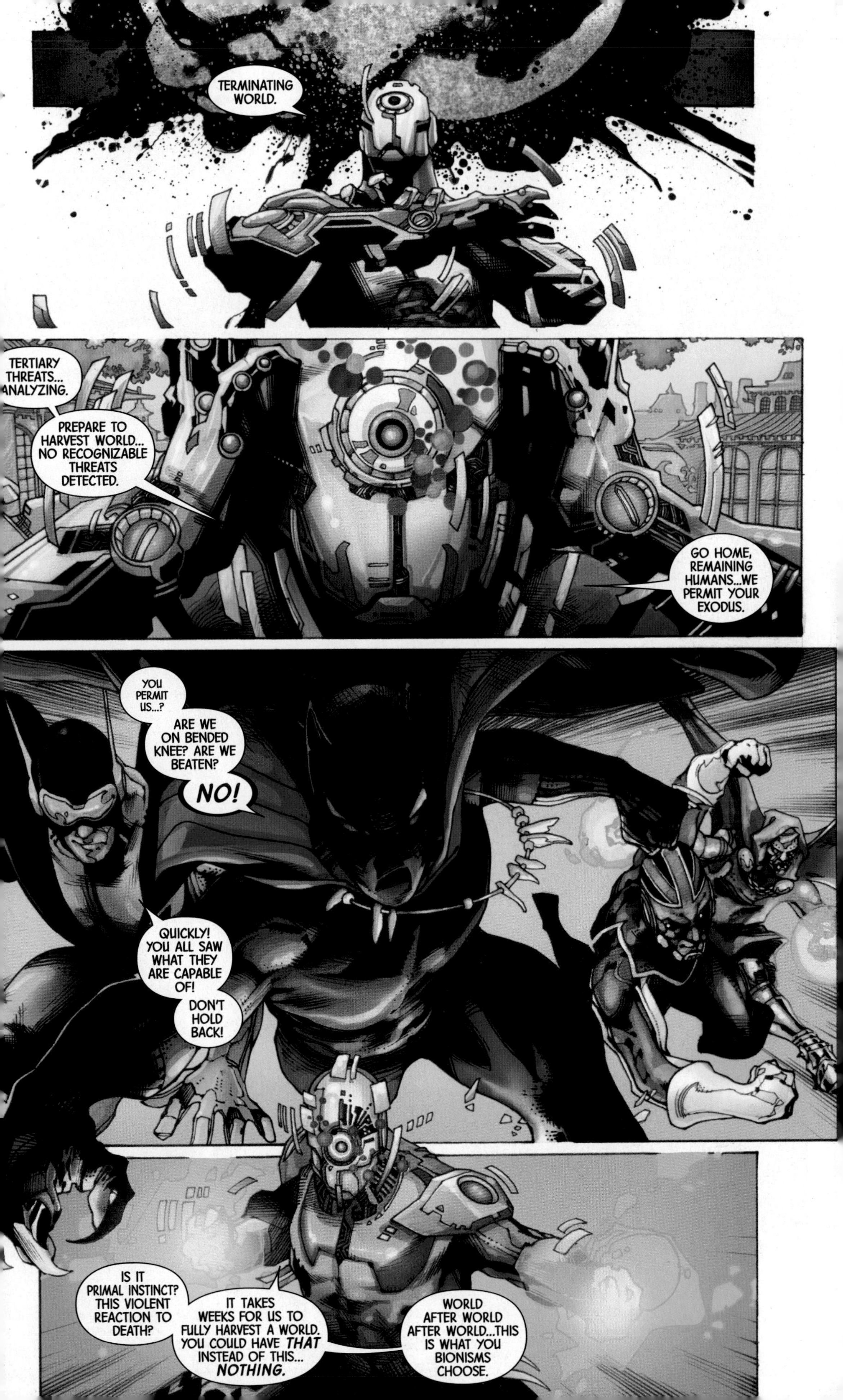

TERMINATING WORLD.
TERTIARY THREATS... ANALYZING.
PREPARE TO HARVEST WORLD... NO RECOGNIZABLE THREATS DETECTED.
GO HOME, REMAINING HUMANS...WE PERMIT YOUR EXODUS.
YOU PERMIT US...?
ARE WE ON BENDED KNEE? ARE WE BEATEN?
NO!
QUICKLY! YOU ALL SAW WHAT THEY ARE CAPABLE OF!
DON'T HOLD BACK!
IS IT PRIMAL INSTINCT? THIS VIOLENT REACTION TO DEATH?
IT TAKES WEEKS FOR US TO FULLY HARVEST A WORLD. YOU COULD HAVE THAT INSTEAD OF THIS... NOTHING.
WORLD AFTER WORLD AFTER WORLD...THIS IS WHAT YOU BIONISMS CHOOSE.

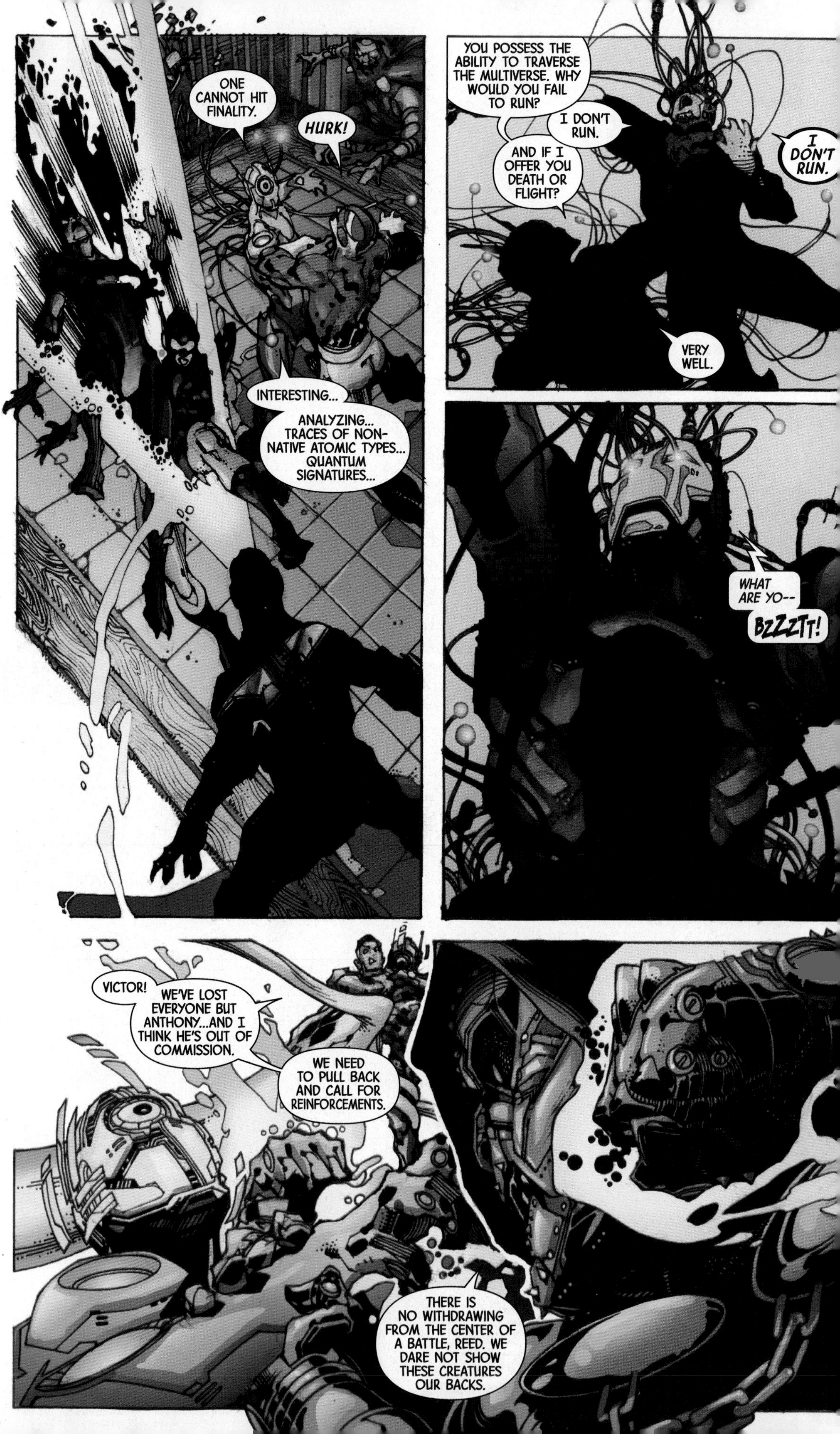
ONE CANNOT HIT FINALITY.
HURK!
INTERESTING...
ANALYZING... TRACES OF NON-NATIVE ATOMIC TYPES... QUANTUM SIGNATURES...
YOU POSSESS THE ABILITY TO TRAVERSE THE MULTIVERSE. WHY WOULD YOU FAIL TO RUN?
I DON'T RUN.
AND IF I OFFER YOU DEATH OR FLIGHT?
I DON'T RUN.
VERY WELL.
WHAT ARE YO--
BZZZTT!
VICTOR!
WE'VE LOST EVERYONE BUT ANTHONY...AND I THINK HE'S OUT OF COMMISSION.
WE NEED TO PULL BACK AND CALL FOR REINFORCEMENTS.
THERE IS NO WITHDRAWING FROM THE CENTER OF A BATTLE, REED. WE DARE NOT SHOW THESE CREATURES OUR BACKS.

BESIDES...

WHY FLEE FROM THAT WHICH CAN BE CONQUERED?

OMEGA-LEVEL THREAT DETECTED.

THAT MAKER ACHIEVED CONSCIOUSNESS ONE HUNDRED CYCLES AGO. IT MAPPED THOUSANDS OF EARTHS.

IT WAS... IRREPLACEABLE.

PRIORITY OVERRIDE.

LOSS OF FULL HARVEST... ACCEPTABLE.

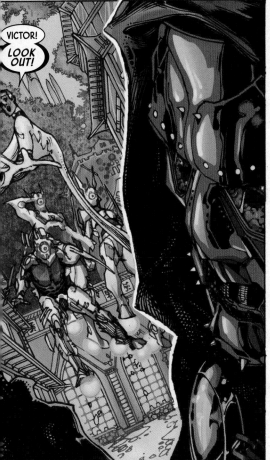

VICTOR! LOOK OUT!

AIEEEEEEEEEE!

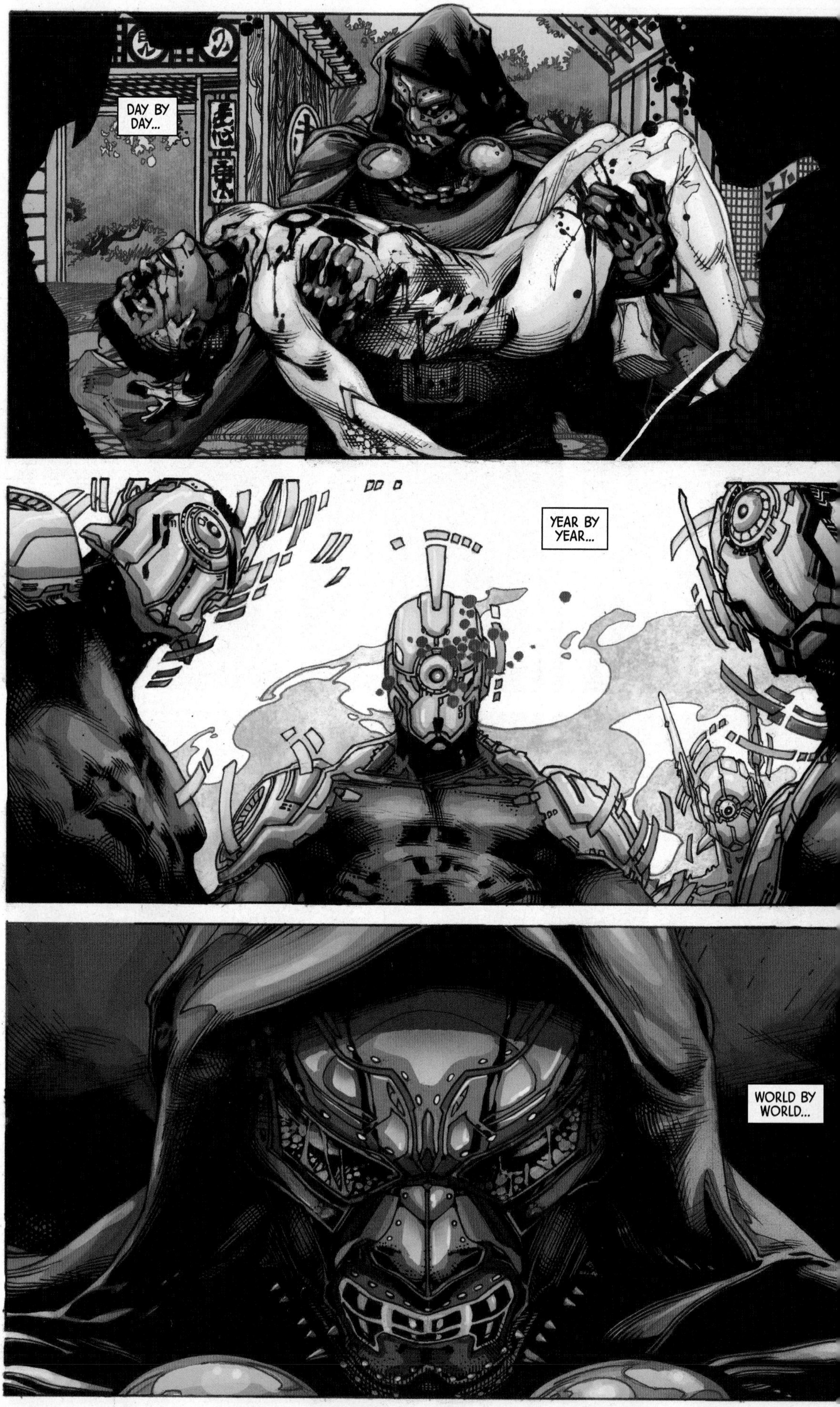
DAY BY DAY...
YEAR BY YEAR...
WORLD BY WORLD...

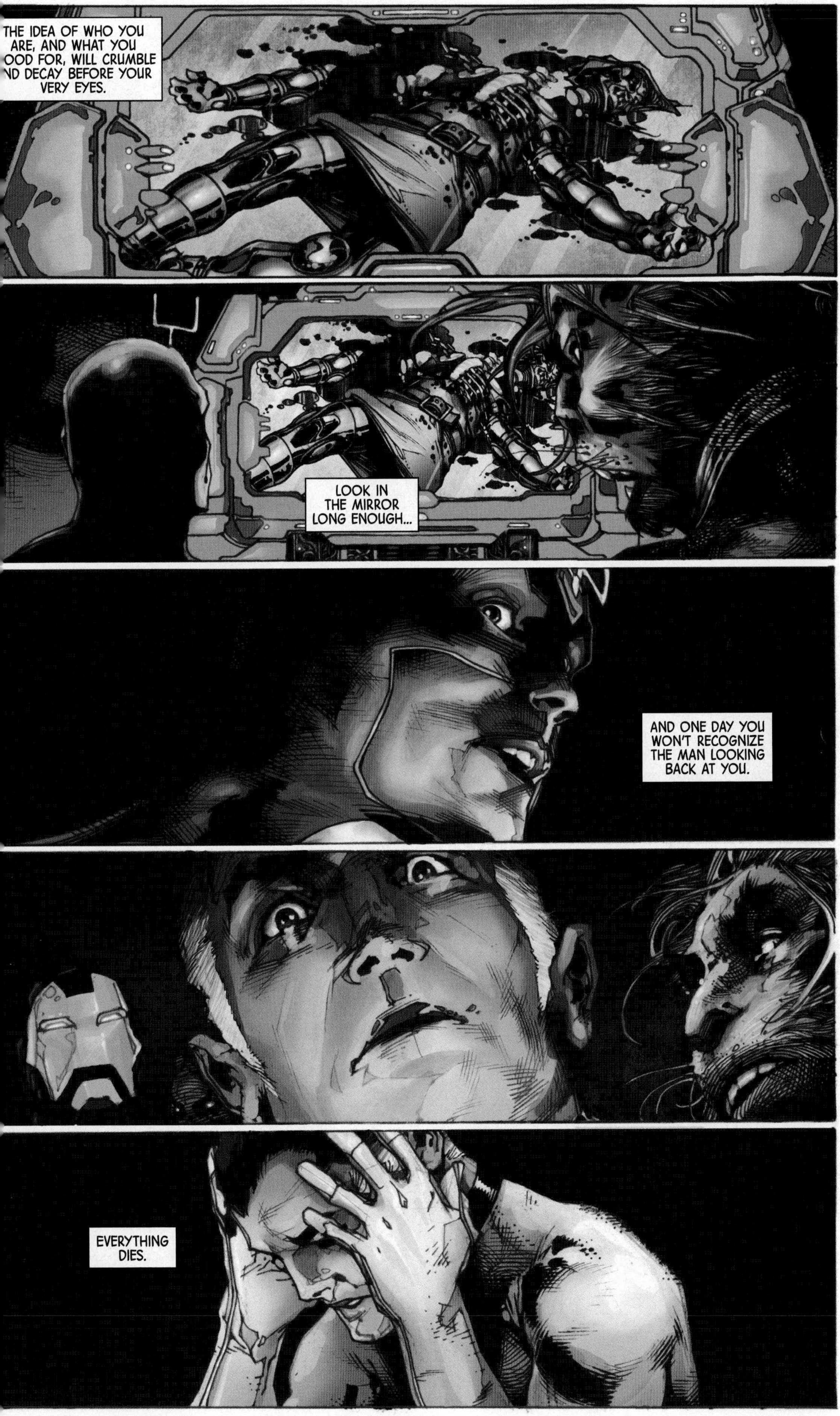
THE IDEA OF WHO YOU
ARE, AND WHAT YOU
OOD FOR, WILL CRUMBLE
ND DECAY BEFORE YOUR
VERY EYES.
LOOK IN
THE MIRROR
LONG ENOUGH...
AND ONE DAY YOU
WON'T RECOGNIZE
THE MAN LOOKING
BACK AT YOU.
EVERYTHING
DIES.

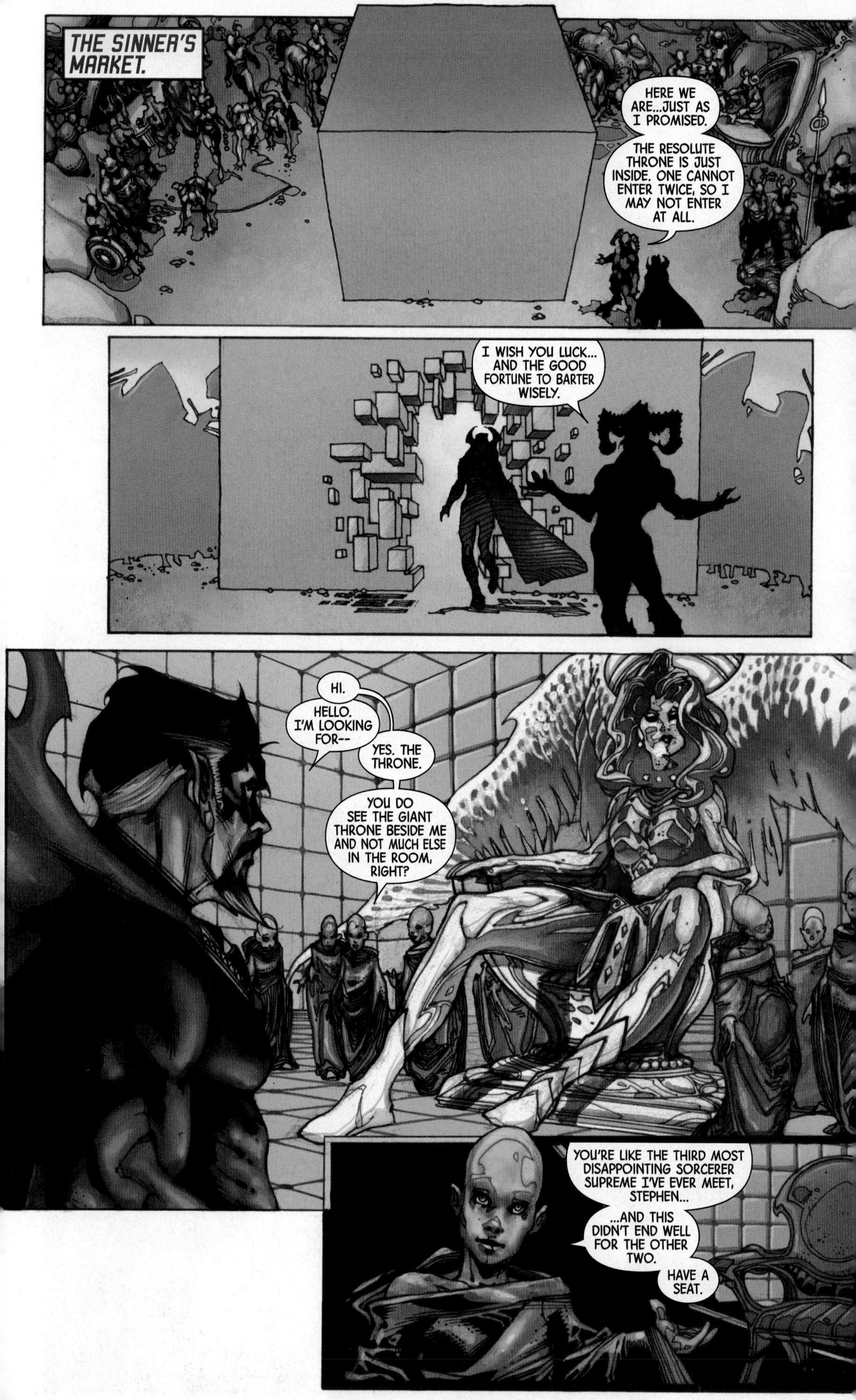
THE SINNER'S MARKET.
HERE WE ARE...JUST AS I PROMISED.
THE RESOLUTE THRONE IS JUST INSIDE. ONE CANNOT ENTER TWICE, SO I MAY NOT ENTER AT ALL.
I WISH YOU LUCK... AND THE GOOD FORTUNE TO BARTER WISELY.
HI.
HELLO. I'M LOOKING FOR--
YES. THE THRONE.
YOU DO SEE THE GIANT THRONE BESIDE ME AND NOT MUCH ELSE IN THE ROOM, RIGHT?
YOU'RE LIKE THE THIRD MOST DISAPPOINTING SORCERER SUPREME I'VE EVER MEET, STEPHEN...
...AND THIS DIDN'T END WELL FOR THE OTHER TWO.
HAVE A SEAT.

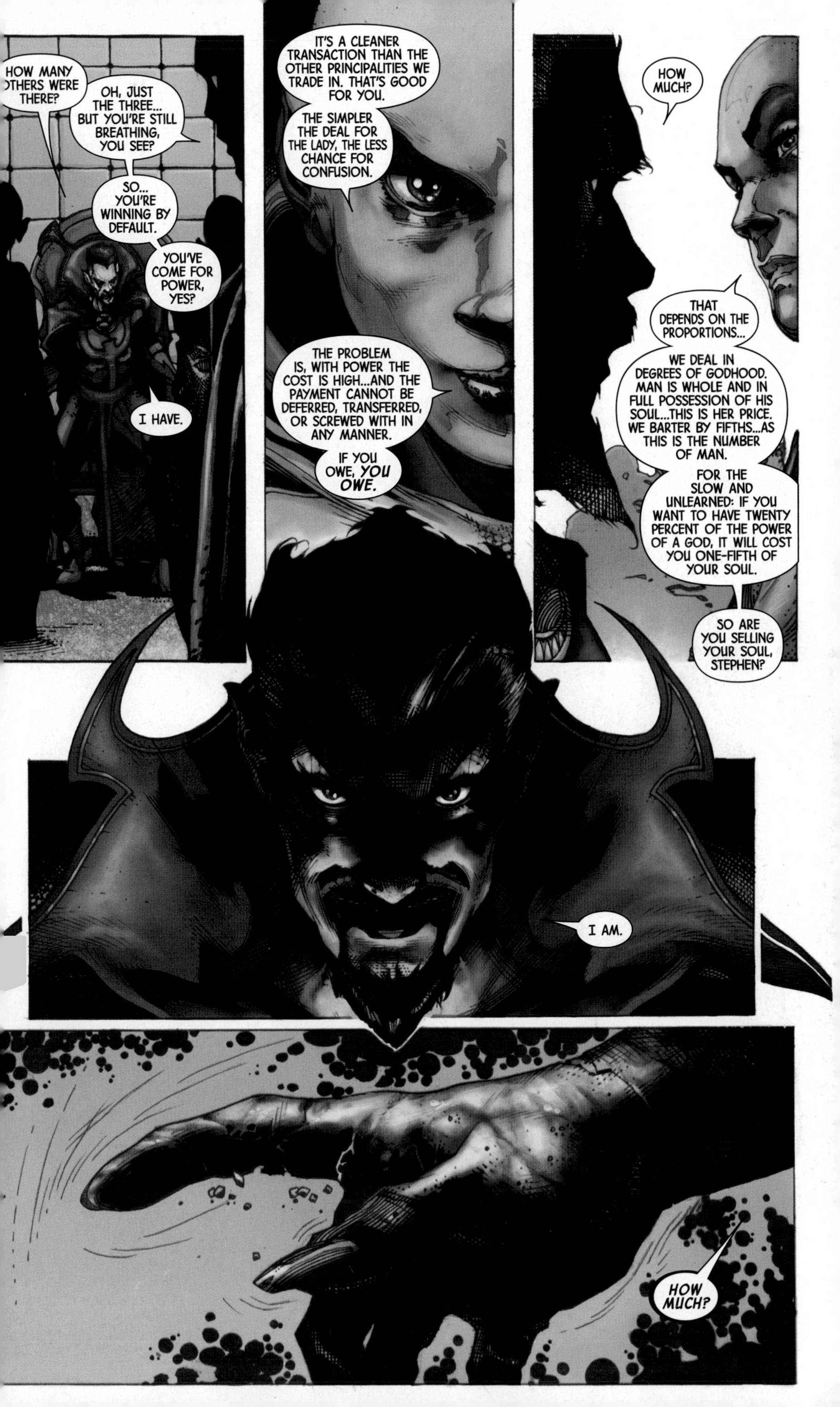

HOW MANY OTHERS WERE THERE?
OH, JUST THE THREE... BUT YOU'RE STILL BREATHING, YOU SEE?
SO... YOU'RE WINNING BY DEFAULT.
YOU'VE COME FOR POWER, YES?
I HAVE.
IT'S A CLEANER TRANSACTION THAN THE OTHER PRINCIPALITIES WE TRADE IN. THAT'S GOOD FOR YOU.
THE SIMPLER THE DEAL FOR THE LADY, THE LESS CHANCE FOR CONFUSION.
THE PROBLEM IS, WITH POWER THE COST IS HIGH...AND THE PAYMENT CANNOT BE DEFERRED, TRANSFERRED, OR SCREWED WITH IN ANY MANNER.
IF YOU OWE, YOU OWE.
HOW MUCH?
THAT DEPENDS ON THE PROPORTIONS...
WE DEAL IN DEGREES OF GODHOOD. MAN IS WHOLE AND IN FULL POSSESSION OF HIS SOUL...THIS IS HER PRICE. WE BARTER BY FIFTHS...AS THIS IS THE NUMBER OF MAN.
FOR THE SLOW AND UNLEARNED: IF YOU WANT TO HAVE TWENTY PERCENT OF THE POWER OF A GOD, IT WILL COST YOU ONE-FIFTH OF YOUR SOUL.
SO ARE YOU SELLING YOUR SOUL, STEPHEN?
I AM.
HOW MUCH?

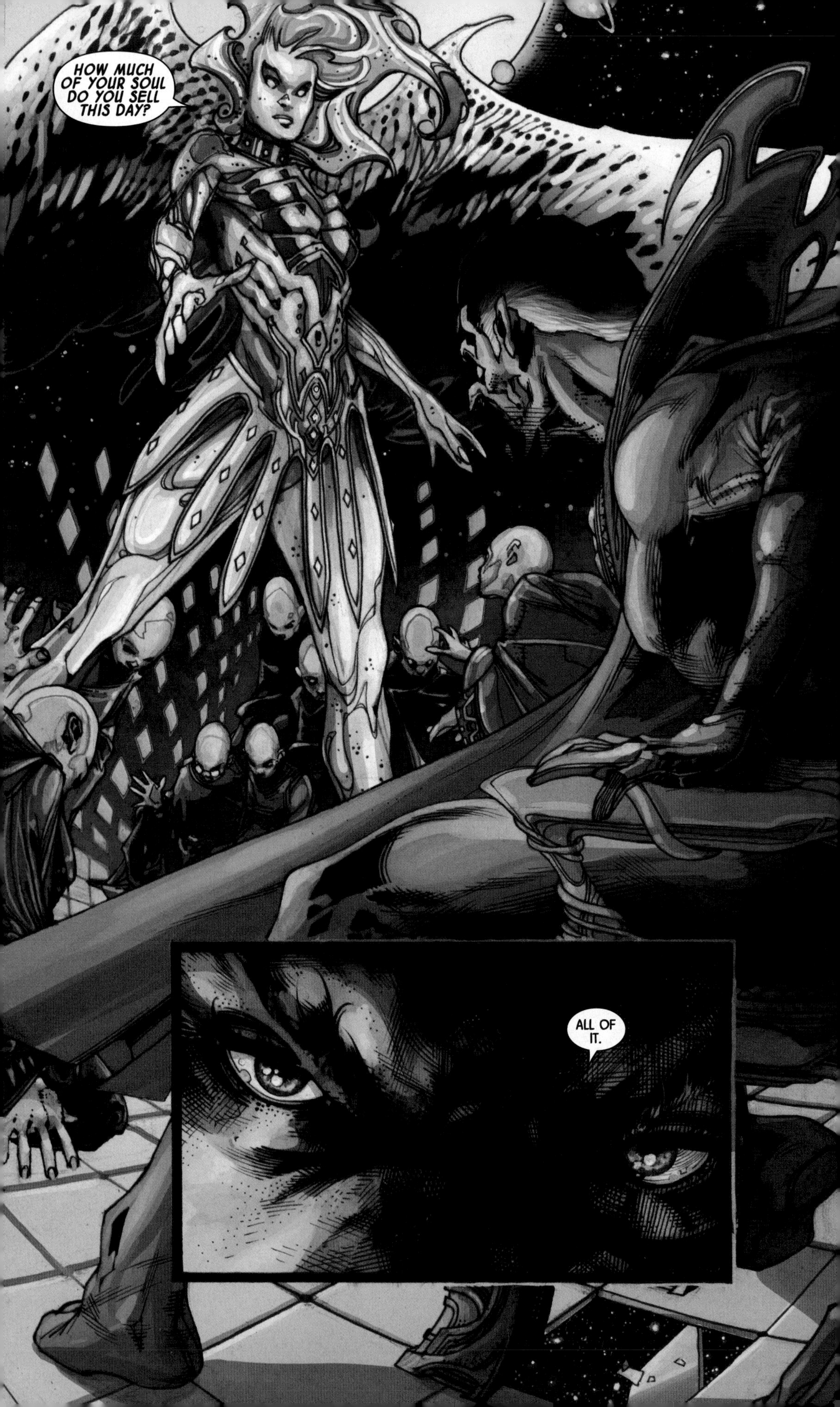
HOW MUCH OF YOUR SOUL DO YOU SELL THIS DAY?
ALL OF IT.

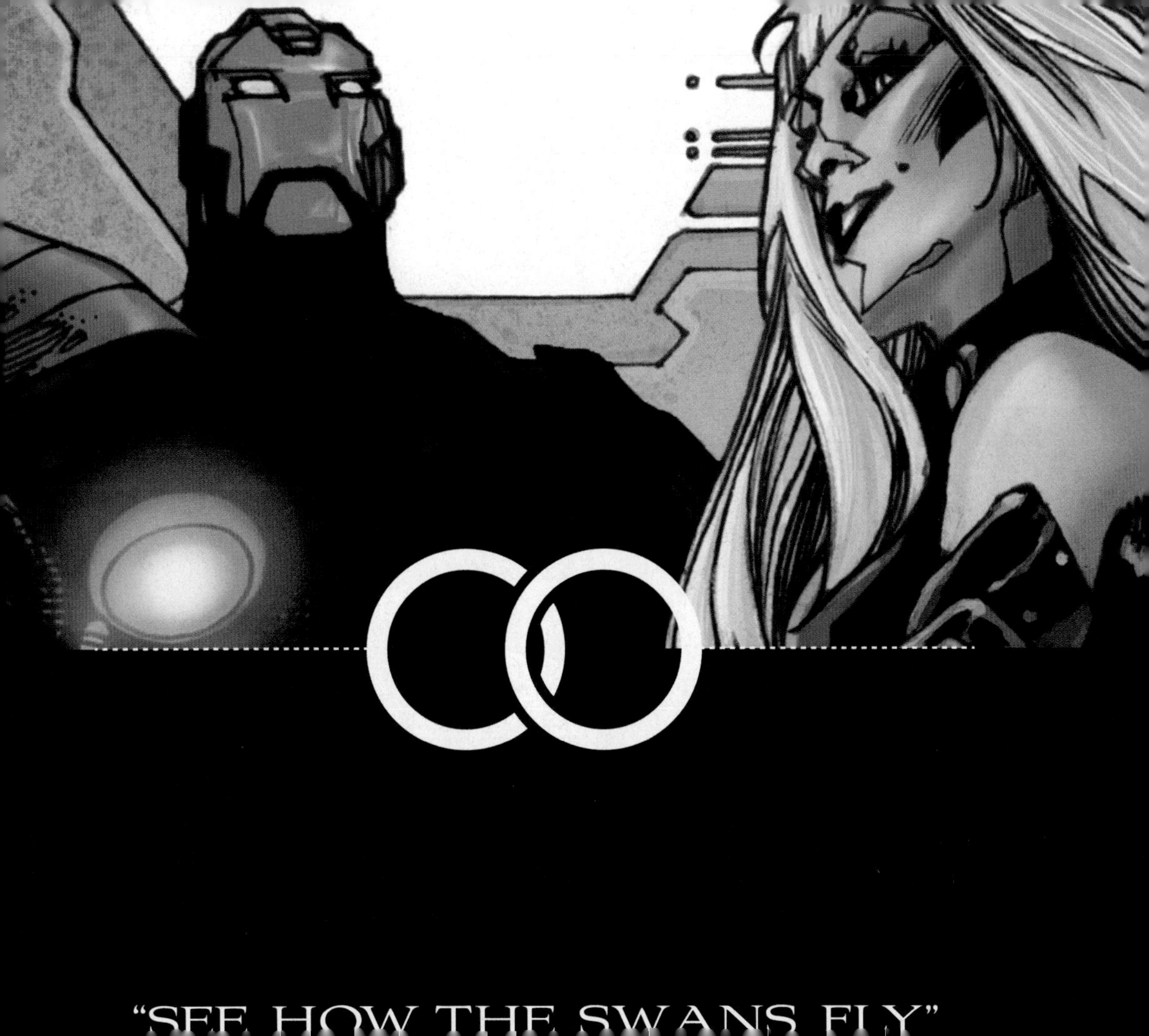

"SEE HOW THE SWANS FLY"

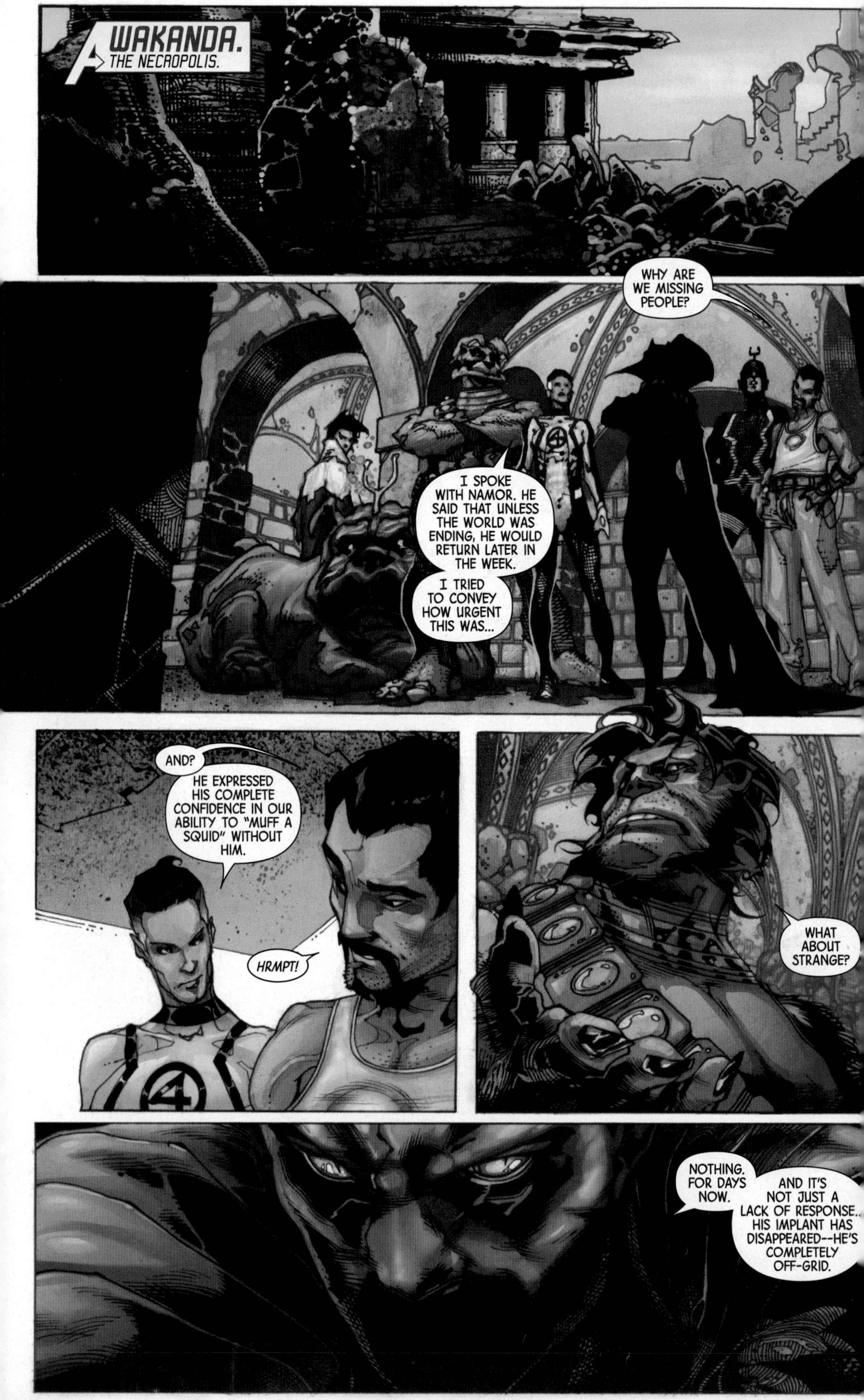
WAKANDA.
THE NECROPOLIS.
WHY ARE WE MISSING PEOPLE?
I SPOKE WITH NAMOR. HE SAID THAT UNLESS THE WORLD WAS ENDING, HE WOULD RETURN LATER IN THE WEEK.
I TRIED TO CONVEY HOW URGENT THIS WAS...
AND?
HE EXPRESSED HIS COMPLETE CONFIDENCE IN OUR ABILITY TO "MUFF A SQUID" WITHOUT HIM.
HRMPT!
WHAT ABOUT STRANGE?
NOTHING. FOR DAYS NOW.
AND IT'S NOT JUST A LACK OF RESPONSE. HIS IMPLANT HAS DISAPPEARED--HE'S COMPLETELY OFF-GRID.

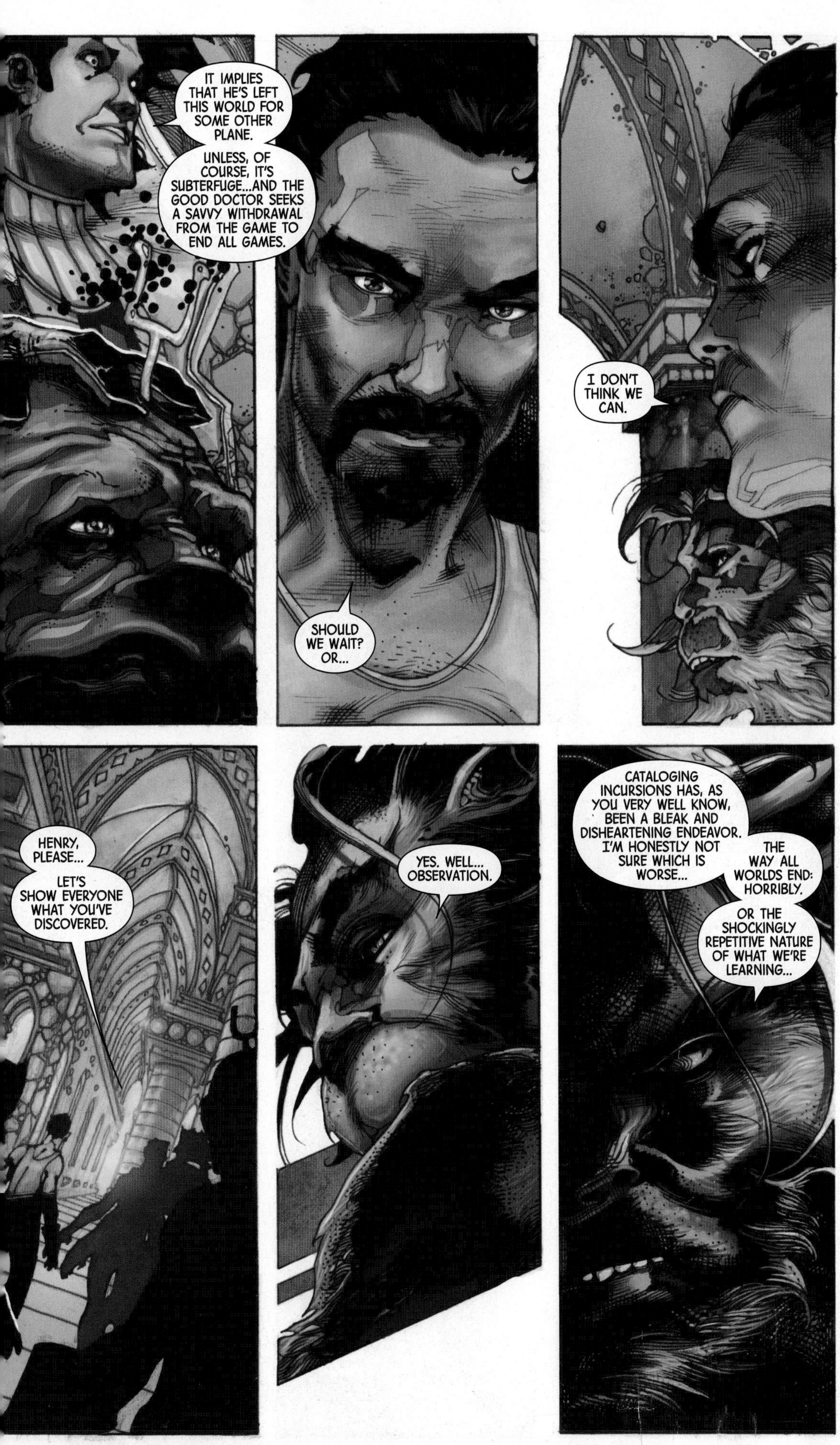

IT IMPLIES THAT HE'S LEFT THIS WORLD FOR SOME OTHER PLANE.
UNLESS, OF COURSE, IT'S SUBTERFUGE...AND THE GOOD DOCTOR SEEKS A SAVVY WITHDRAWAL FROM THE GAME TO END ALL GAMES.
SHOULD WE WAIT? OR...
I DON'T THINK WE CAN.
HENRY, PLEASE...
LET'S SHOW EVERYONE WHAT YOU'VE DISCOVERED.
YES. WELL... OBSERVATION.
CATALOGING INCURSIONS HAS, AS YOU VERY WELL KNOW, BEEN A BLEAK AND DISHEARTENING ENDEAVOR. I'M HONESTLY NOT SURE WHICH IS WORSE...
THE WAY ALL WORLDS END: HORRIBLY.
OR THE SHOCKINGLY REPETITIVE NATURE OF WHAT WE'RE LEARNING...

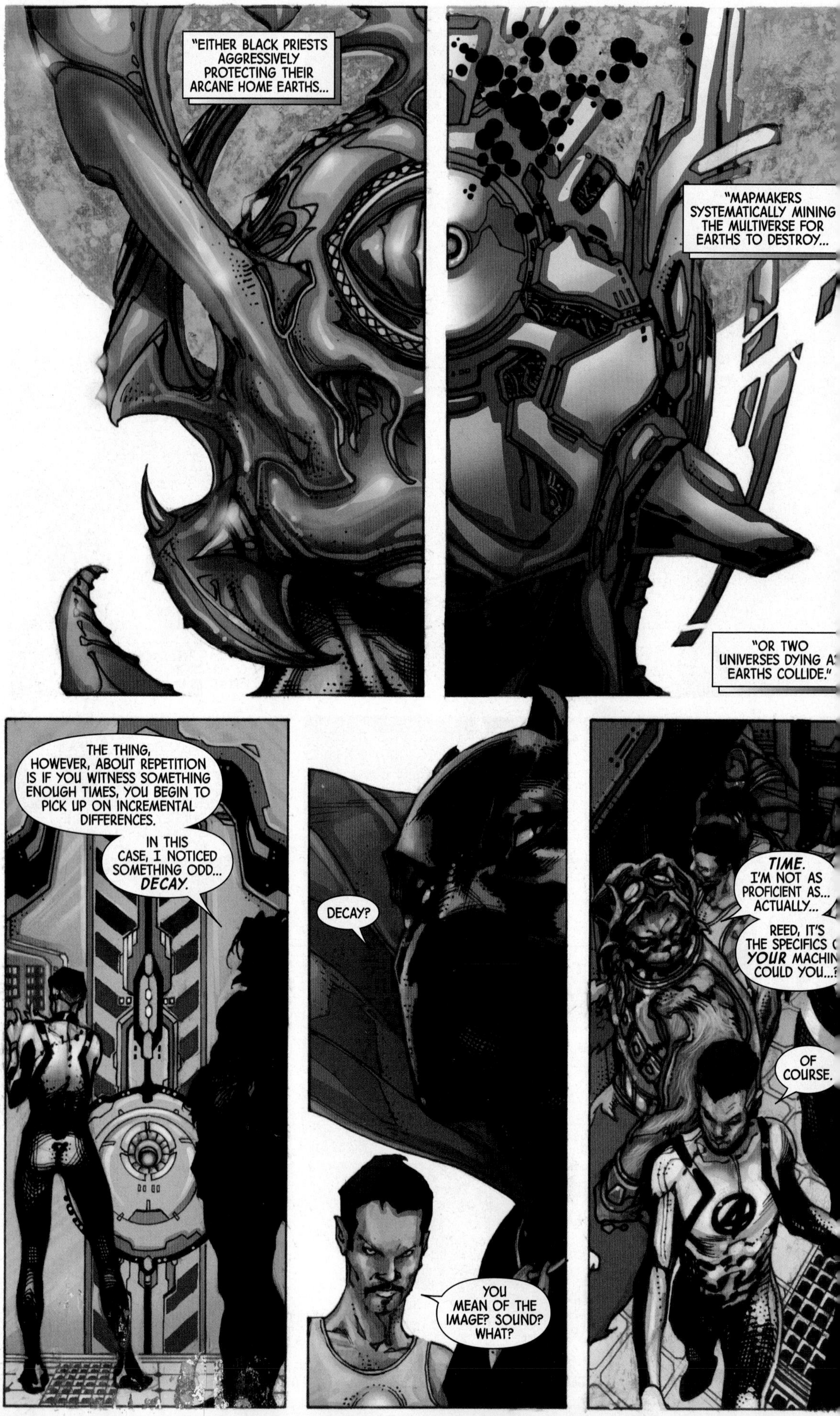

"EITHER BLACK PRIESTS AGGRESSIVELY PROTECTING THEIR ARCANE HOME EARTHS...
"MAPMAKERS SYSTEMATICALLY MINING THE MULTIVERSE FOR EARTHS TO DESTROY...
"OR TWO UNIVERSES DYING A
EARTHS COLLIDE."
THE THING, HOWEVER, ABOUT REPETITION IS IF YOU WITNESS SOMETHING ENOUGH TIMES, YOU BEGIN TO PICK UP ON INCREMENTAL DIFFERENCES.
IN THIS CASE, I NOTICED SOMETHING ODD... *DECAY*.
DECAY?
YOU MEAN OF THE IMAGE? SOUND? WHAT?
TIME. I'M NOT AS PROFICIENT AS... ACTUALLY...
REED, IT'S THE SPECIFICS
YOUR MACHIN
COULD YOU...
OF COURSE.

THINK OF IT LIKE DOPPLER SHIFT.

THE SAME NOISE SOUNDS DIFFERENT APPROACHING YOU THAN MOVING AWAY FROM YOU.

ROUGHLY THE SAME PRINCIPLE APPLIES CELESTIALLY-- RED AND BLUE SHIFT FOR THE CONTRACTION AND EXPANSION OF THE UNIVERSE.

WHAT HENRY NOTICED IS, FUNDAMENTALLY, THIS SAME CONCEPT.

AS YOU KNOW, THE BRIDGE PRIMARILY FUNCTIONS AS AN OBSERVATION DEVICE.

THE DATA SET FOR RUNNING A SEARCH THROUGH BOTH ALL REALITIES AND ALL TIMES IS INFINITE, AND THEREFORE NOT OBSERVABLE. WELL, OBSERVABLE IN THE SENSE THAT--

YOU'RE MAKING MY TEETH HURT, REED.

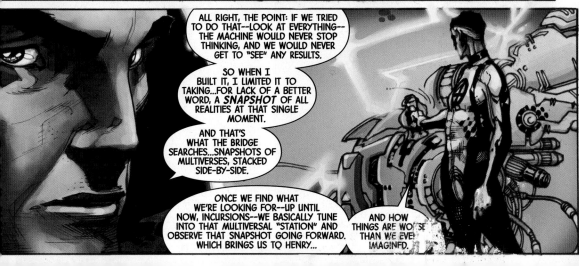

ALL RIGHT, THE POINT: IF WE TRIED TO DO THAT--LOOK AT EVERYTHING-- THE MACHINE WOULD NEVER STOP THINKING, AND WE WOULD NEVER GET TO "SEE" ANY RESULTS.

SO WHEN I BUILT IT, I LIMITED IT TO TAKING...FOR LACK OF A BETTER WORD, A *SNAPSHOT* OF ALL REALITIES AT THAT SINGLE MOMENT.

AND THAT'S WHAT THE BRIDGE SEARCHES...SNAPSHOTS OF MULTIVERSES, STACKED SIDE-BY-SIDE.

ONCE WE FIND WHAT WE'RE LOOKING FOR--UP UNTIL NOW, INCURSIONS--WE BASICALLY TUNE INTO THAT MULTIVERSAL "STATION" AND OBSERVE THAT SNAPSHOT GOING FORWARD. WHICH BRINGS US TO HENRY...

AND HOW THINGS ARE WORSE THAN WE EVER IMAGINED.

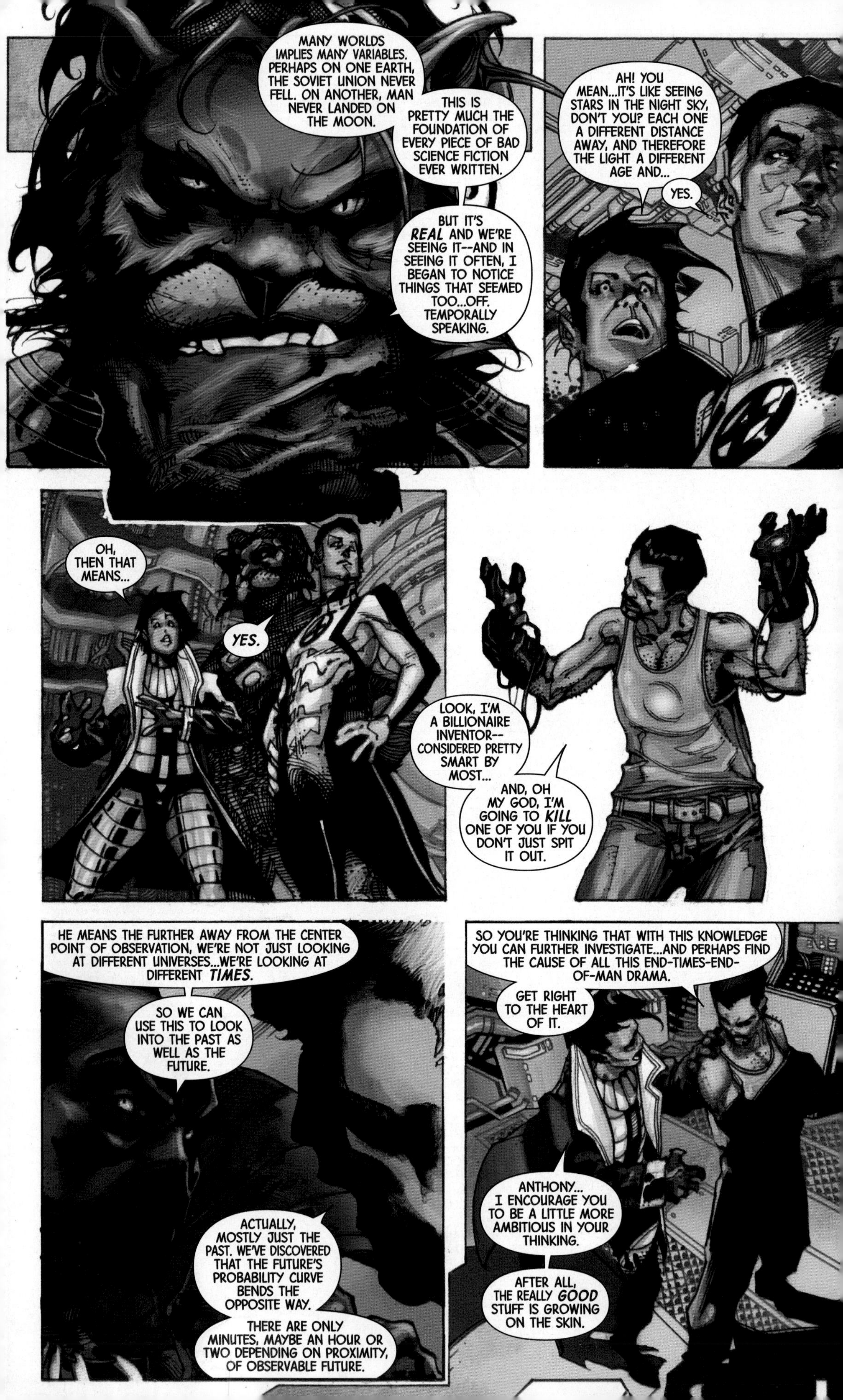
MANY WORLDS IMPLIES MANY VARIABLES. PERHAPS ON ONE EARTH, THE SOVIET UNION NEVER FELL. ON ANOTHER, MAN NEVER LANDED ON THE MOON.
THIS IS PRETTY MUCH THE FOUNDATION OF EVERY PIECE OF BAD SCIENCE FICTION EVER WRITTEN.
BUT IT'S *REAL* AND WE'RE SEEING IT--AND IN SEEING IT OFTEN, I BEGAN TO NOTICE THINGS THAT SEEMED TOO...OFF. TEMPORALLY SPEAKING.
AH! YOU MEAN...IT'S LIKE SEEING STARS IN THE NIGHT SKY, DON'T YOU? EACH ONE A DIFFERENT DISTANCE AWAY, AND THEREFORE THE LIGHT A DIFFERENT AGE AND...
YES.
OH, THEN THAT MEANS...
YES.
LOOK, I'M A BILLIONAIRE INVENTOR-- CONSIDERED PRETTY SMART BY MOST...
AND, OH MY GOD, I'M GOING TO *KILL* ONE OF YOU IF YOU DON'T JUST SPIT IT OUT.
HE MEANS THE FURTHER AWAY FROM THE CENTER POINT OF OBSERVATION, WE'RE NOT JUST LOOKING AT DIFFERENT UNIVERSES...WE'RE LOOKING AT DIFFERENT *TIMES*.
SO WE CAN USE THIS TO LOOK INTO THE PAST AS WELL AS THE FUTURE.
ACTUALLY, MOSTLY JUST THE PAST. WE'VE DISCOVERED THAT THE FUTURE'S PROBABILITY CURVE BENDS THE OPPOSITE WAY.
THERE ARE ONLY MINUTES, MAYBE AN HOUR OR TWO DEPENDING ON PROXIMITY, OF OBSERVABLE FUTURE.
SO YOU'RE THINKING THAT WITH THIS KNOWLEDGE YOU CAN FURTHER INVESTIGATE...AND PERHAPS FIND THE CAUSE OF ALL THIS END-TIMES-END-OF-MAN DRAMA.
GET RIGHT TO THE HEART OF IT.
ANTHONY... I ENCOURAGE YOU TO BE A LITTLE MORE AMBITIOUS IN YOUR THINKING.
AFTER ALL, THE REALLY *GOOD* STUFF IS GROWING ON THE SKIN.

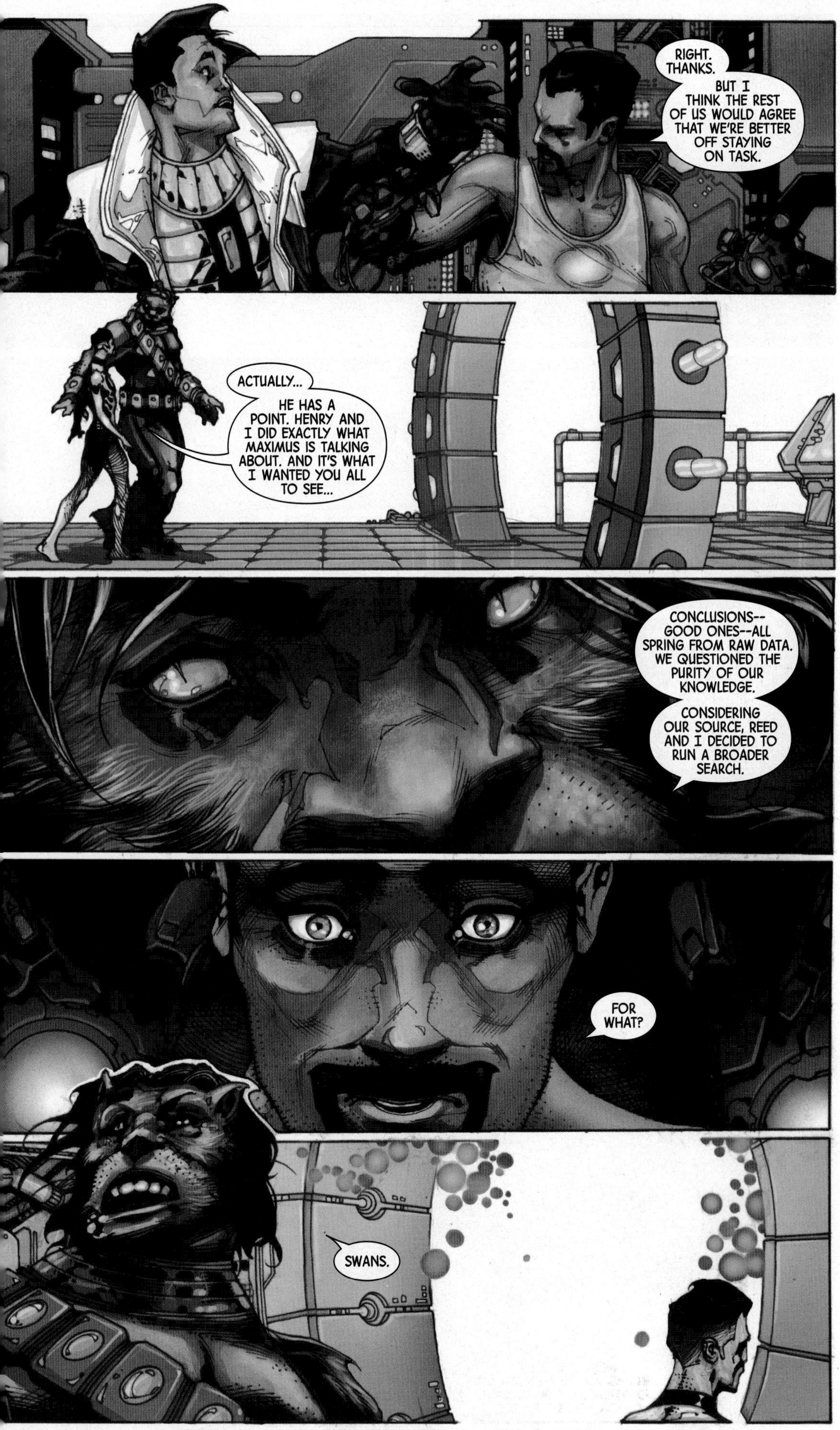
RIGHT. THANKS.
BUT I THINK THE REST OF US WOULD AGREE THAT WE'RE BETTER OFF STAYING ON TASK.
ACTUALLY...
HE HAS A POINT. HENRY AND I DID EXACTLY WHAT MAXIMUS IS TALKING ABOUT. AND IT'S WHAT I WANTED YOU ALL TO SEE...
CONCLUSIONS--GOOD ONES--ALL SPRING FROM RAW DATA. WE QUESTIONED THE PURITY OF OUR KNOWLEDGE.
CONSIDERING OUR SOURCE, REED AND I DECIDED TO RUN A BROADER SEARCH.
FOR WHAT?
SWANS.

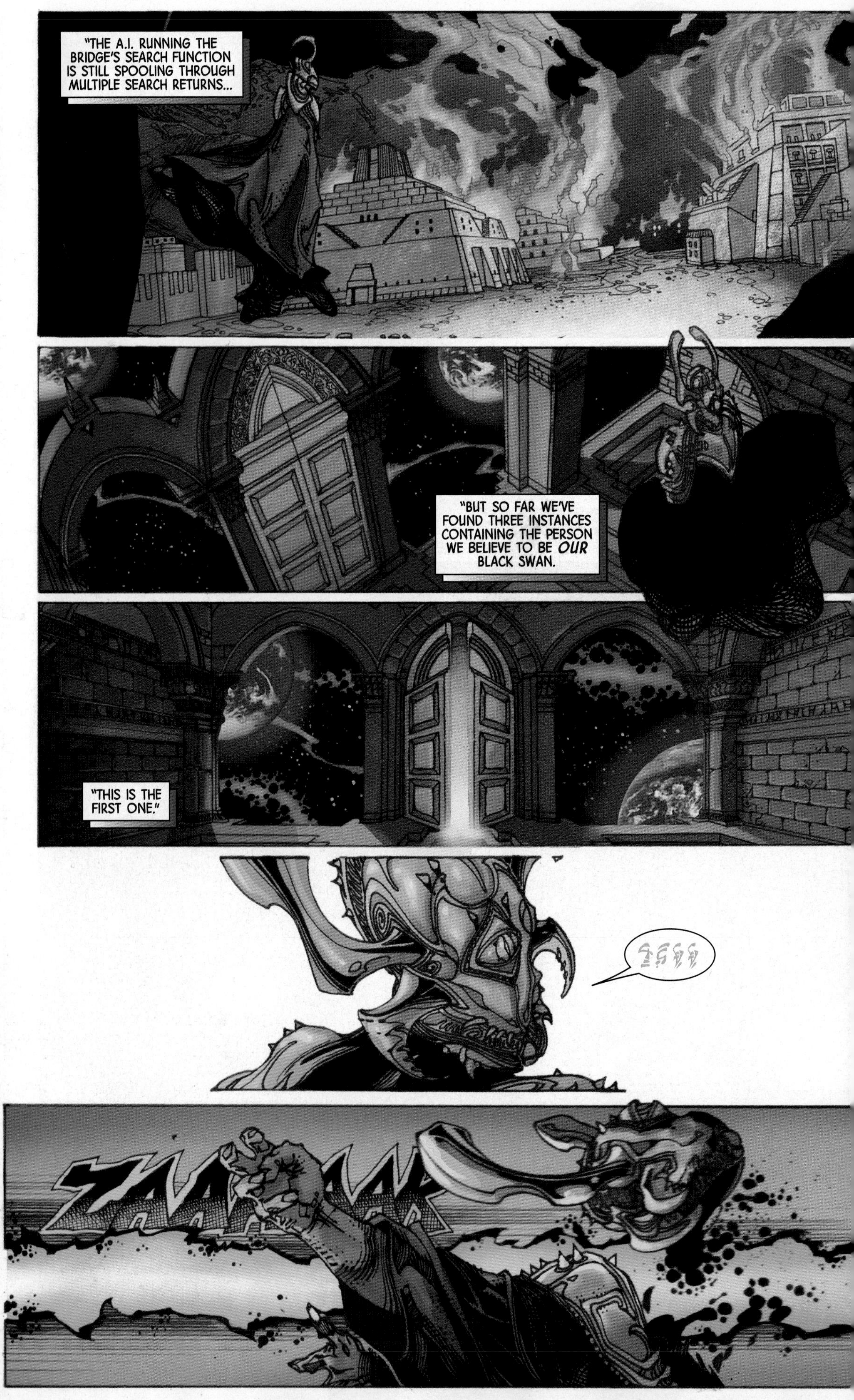
"THE A.I. RUNNING THE BRIDGE'S SEARCH FUNCTION IS STILL SPOOLING THROUGH MULTIPLE SEARCH RETURNS...
"BUT SO FAR WE'VE FOUND THREE INSTANCES CONTAINING THE PERSON WE BELIEVE TO BE *OUR* BLACK SWAN.
"THIS IS THE FIRST ONE."

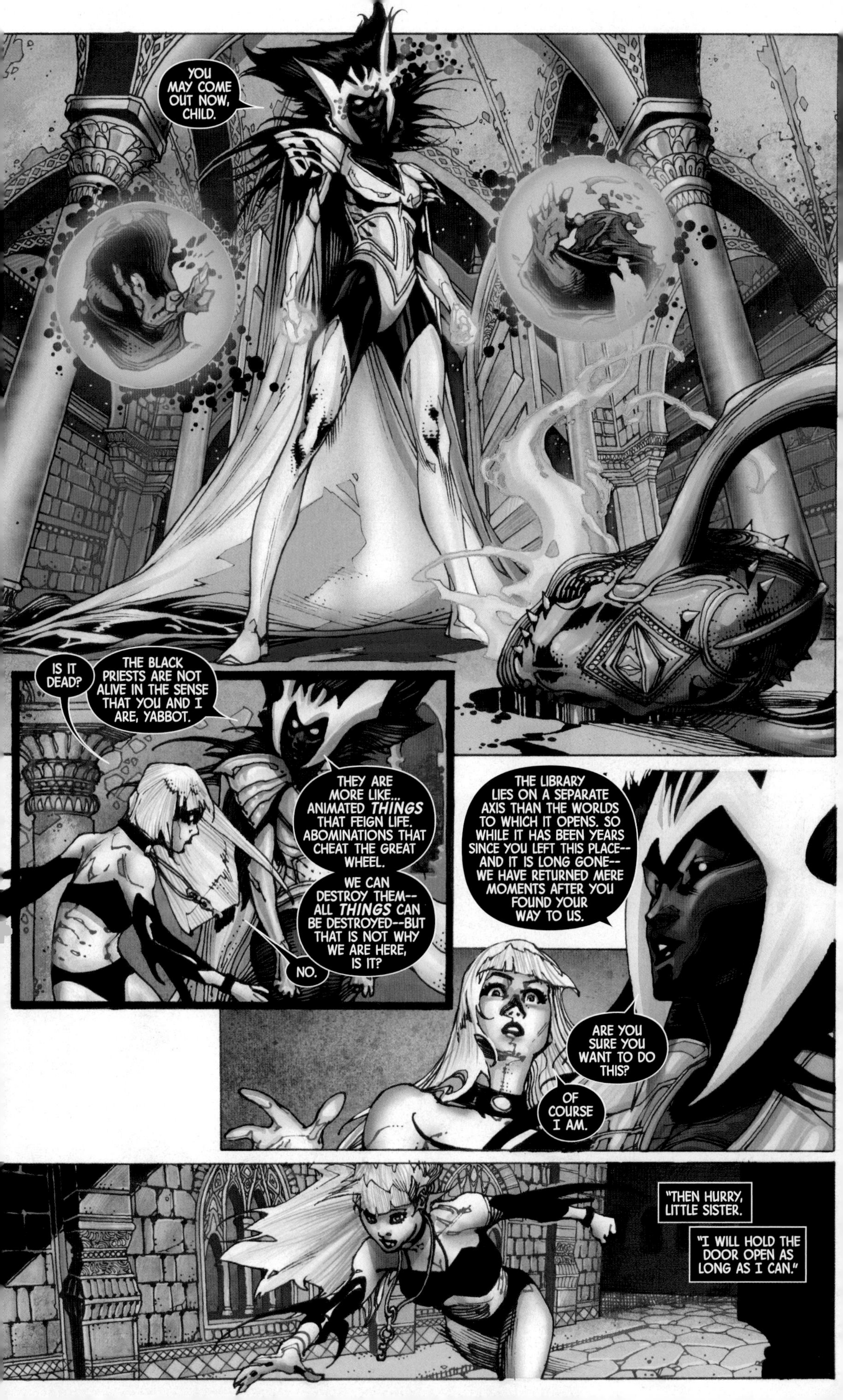

YOU MAY COME OUT NOW, CHILD.
IS IT DEAD?
THE BLACK PRIESTS ARE NOT ALIVE IN THE SENSE THAT YOU AND I ARE, YABBOT.
THEY ARE MORE LIKE... ANIMATED THINGS THAT FEIGN LIFE. ABOMINATIONS THAT CHEAT THE GREAT WHEEL.
WE CAN DESTROY THEM--ALL THINGS CAN BE DESTROYED--BUT THAT IS NOT WHY WE ARE HERE, IS IT?
NO.
THE LIBRARY LIES ON A SEPARATE AXIS THAN THE WORLDS TO WHICH IT OPENS. SO WHILE IT HAS BEEN YEARS SINCE YOU LEFT THIS PLACE--AND IT IS LONG GONE--WE HAVE RETURNED MERE MOMENTS AFTER YOU FOUND YOUR WAY TO US.
ARE YOU SURE YOU WANT TO DO THIS?
OF COURSE I AM.
"THEN HURRY, LITTLE SISTER.
"I WILL HOLD THE DOOR OPEN AS LONG AS I CAN."

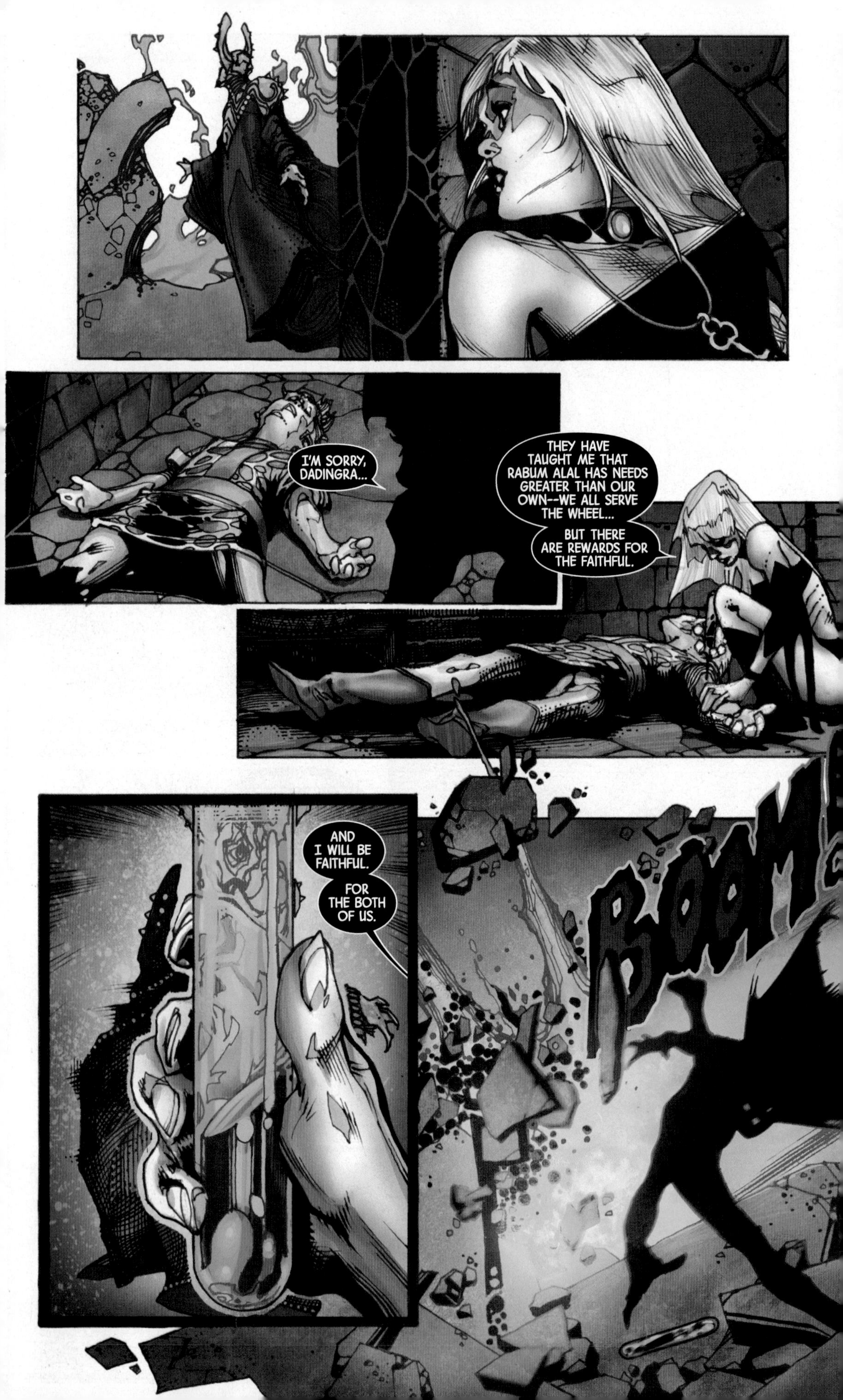
I'M SORRY, DADINGRA...
THEY HAVE TAUGHT ME THAT RABUM ALAL HAS NEEDS GREATER THAN OUR OWN--WE ALL SERVE THE WHEEL...
BUT THERE ARE REWARDS FOR THE FAITHFUL.
AND I WILL BE FAITHFUL.
FOR THE BOTH OF US.
BOOM

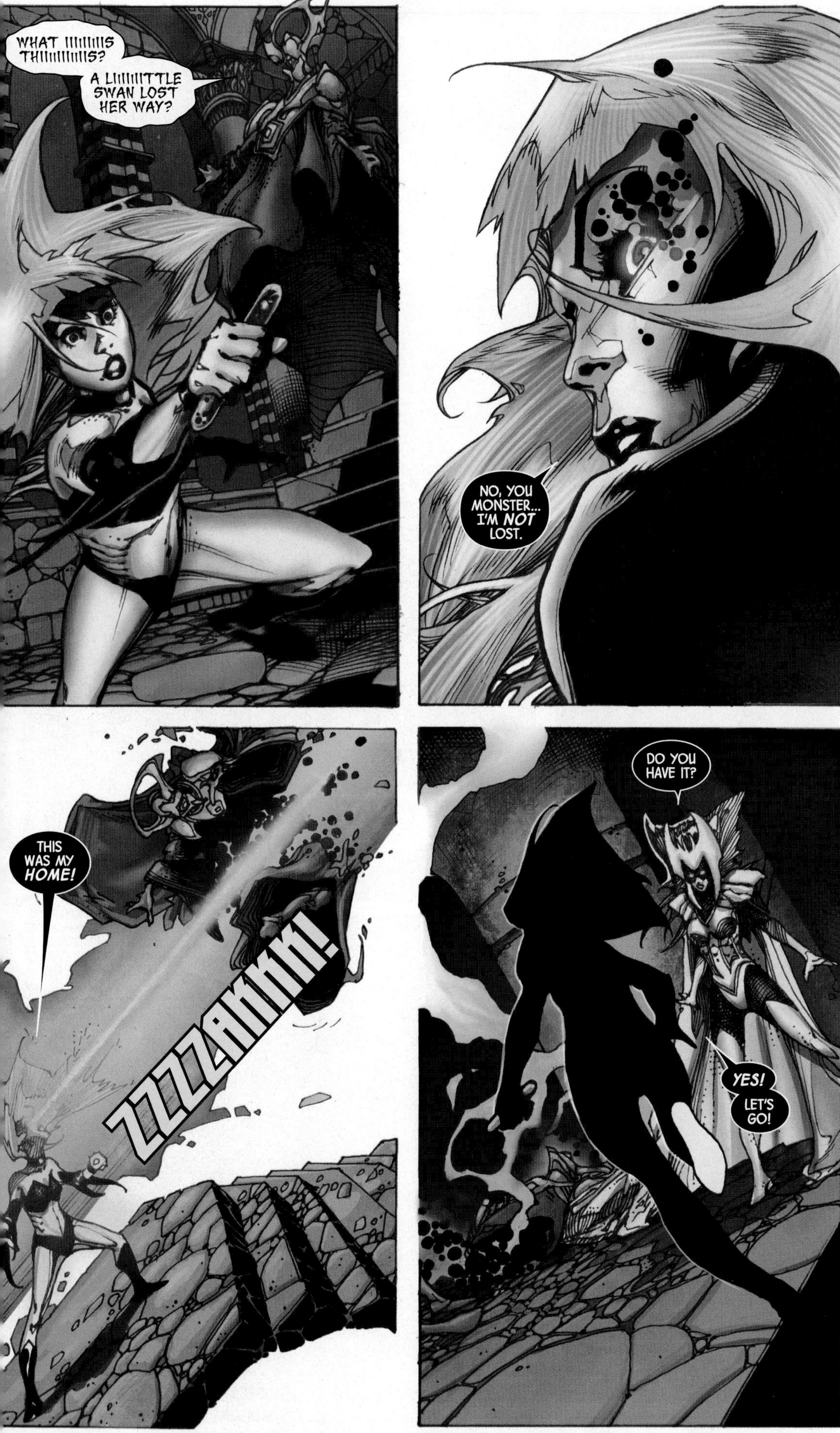
WHAT IIIIIIIIS THIIIIIIIIIIS?
A LIIIIIIITTLE SWAN LOST HER WAY?
NO, YOU MONSTER... I'M *NOT* LOST.
THIS WAS MY *HOME!*
ZZZZZAKKKK!
DO YOU HAVE IT?
YES!
LET'S GO!

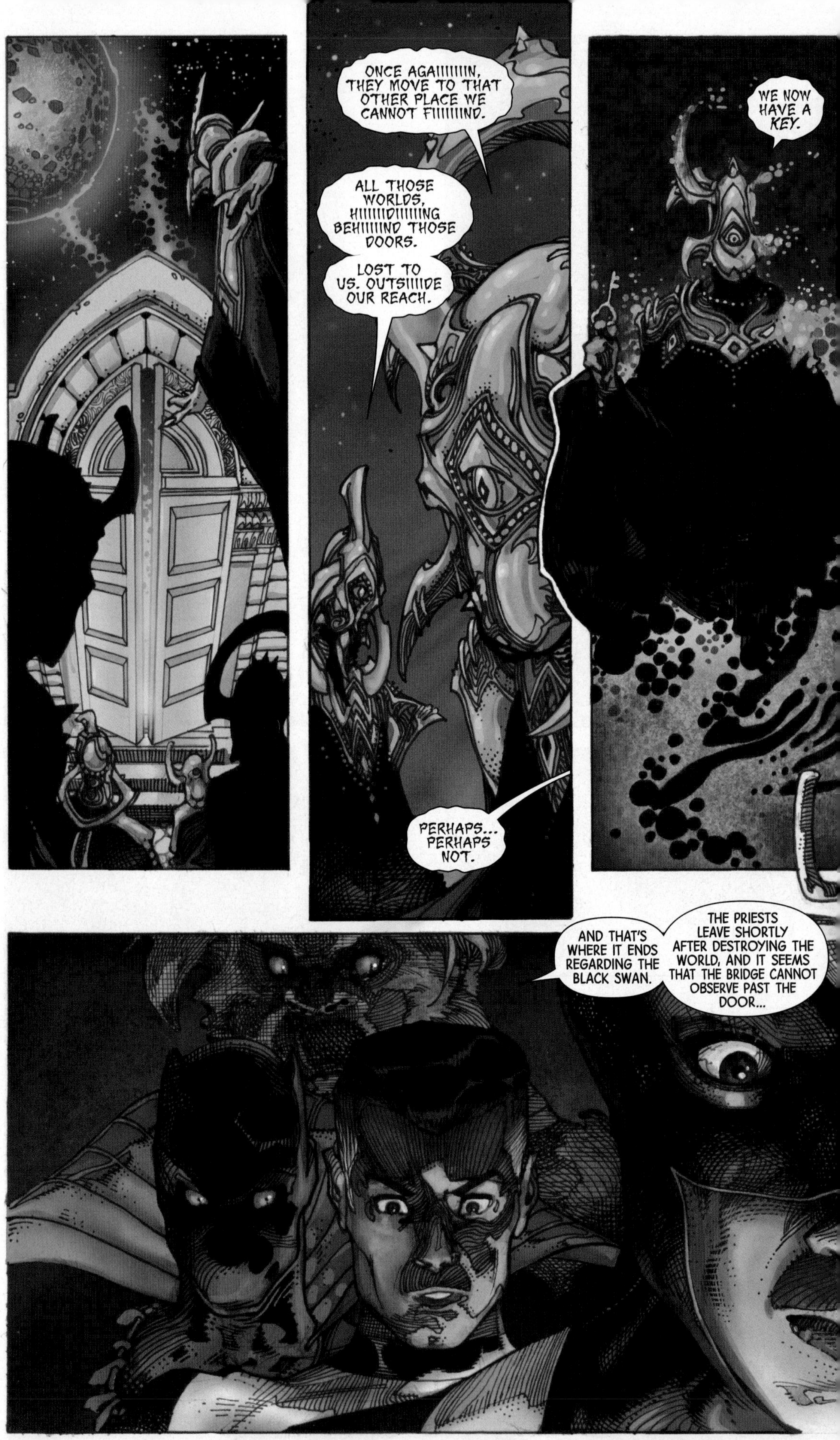
ONCE AGAIIIIIIIN, THEY MOVE TO THAT OTHER PLACE WE CANNOT FIIIIIIIND.
ALL THOSE WORLDS, HIIIIIIDIIIIIING BEHIIIIIND THOSE DOORS.
LOST TO US. OUTSIIIIIDE OUR REACH.
PERHAPS... PERHAPS NOT.
WE NOW HAVE A KEY.
AND THAT'S WHERE IT ENDS REGARDING THE BLACK SWAN.
THE PRIESTS LEAVE SHORTLY AFTER DESTROYING THE WORLD, AND IT SEEMS THAT THE BRIDGE CANNOT OBSERVE PAST THE DOOR...

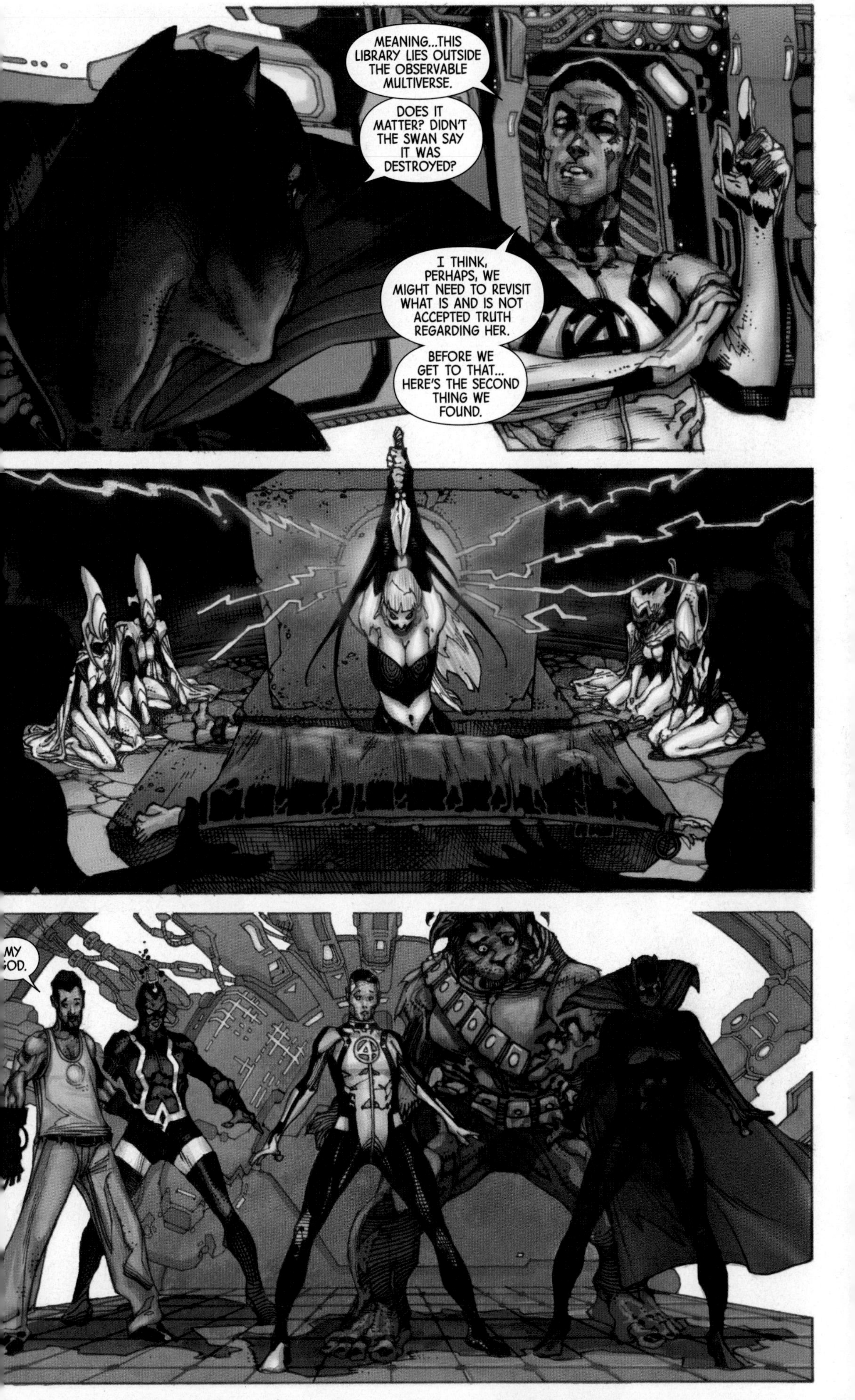

MEANING...THIS LIBRARY LIES OUTSIDE THE OBSERVABLE MULTIVERSE.
DOES IT MATTER? DIDN'T THE SWAN SAY IT WAS DESTROYED?
I THINK, PERHAPS, WE MIGHT NEED TO REVISIT WHAT IS AND IS NOT ACCEPTED TRUTH REGARDING HER.
BEFORE WE GET TO THAT... HERE'S THE SECOND THING WE FOUND.
MY GOD.

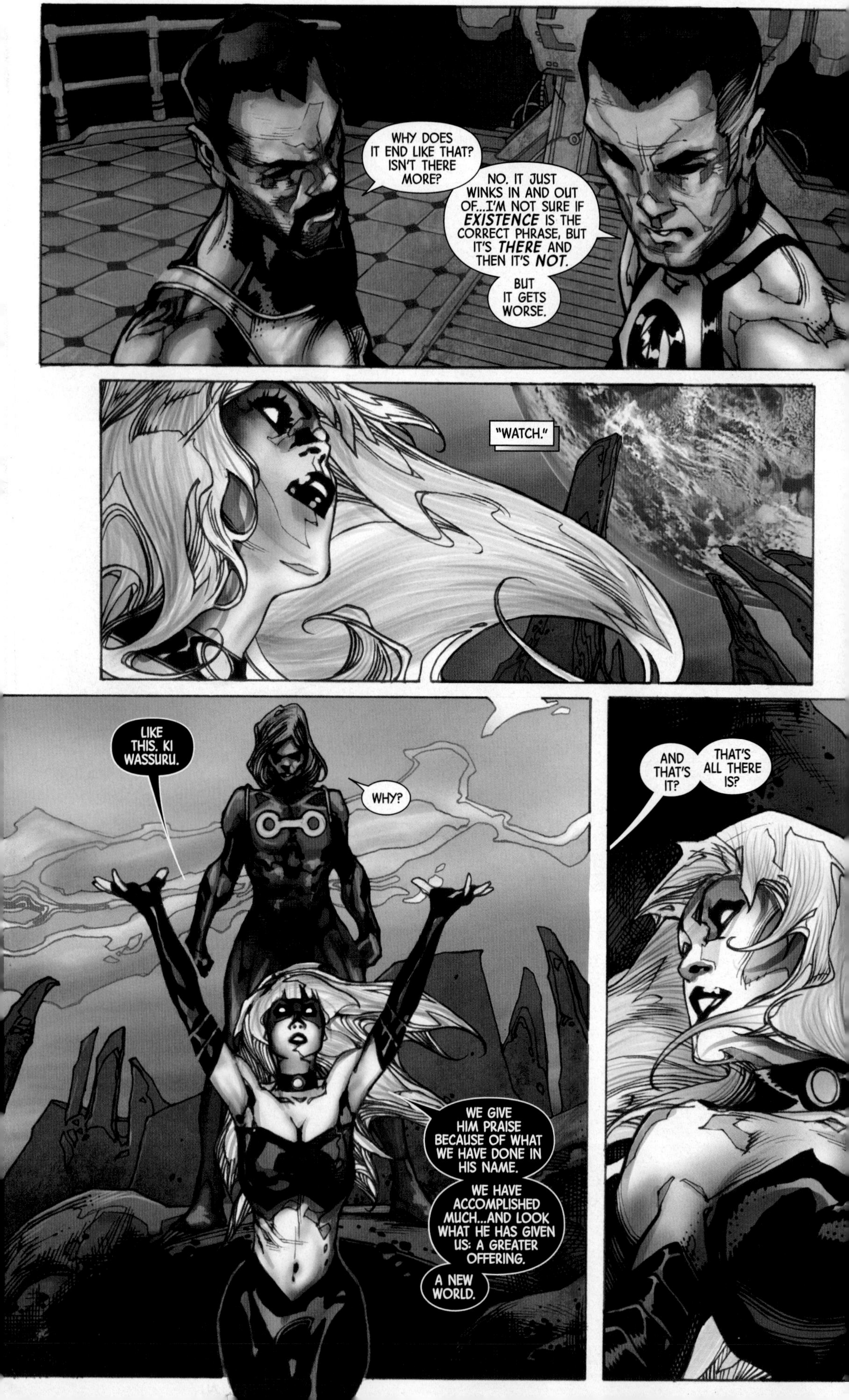
WHY DOES IT END LIKE THAT? ISN'T THERE MORE?
NO. IT JUST WINKS IN AND OUT OF...I'M NOT SURE IF EXISTENCE IS THE CORRECT PHRASE, BUT IT'S THERE AND THEN IT'S NOT.
BUT IT GETS WORSE.
"WATCH."
LIKE THIS, KI WASSURU.
WHY?
WE GIVE HIM PRAISE BECAUSE OF WHAT WE HAVE DONE IN HIS NAME.
WE HAVE ACCOMPLISHED MUCH...AND LOOK WHAT HE HAS GIVEN US: A GREATER OFFERING.
A NEW WORLD.
AND THAT'S IT?
THAT'S ALL THERE IS?

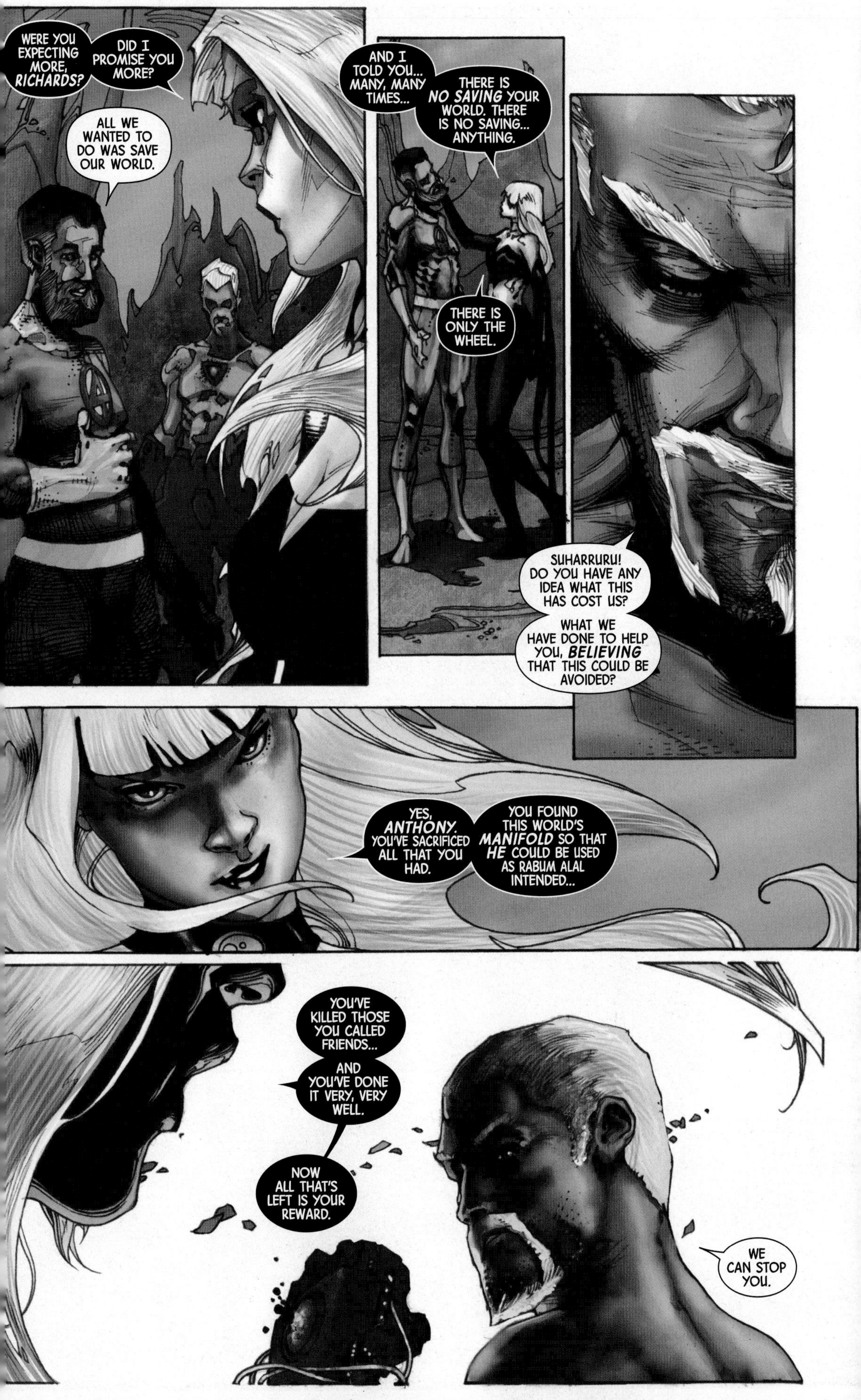
WERE YOU EXPECTING MORE, RICHARDS?
DID I PROMISE YOU MORE?
ALL WE WANTED TO DO WAS SAVE OUR WORLD.
AND I TOLD YOU... MANY, MANY TIMES...
THERE IS NO SAVING YOUR WORLD. THERE IS NO SAVING... ANYTHING.
THERE IS ONLY THE WHEEL.
SUHARRURU! DO YOU HAVE ANY IDEA WHAT THIS HAS COST US?
WHAT WE HAVE DONE TO HELP YOU, BELIEVING THAT THIS COULD BE AVOIDED?
YES, ANTHONY. YOU'VE SACRIFICED ALL THAT YOU HAD.
YOU FOUND THIS WORLD'S MANIFOLD SO THAT HE COULD BE USED AS RABUM ALAL INTENDED...
YOU'VE KILLED THOSE YOU CALLED FRIENDS...
AND YOU'VE DONE IT VERY, VERY WELL.
NOW ALL THAT'S LEFT IS YOUR REWARD.
WE CAN STOP YOU.

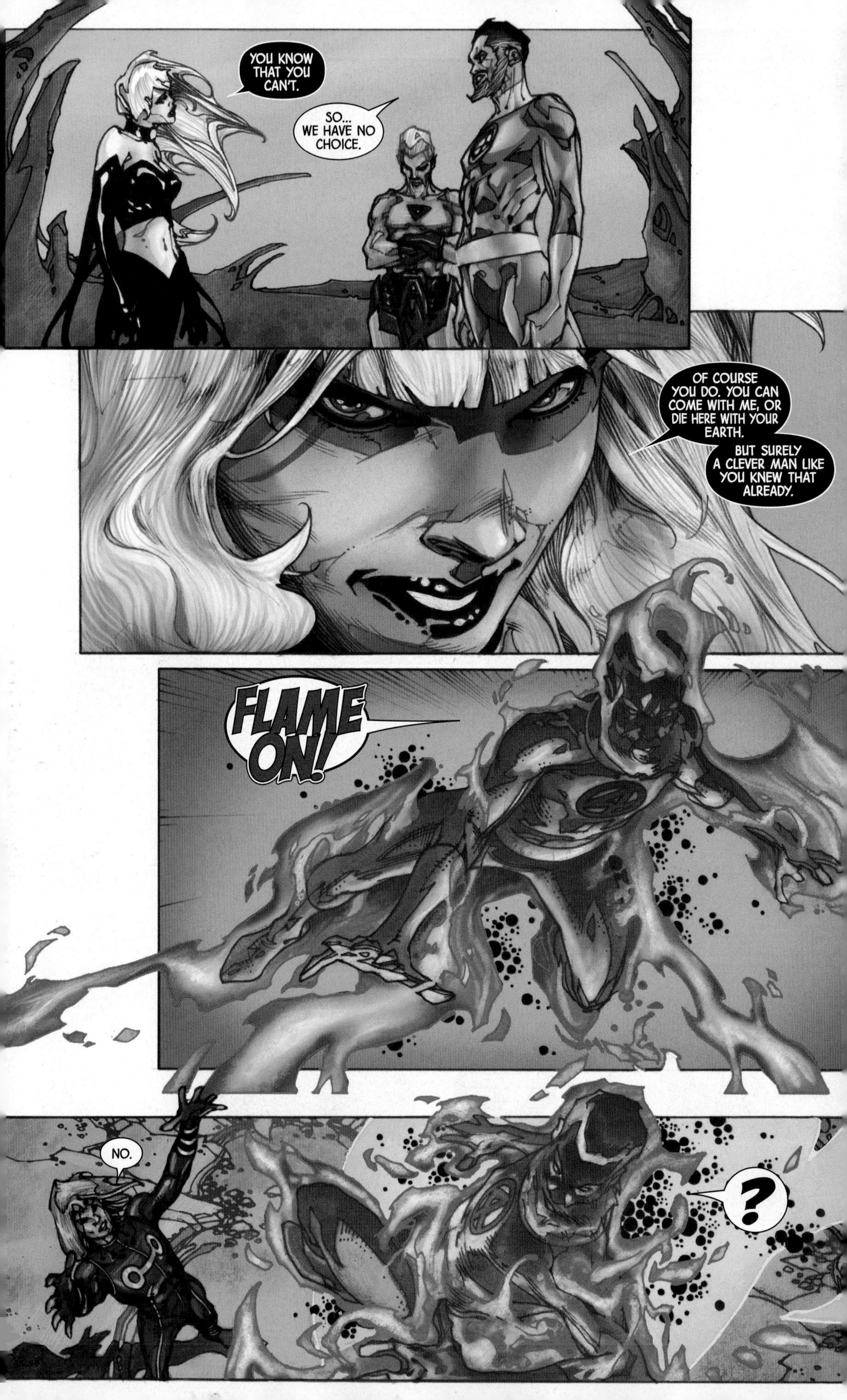
YOU KNOW THAT YOU CAN'T.
SO... WE HAVE NO CHOICE.
OF COURSE YOU DO. YOU CAN COME WITH ME, OR DIE HERE WITH YOUR EARTH.
BUT SURELY A CLEVER MAN LIKE YOU KNEW THAT ALREADY.
FLAME ON!
NO.
?

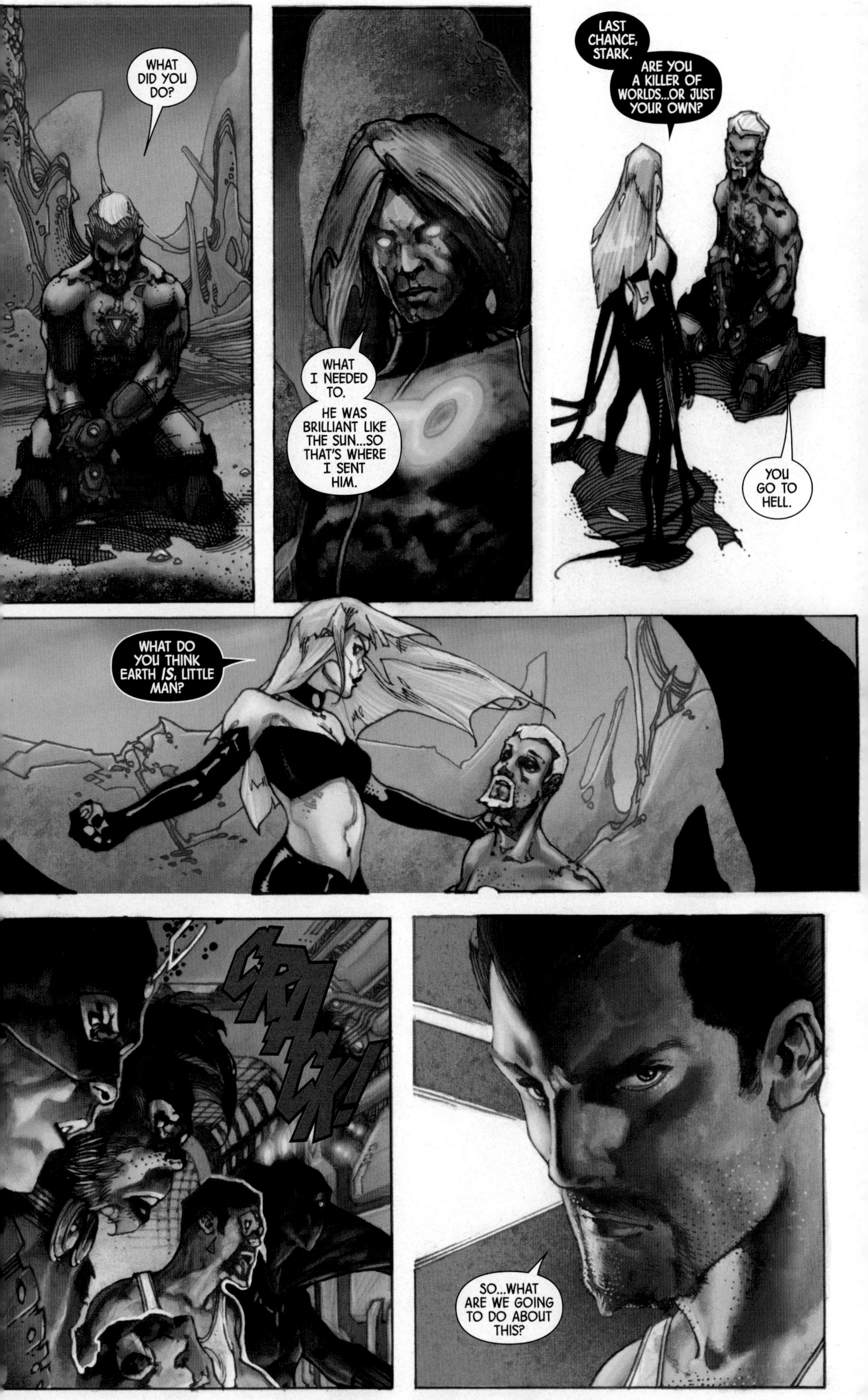
WHAT DID YOU DO?
WHAT I NEEDED TO.
HE WAS BRILLIANT LIKE THE SUN...SO THAT'S WHERE I SENT HIM.
LAST CHANCE, STARK.
ARE YOU A KILLER OF WORLDS...OR JUST YOUR OWN?
YOU GO TO HELL.
WHAT DO YOU THINK EARTH *IS*, LITTLE MAN?
CRACK!
SO...WHAT ARE WE GOING TO DO ABOUT THIS?

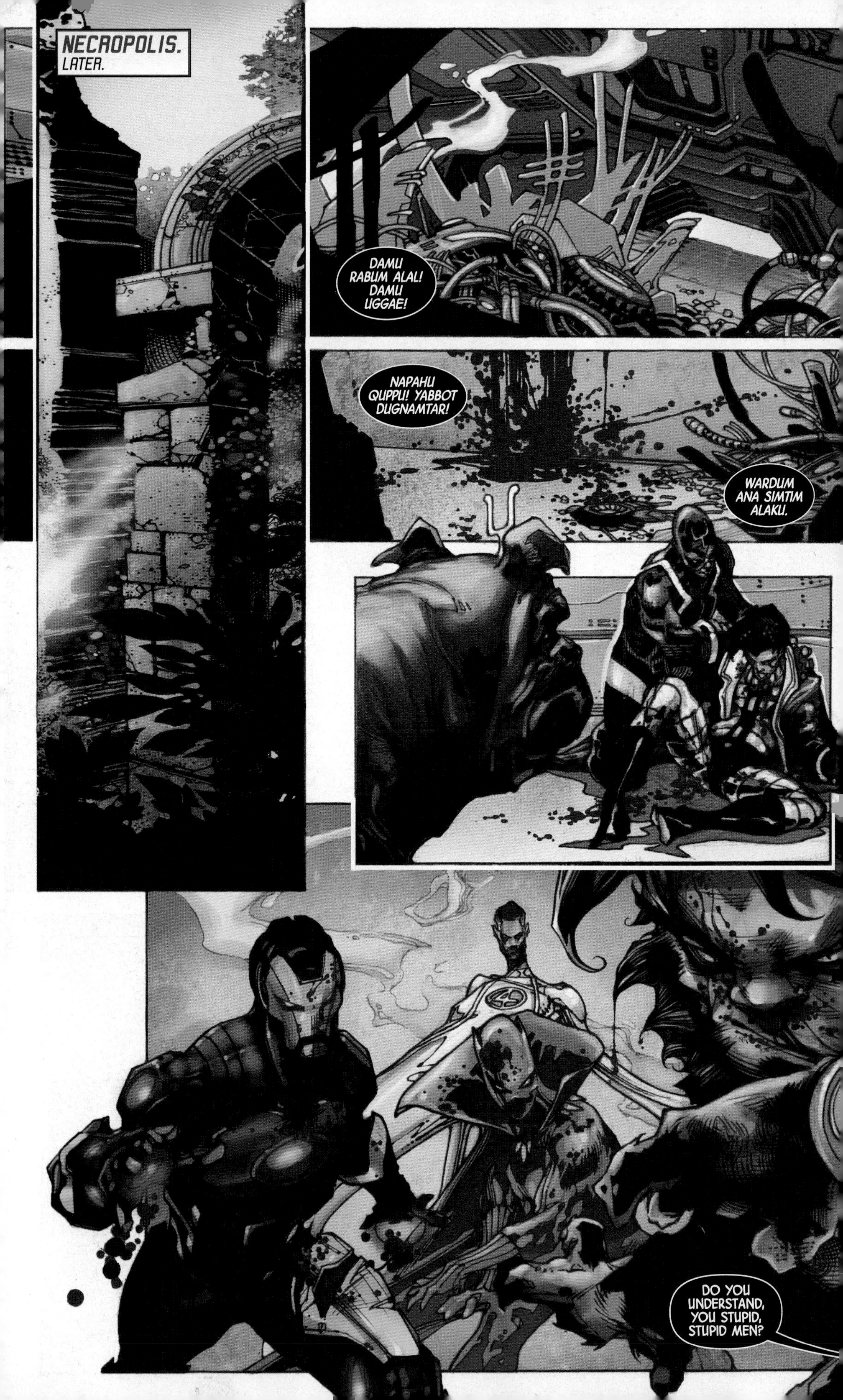
NECROPOLIS.
LATER.
DAMU RABUM ALAL! DAMU UGGAE!
NAPAHU QUPPU! YABBOT DUGNAMTAR!
WARDUM ANA SIMTIM ALAKU.
DO YOU UNDERSTAND, YOU STUPID, STUPID MEN?

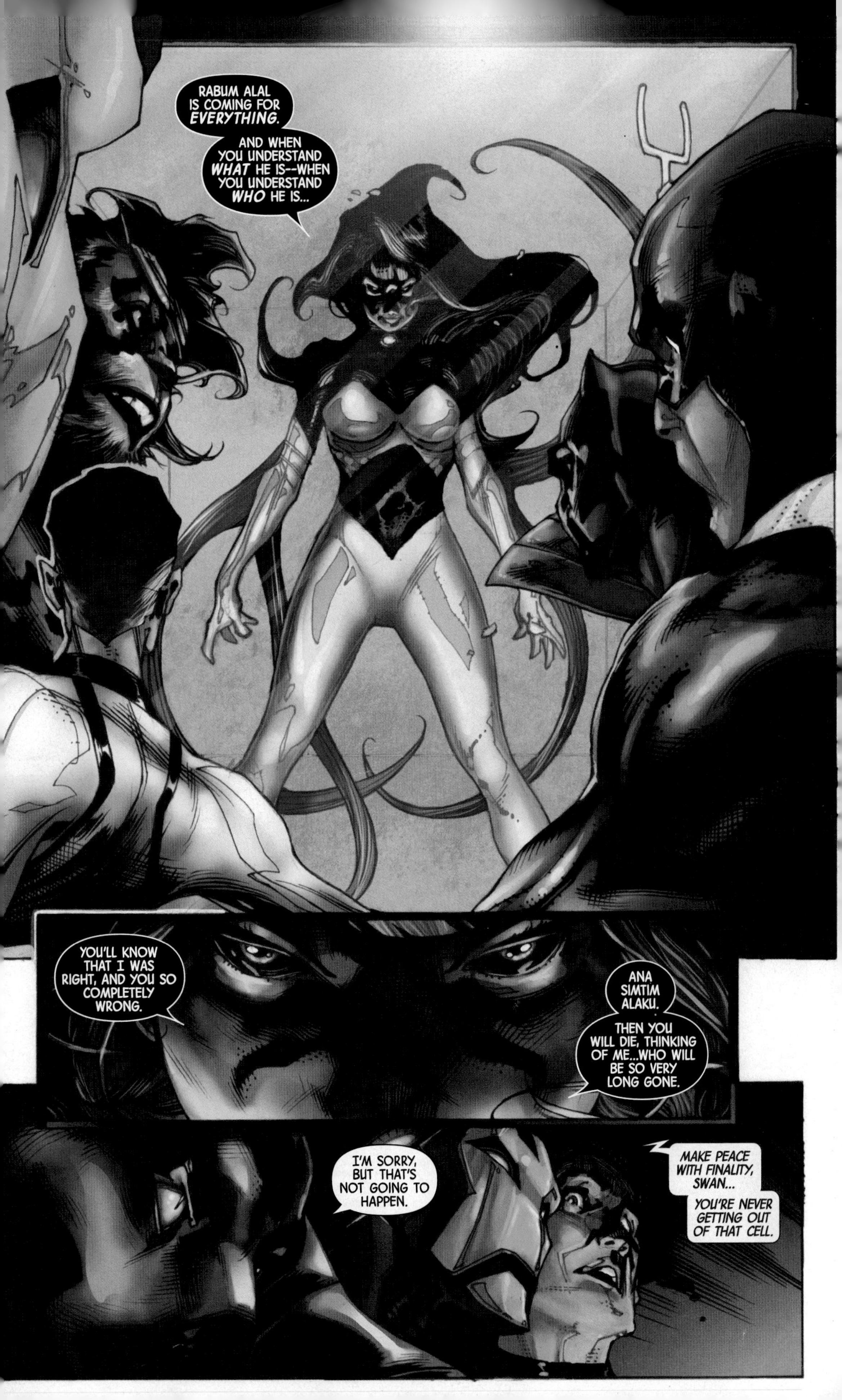
RABUM ALAL IS COMING FOR *EVERYTHING*.
AND WHEN YOU UNDERSTAND *WHAT* HE IS--WHEN YOU UNDERSTAND *WHO* HE IS...
YOU'LL KNOW THAT I WAS RIGHT, AND YOU SO COMPLETELY WRONG.
ANA SIMTIM ALAKU.
THEN YOU WILL DIE, THINKING OF ME...WHO WILL BE SO VERY LONG GONE.
I'M SORRY, BUT THAT'S NOT GOING TO HAPPEN.
MAKE PEACE WITH FINALITY, SWAN...
YOU'RE NEVER GETTING OUT OF THAT CELL.

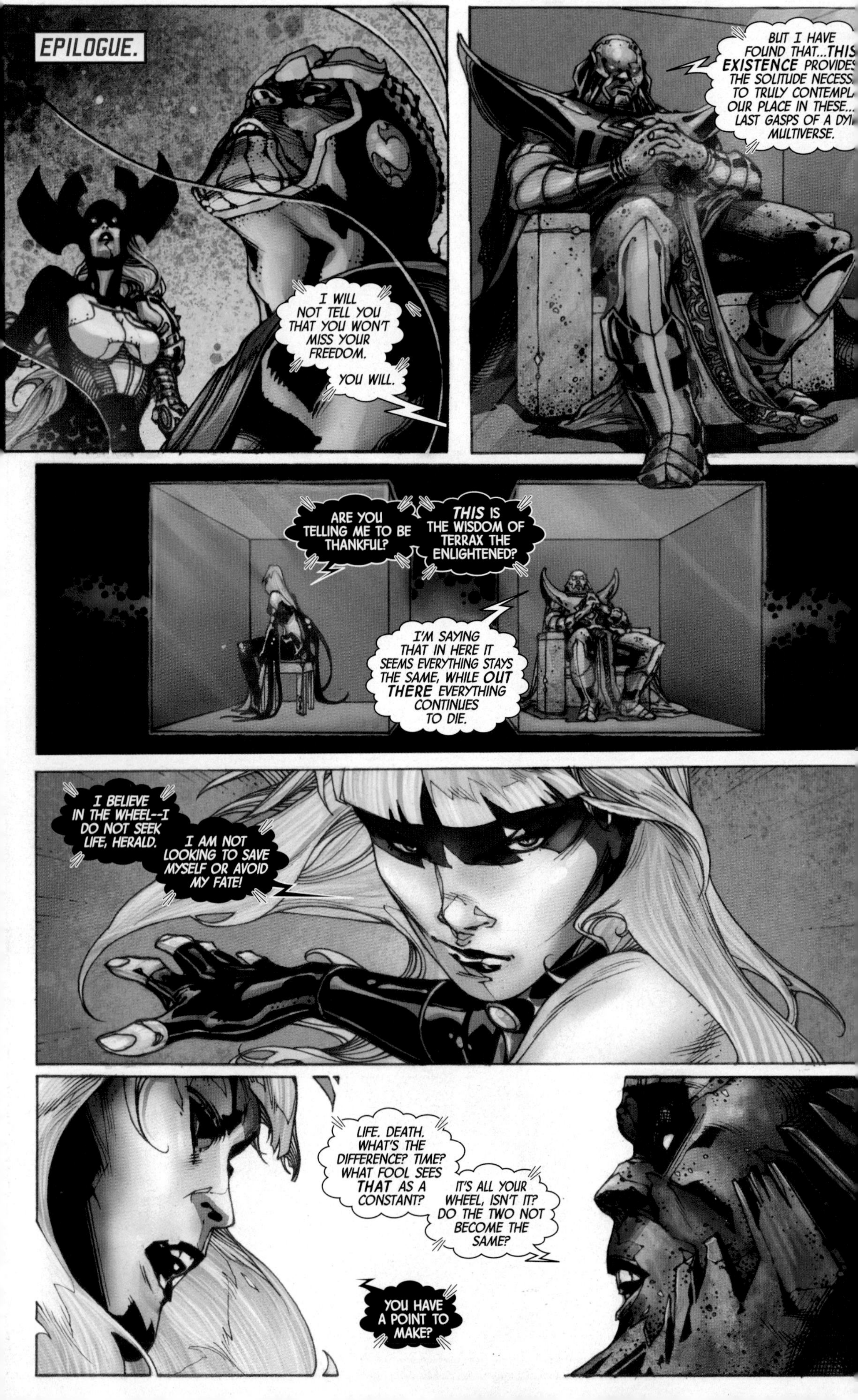
EPILOGUE.
I WILL NOT TELL YOU THAT YOU WON'T MISS YOUR FREEDOM.
YOU WILL.
BUT I HAVE FOUND THAT...THIS EXISTENCE PROVIDES THE SOLITUDE NECESS TO TRULY CONTEMPL OUR PLACE IN THESE... LAST GASPS OF A DYI MULTIVERSE.
ARE YOU TELLING ME TO BE THANKFUL?
THIS IS THE WISDOM OF TERRAX THE ENLIGHTENED?
I'M SAYING THAT IN HERE IT SEEMS EVERYTHING STAYS THE SAME, WHILE OUT THERE EVERYTHING CONTINUES TO DIE.
I BELIEVE IN THE WHEEL--I DO NOT SEEK LIFE, HERALD.
I AM NOT LOOKING TO SAVE MYSELF OR AVOID MY FATE!
LIFE. DEATH. WHAT'S THE DIFFERENCE? TIME? WHAT FOOL SEES THAT AS A CONSTANT?
IT'S ALL YOUR WHEEL, ISN'T IT? DO THE TWO NOT BECOME THE SAME?
YOU HAVE A POINT TO MAKE?

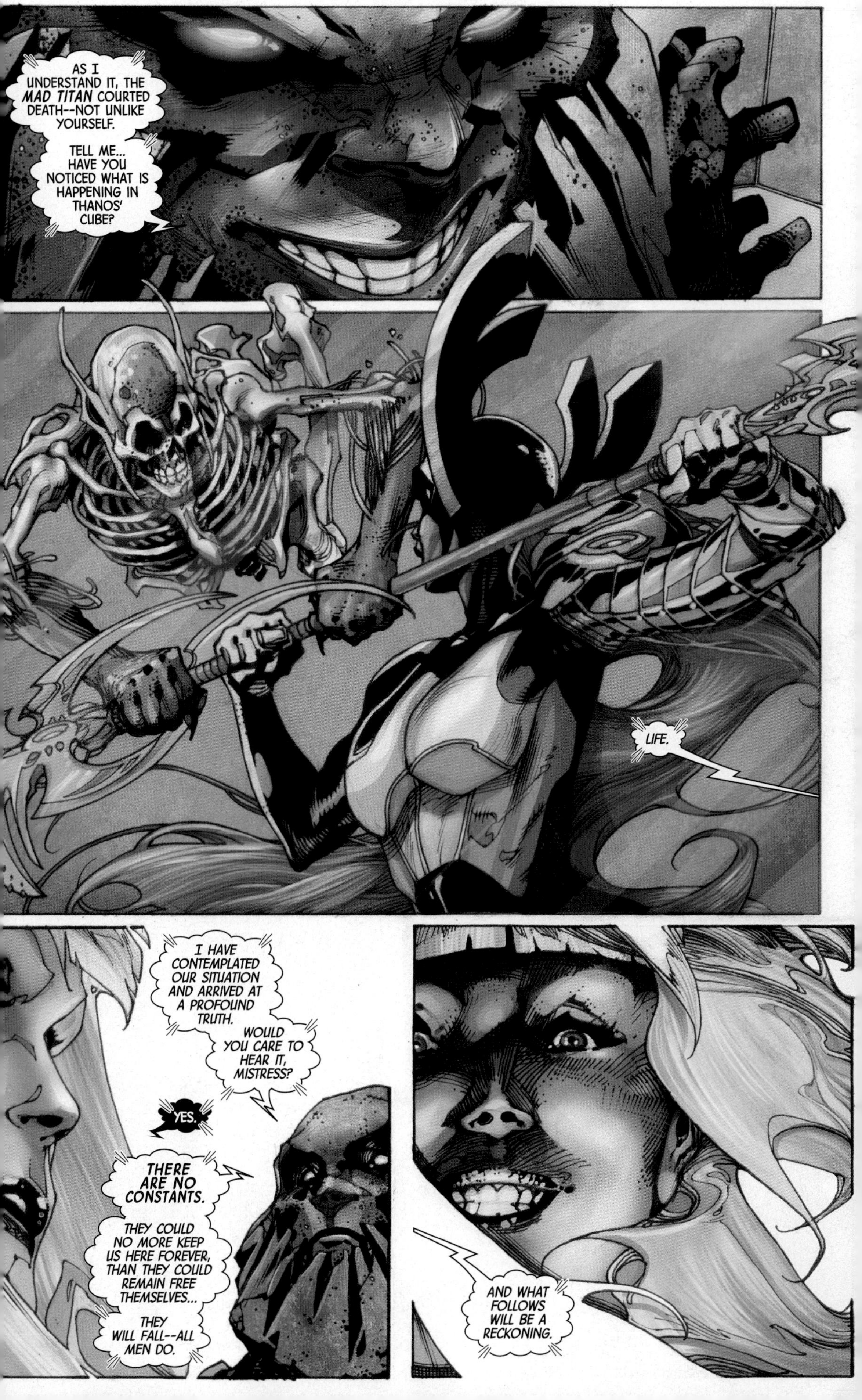

AS I UNDERSTAND IT, THE MAD TITAN COURTED DEATH--NOT UNLIKE YOURSELF.
TELL ME... HAVE YOU NOTICED WHAT IS HAPPENING IN THANOS' CUBE?
LIFE.
I HAVE CONTEMPLATED OUR SITUATION AND ARRIVED AT A PROFOUND TRUTH.
WOULD YOU CARE TO HEAR IT, MISTRESS?
YES.
THERE ARE NO CONSTANTS.
THEY COULD NO MORE KEEP US HERE FOREVER, THAN THEY COULD REMAIN FREE THEMSELVES...
THEY WILL FALL--ALL MEN DO.
AND WHAT FOLLOWS WILL BE A RECKONING.

"A PERFECT WORLD"

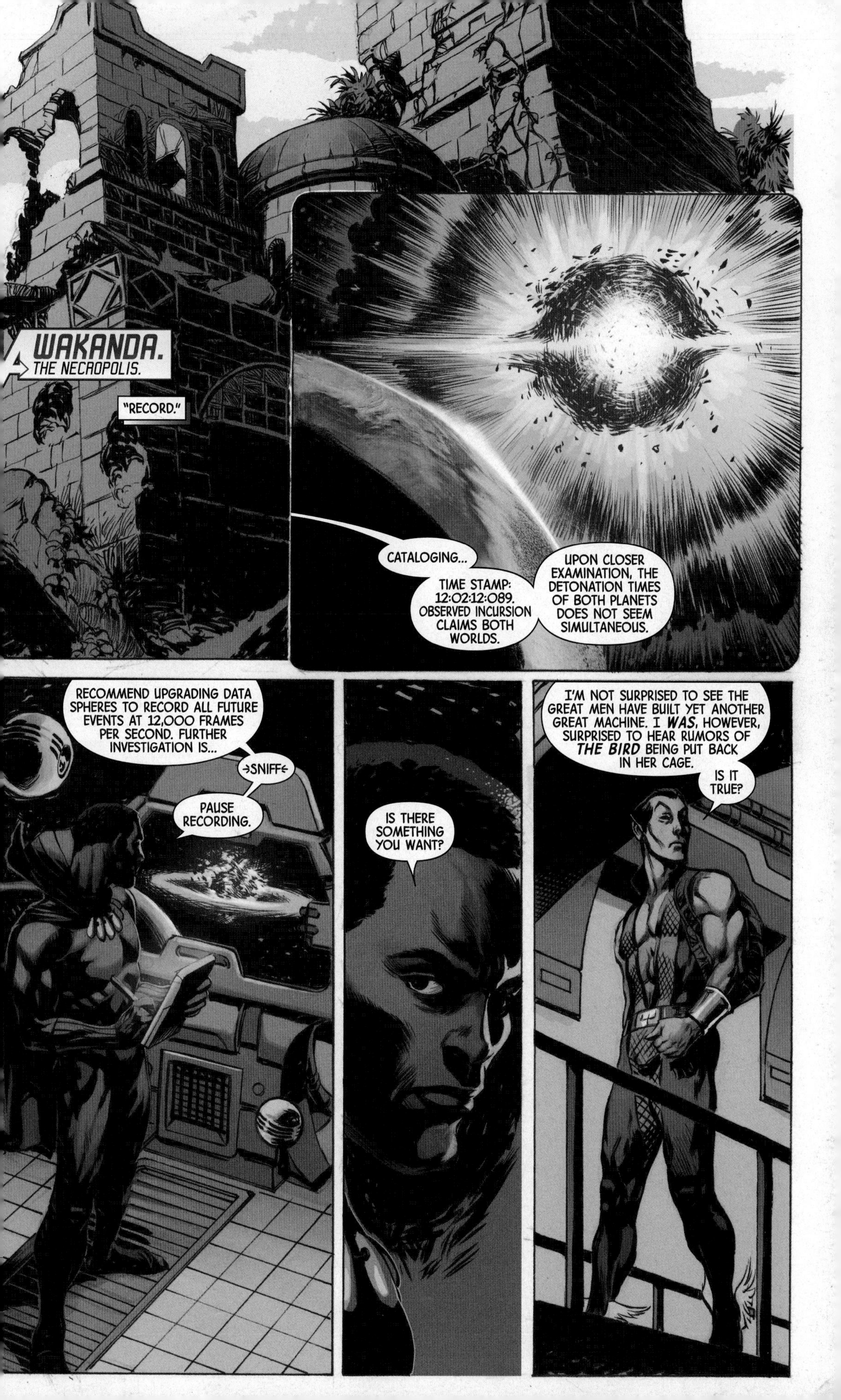
WAKANDA.
THE NECROPOLIS.
"RECORD."
CATALOGING...
TIME STAMP: 12:02:12:089. OBSERVED INCURSION CLAIMS BOTH WORLDS.
UPON CLOSER EXAMINATION, THE DETONATION TIMES OF BOTH PLANETS DOES NOT SEEM SIMULTANEOUS.
RECOMMEND UPGRADING DATA SPHERES TO RECORD ALL FUTURE EVENTS AT 12,000 FRAMES PER SECOND. FURTHER INVESTIGATION IS...
→SNIFF←
PAUSE RECORDING.
IS THERE SOMETHING YOU WANT?
I'M NOT SURPRISED TO SEE THE GREAT MEN HAVE BUILT YET ANOTHER GREAT MACHINE. I WAS, HOWEVER, SURPRISED TO HEAR RUMORS OF THE BIRD BEING PUT BACK IN HER CAGE.
IS IT TRUE?

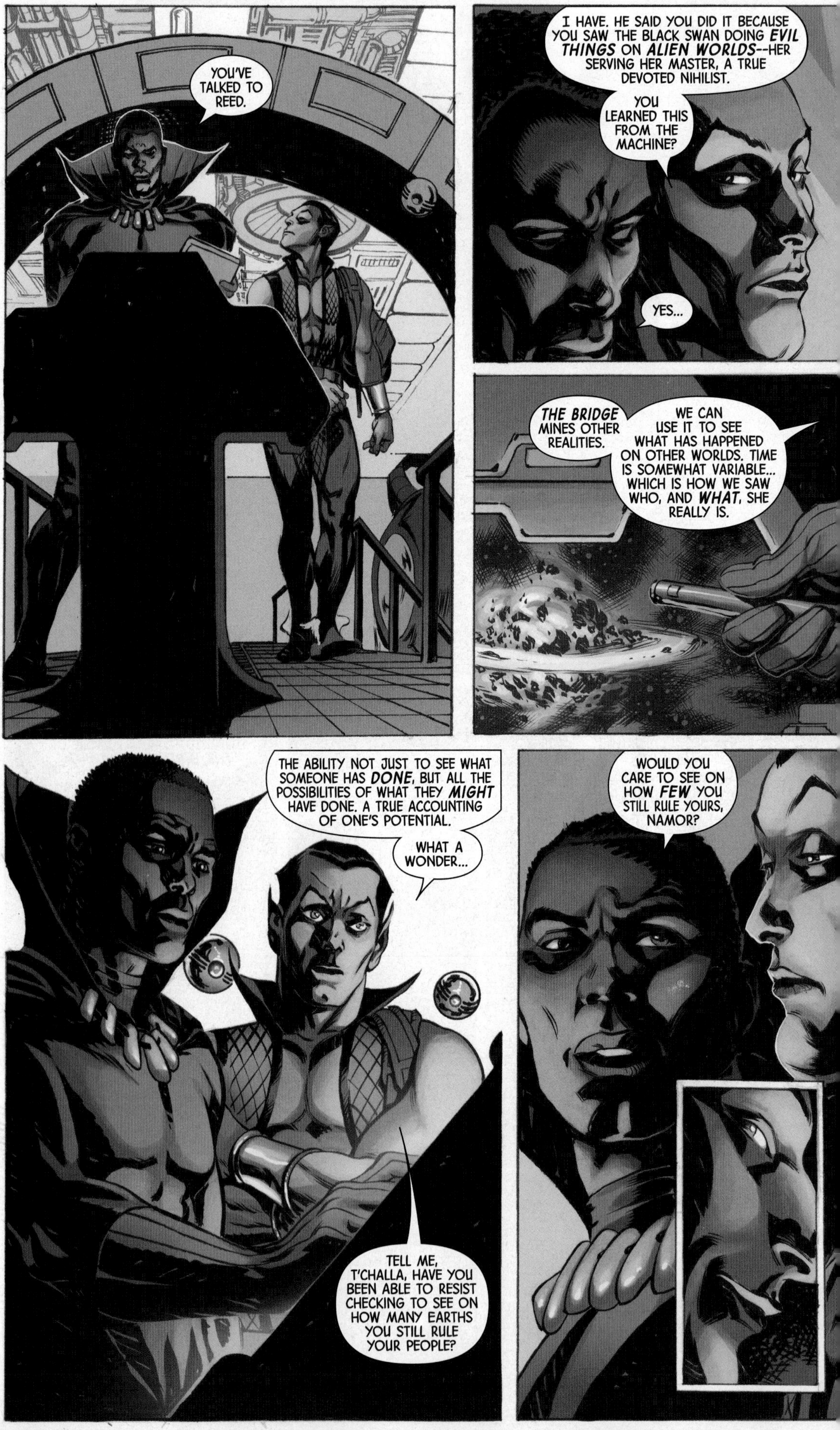
YOU'VE TALKED TO REED.
I HAVE. HE SAID YOU DID IT BECAUSE YOU SAW THE BLACK SWAN DOING EVIL THINGS ON ALIEN WORLDS--HER SERVING HER MASTER, A TRUE DEVOTED NIHILIST.
YOU LEARNED THIS FROM THE MACHINE?
YES...
THE BRIDGE MINES OTHER REALITIES.
WE CAN USE IT TO SEE WHAT HAS HAPPENED ON OTHER WORLDS. TIME IS SOMEWHAT VARIABLE... WHICH IS HOW WE SAW WHO, AND WHAT, SHE REALLY IS.
THE ABILITY NOT JUST TO SEE WHAT SOMEONE HAS DONE, BUT ALL THE POSSIBILITIES OF WHAT THEY MIGHT HAVE DONE. A TRUE ACCOUNTING OF ONE'S POTENTIAL.
WHAT A WONDER...
TELL ME, T'CHALLA, HAVE YOU BEEN ABLE TO RESIST CHECKING TO SEE ON HOW MANY EARTHS YOU STILL RULE YOUR PEOPLE?
WOULD YOU CARE TO SEE ON HOW FEW YOU STILL RULE YOURS, NAMOR?

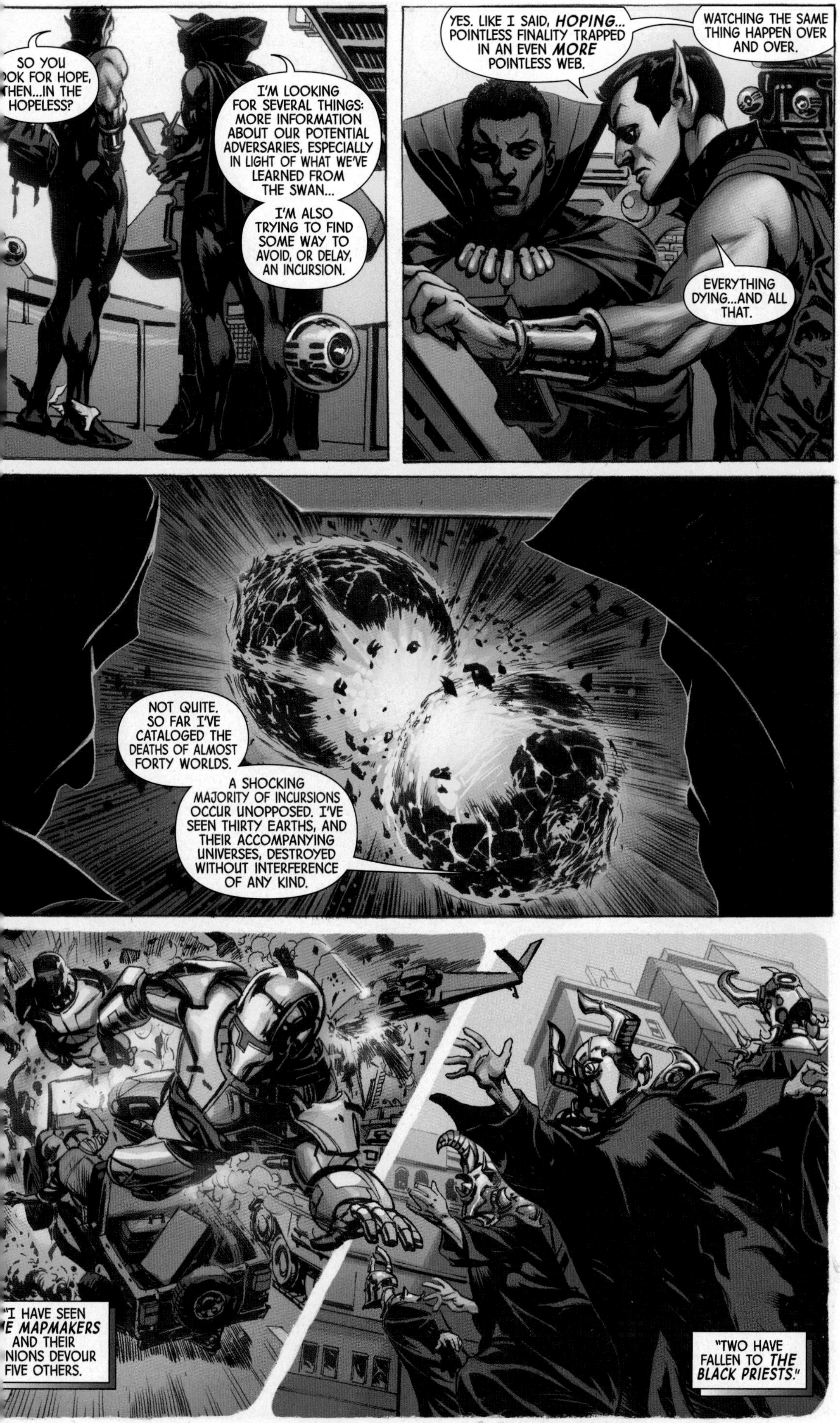

SO YOU
OOK FOR HOPE,
THEN...IN THE
HOPELESS?
I'M LOOKING FOR SEVERAL THINGS: MORE INFORMATION ABOUT OUR POTENTIAL ADVERSARIES, ESPECIALLY IN LIGHT OF WHAT WE'VE LEARNED FROM THE SWAN...
I'M ALSO TRYING TO FIND SOME WAY TO AVOID, OR DELAY, AN INCURSION.
YES. LIKE I SAID, HOPING... POINTLESS FINALITY TRAPPED IN AN EVEN MORE POINTLESS WEB.
WATCHING THE SAME THING HAPPEN OVER AND OVER.
EVERYTHING DYING...AND ALL THAT.
NOT QUITE. SO FAR I'VE CATALOGED THE DEATHS OF ALMOST FORTY WORLDS.
A SHOCKING MAJORITY OF INCURSIONS OCCUR UNOPPOSED. I'VE SEEN THIRTY EARTHS, AND THEIR ACCOMPANYING UNIVERSES, DESTROYED WITHOUT INTERFERENCE OF ANY KIND.
"I HAVE SEEN
E MAPMAKERS
AND THEIR
NIONS DEVOUR
FIVE OTHERS.
"TWO HAVE FALLEN TO THE BLACK PRIESTS."

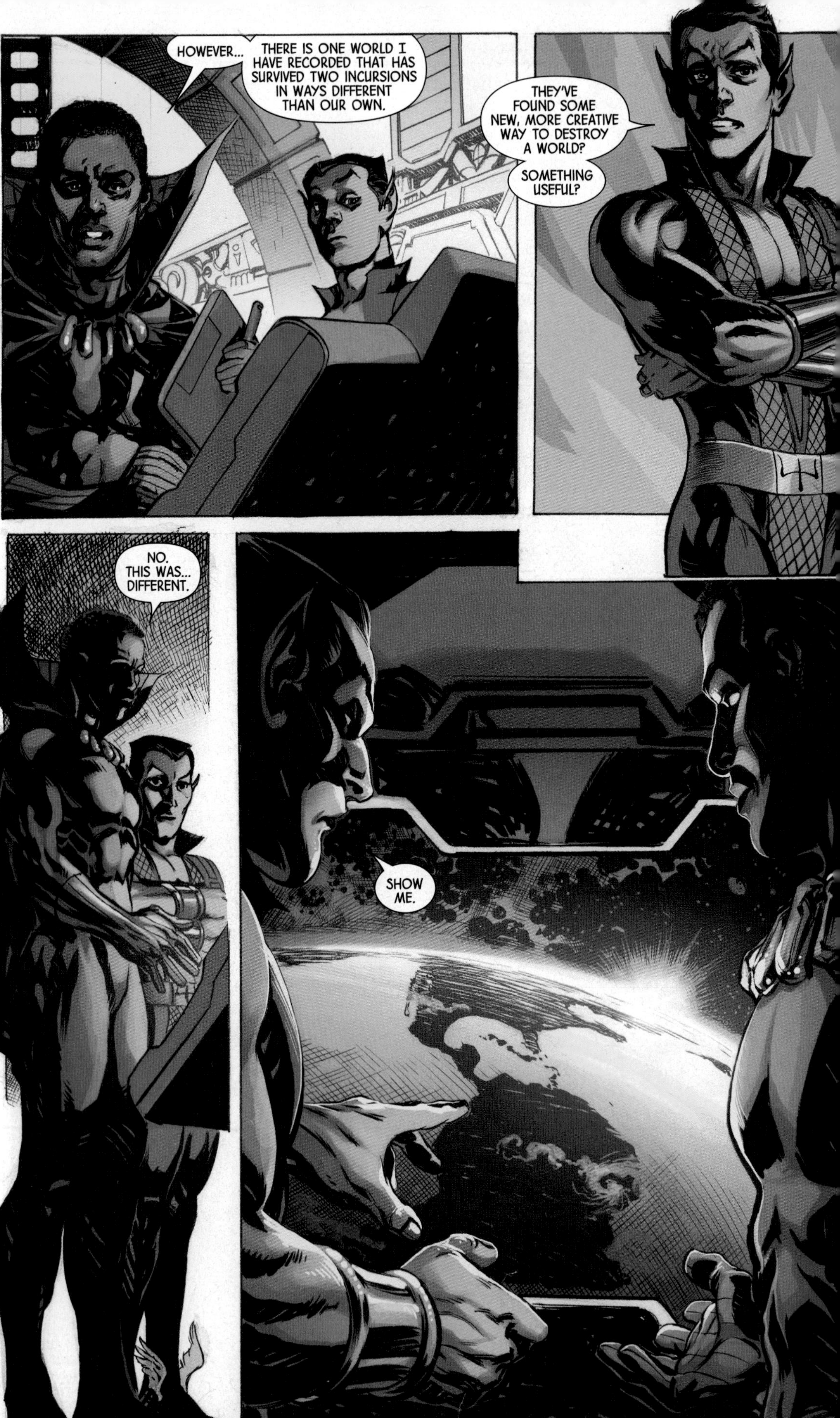
HOWEVER...
THERE IS ONE WORLD I HAVE RECORDED THAT HAS SURVIVED TWO INCURSIONS IN WAYS DIFFERENT THAN OUR OWN.
THEY'VE FOUND SOME NEW, MORE CREATIVE WAY TO DESTROY A WORLD?
SOMETHING USEFUL?
NO. THIS WAS... DIFFERENT.
SHOW ME.

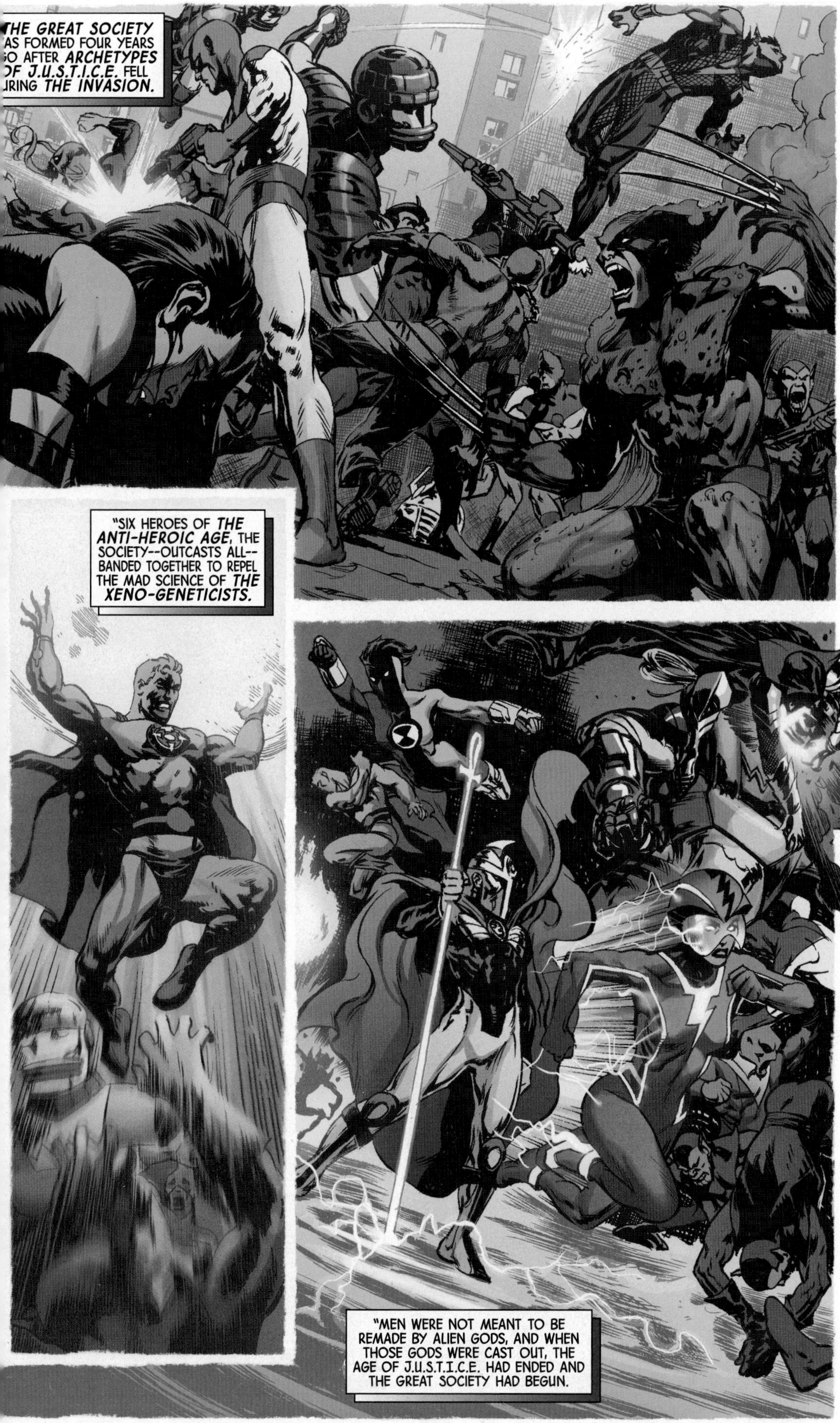
THE GREAT SOCIETY
AS FORMED FOUR YEARS
GO AFTER ARCHETYPES
OF J.U.S.T.I.C.E. FELL
URING THE INVASION.
"SIX HEROES OF THE ANTI-HEROIC AGE, THE SOCIETY--OUTCASTS ALL--BANDED TOGETHER TO REPEL THE MAD SCIENCE OF THE XENO-GENETICISTS.
"MEN WERE NOT MEANT TO BE REMADE BY ALIEN GODS, AND WHEN THOSE GODS WERE CAST OUT, THE AGE OF J.U.S.T.I.C.E. HAD ENDED AND THE GREAT SOCIETY HAD BEGUN.

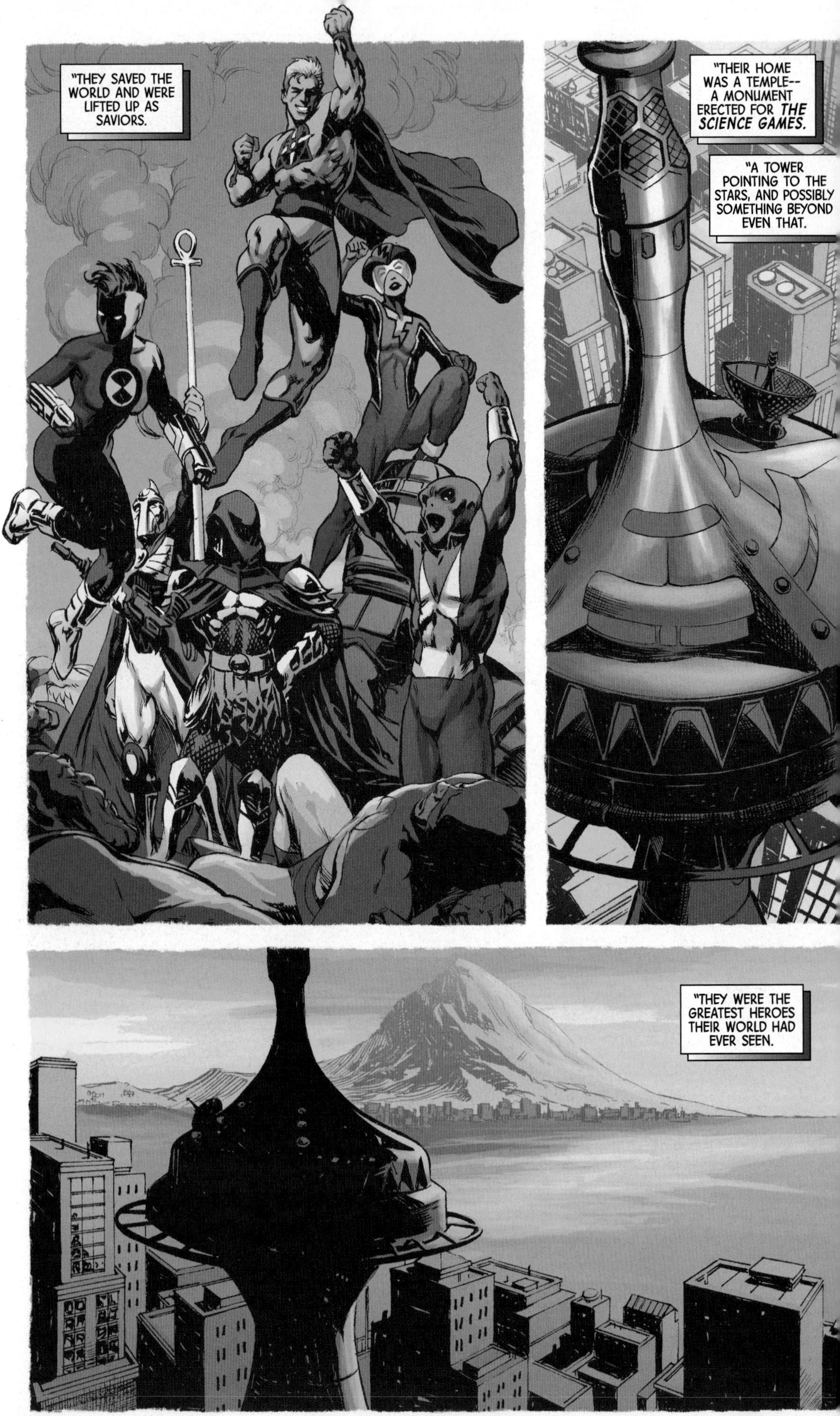
"THEY SAVED THE WORLD AND WERE LIFTED UP AS SAVIORS.
"THEIR HOME WAS A TEMPLE-- A MONUMENT ERECTED FOR *THE SCIENCE GAMES.*
"A TOWER POINTING TO THE STARS, AND POSSIBLY SOMETHING BEYOND EVEN THAT.
"THEY WERE THE GREATEST HEROES THEIR WORLD HAD EVER SEEN.

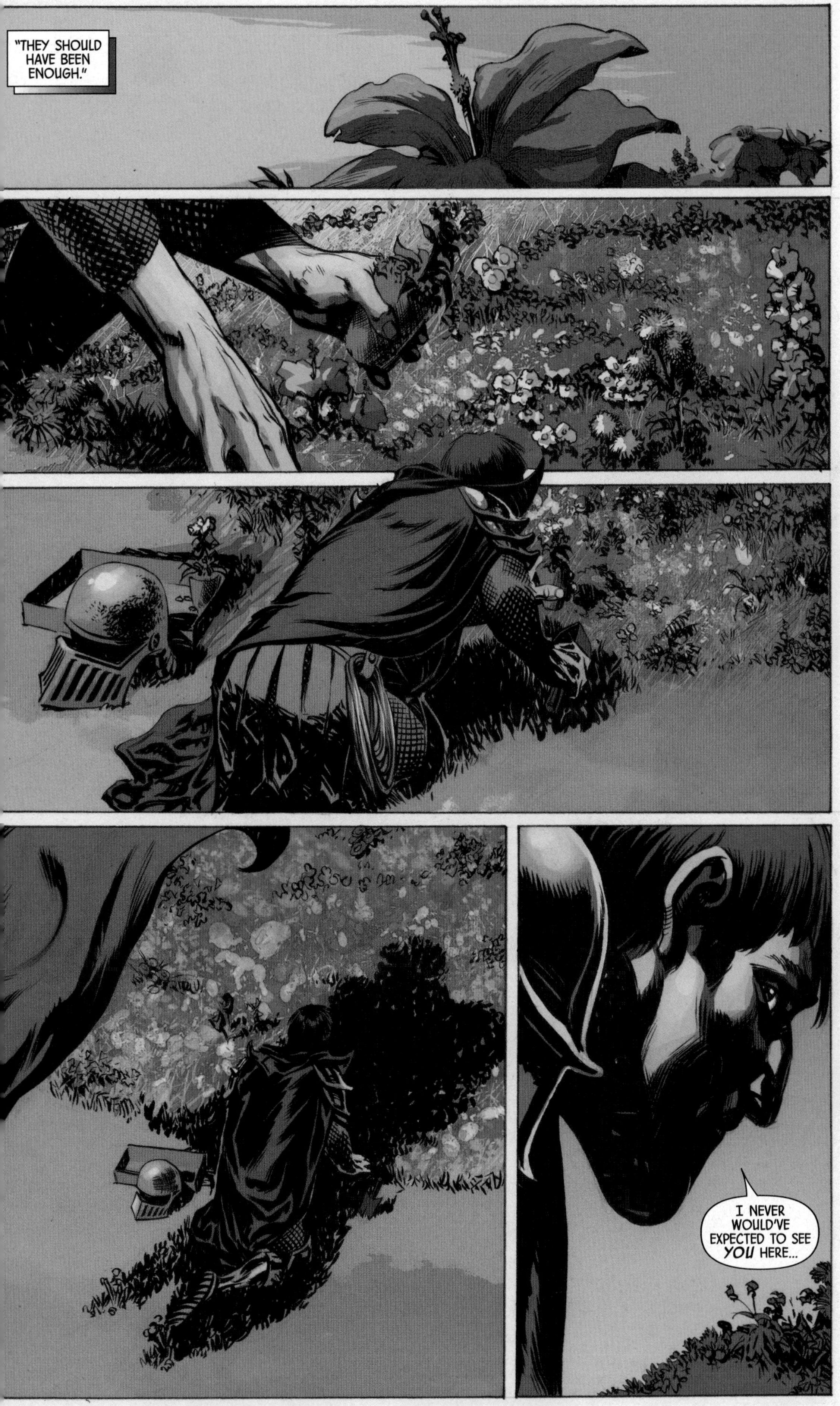
"THEY SHOULD HAVE BEEN ENOUGH."
I NEVER WOULD'VE EXPECTED TO SEE *YOU* HERE...

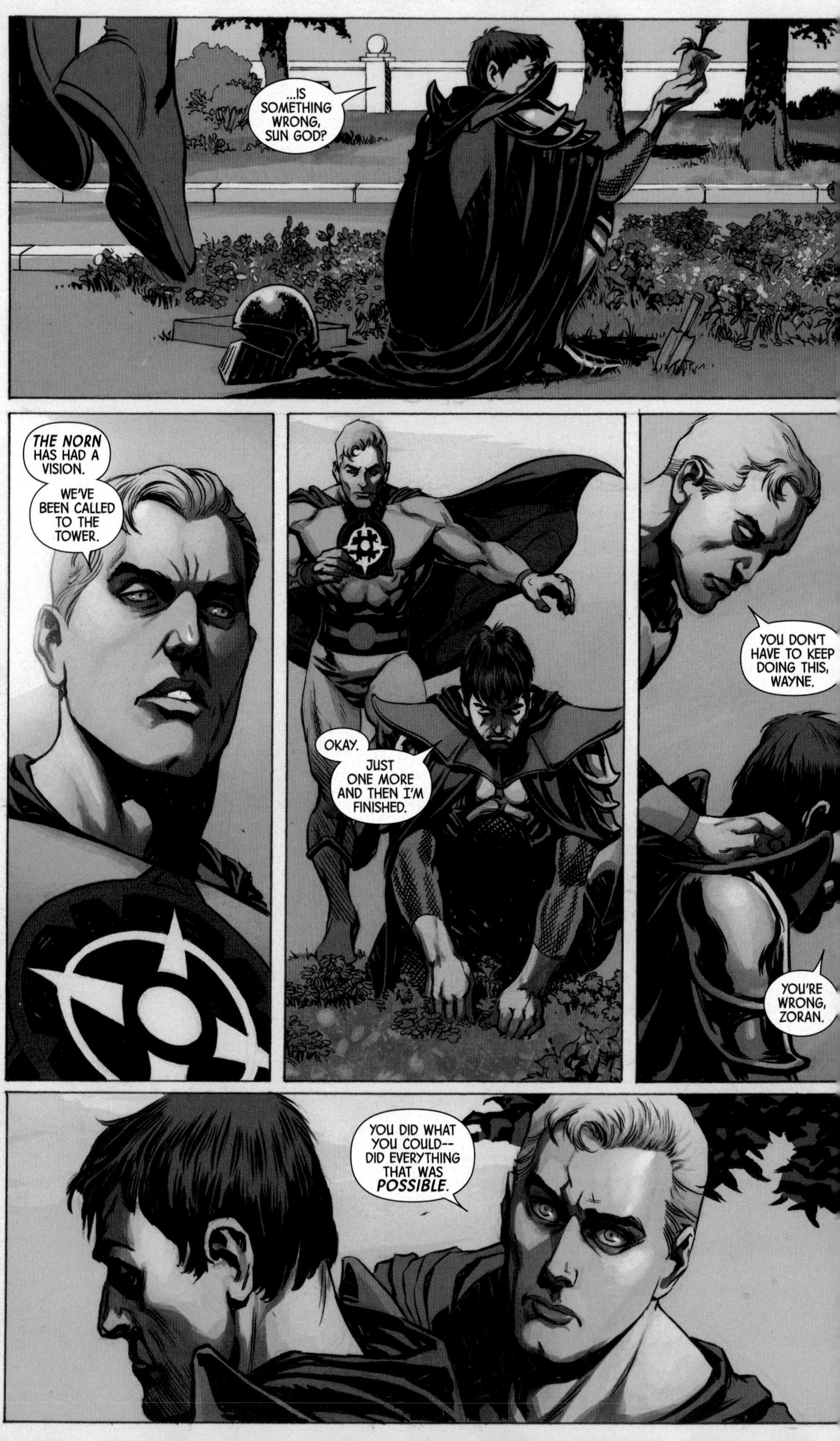
...IS SOMETHING WRONG, SUN GOD?
THE NORN HAS HAD A VISION.
WE'VE BEEN CALLED TO THE TOWER.
OKAY.
JUST ONE MORE AND THEN I'M FINISHED.
YOU DON'T HAVE TO KEEP DOING THIS, WAYNE.
YOU'RE WRONG, ZORAN.
YOU DID WHAT YOU COULD-- DID EVERYTHING THAT WAS POSSIBLE.

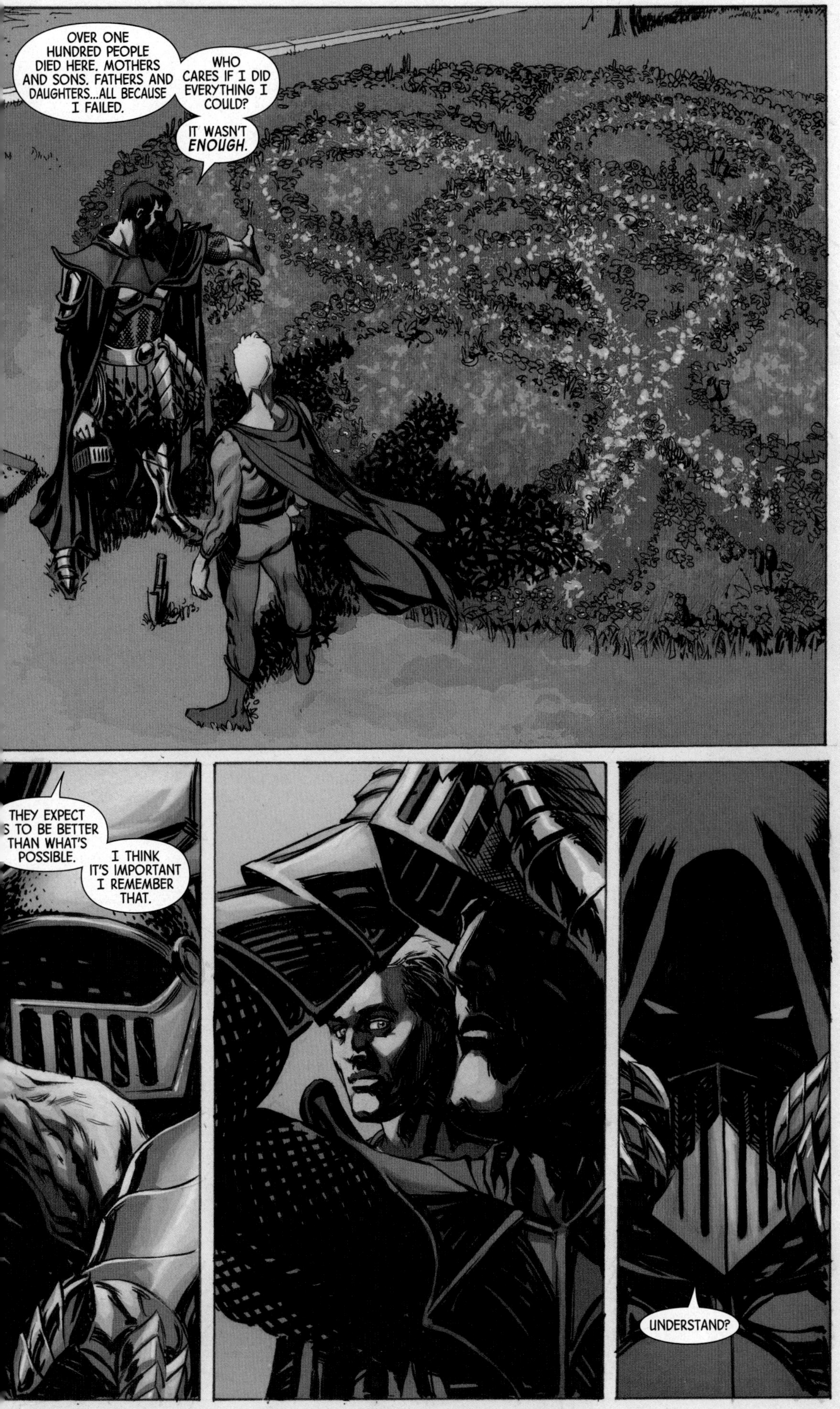
OVER ONE HUNDRED PEOPLE DIED HERE. MOTHERS AND SONS. FATHERS AND DAUGHTERS...ALL BECAUSE I FAILED.
WHO CARES IF I DID EVERYTHING I COULD?
IT WASN'T *ENOUGH*.
THEY EXPECT S TO BE BETTER THAN WHAT'S POSSIBLE.
I THINK IT'S IMPORTANT I REMEMBER THAT.
UNDERSTAND?

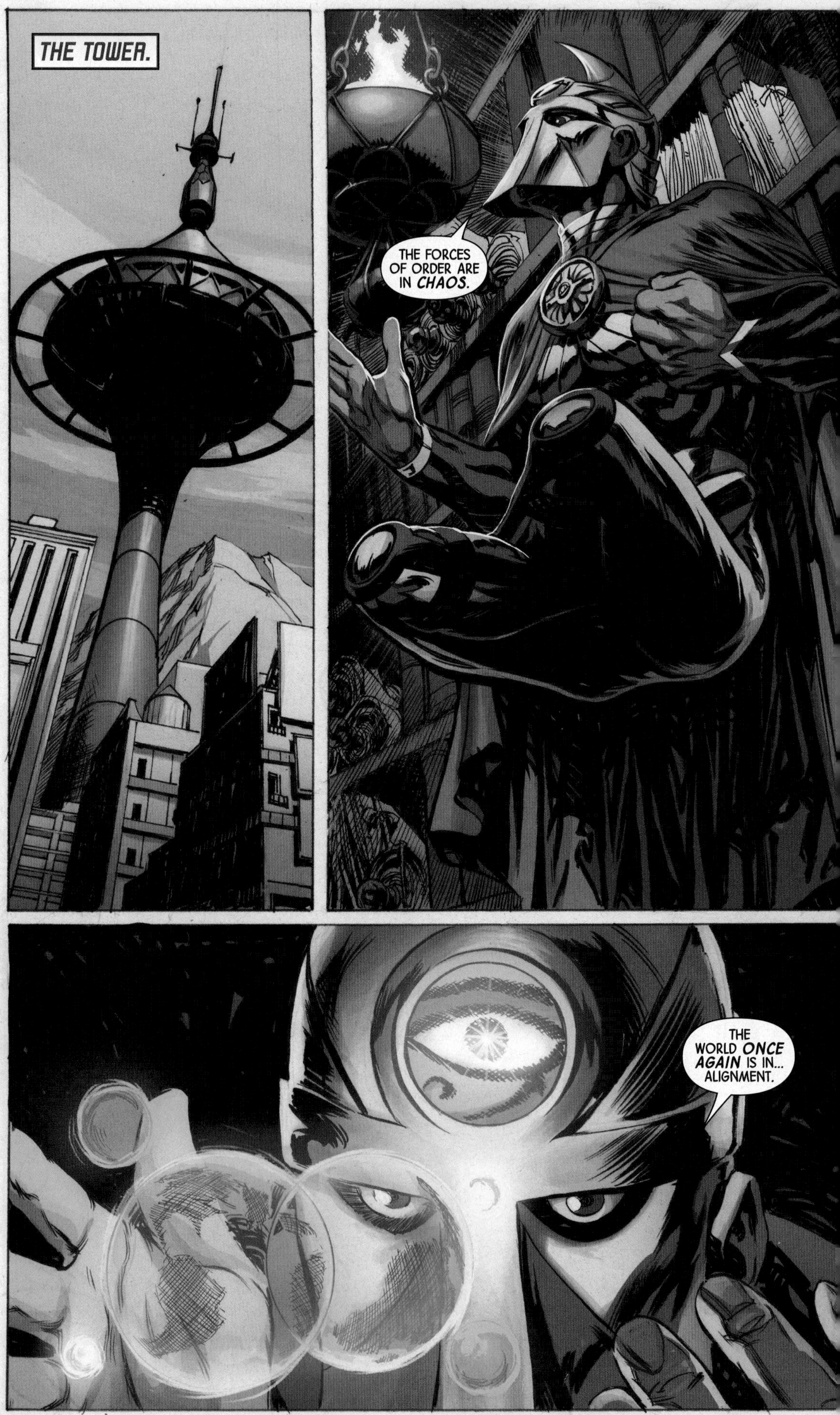
THE TOWER.
THE FORCES OF ORDER ARE IN CHAOS.
THE WORLD ONCE AGAIN IS IN... ALIGNMENT.

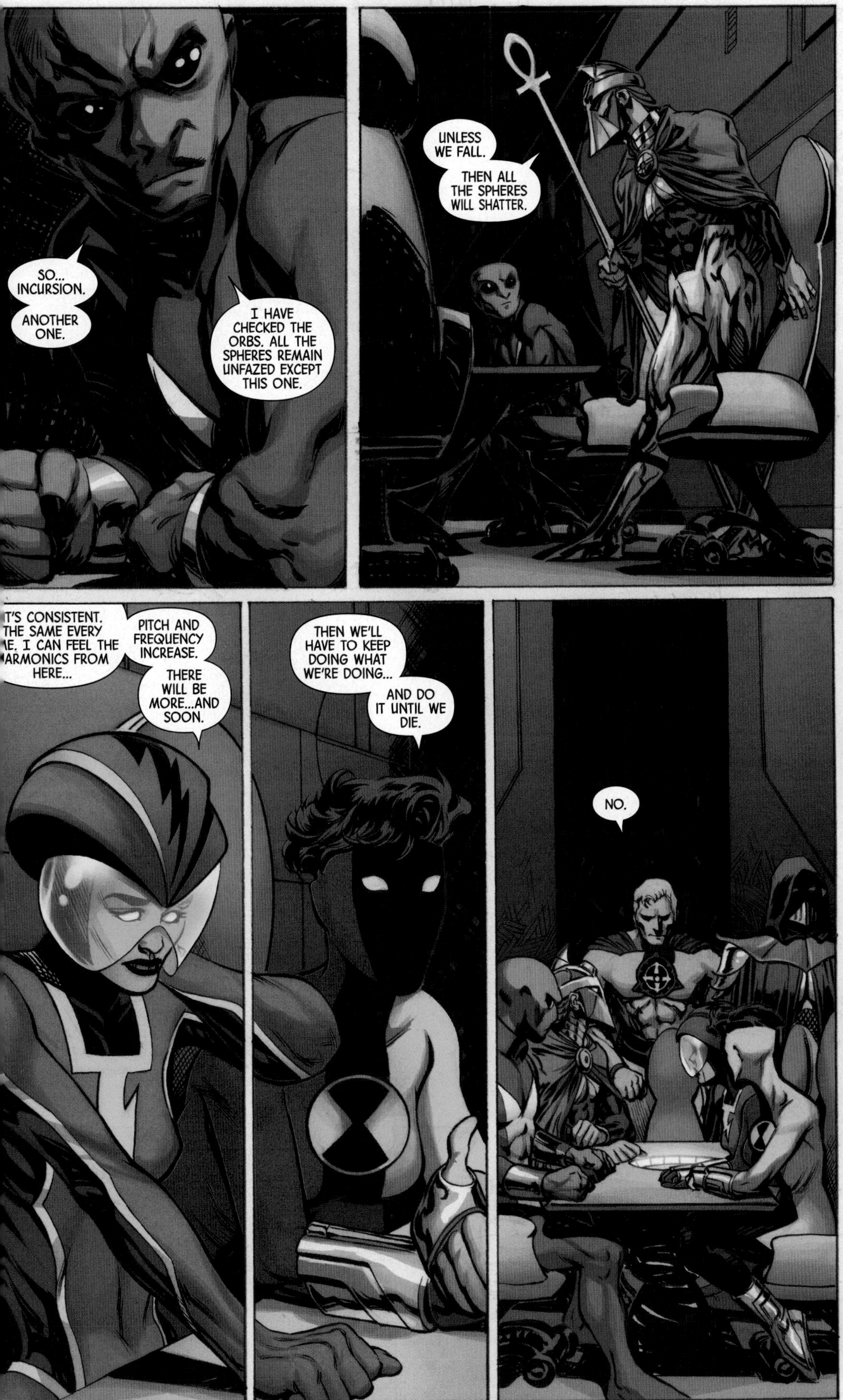
SO... INCURSION.
ANOTHER ONE.
I HAVE CHECKED THE ORBS. ALL THE SPHERES REMAIN UNFAZED EXCEPT THIS ONE.
UNLESS WE FALL.
THEN ALL THE SPHERES WILL SHATTER.
IT'S CONSISTENT. THE SAME EVERY TIME. I CAN FEEL THE HARMONICS FROM HERE...
PITCH AND FREQUENCY INCREASE.
THERE WILL BE MORE...AND SOON.
THEN WE'LL HAVE TO KEEP DOING WHAT WE'RE DOING...
AND DO IT UNTIL WE DIE.
NO.

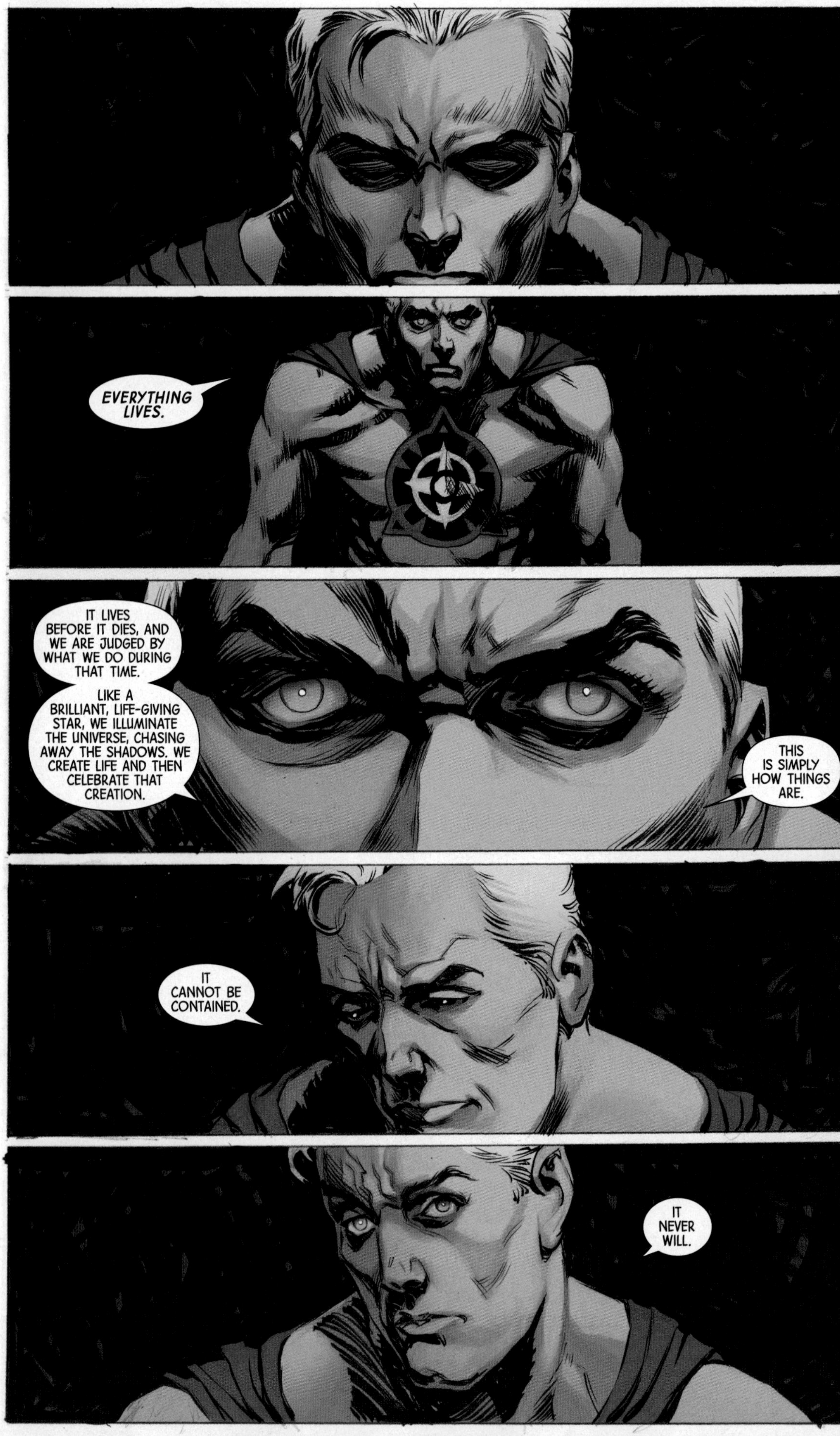
EVERYTHING LIVES.
IT LIVES BEFORE IT DIES, AND WE ARE JUDGED BY WHAT WE DO DURING THAT TIME.
LIKE A BRILLIANT, LIFE-GIVING STAR, WE ILLUMINATE THE UNIVERSE, CHASING AWAY THE SHADOWS. WE CREATE LIFE AND THEN CELEBRATE THAT CREATION.
THIS IS SIMPLY HOW THINGS ARE.
IT CANNOT BE CONTAINED.
IT NEVER WILL.

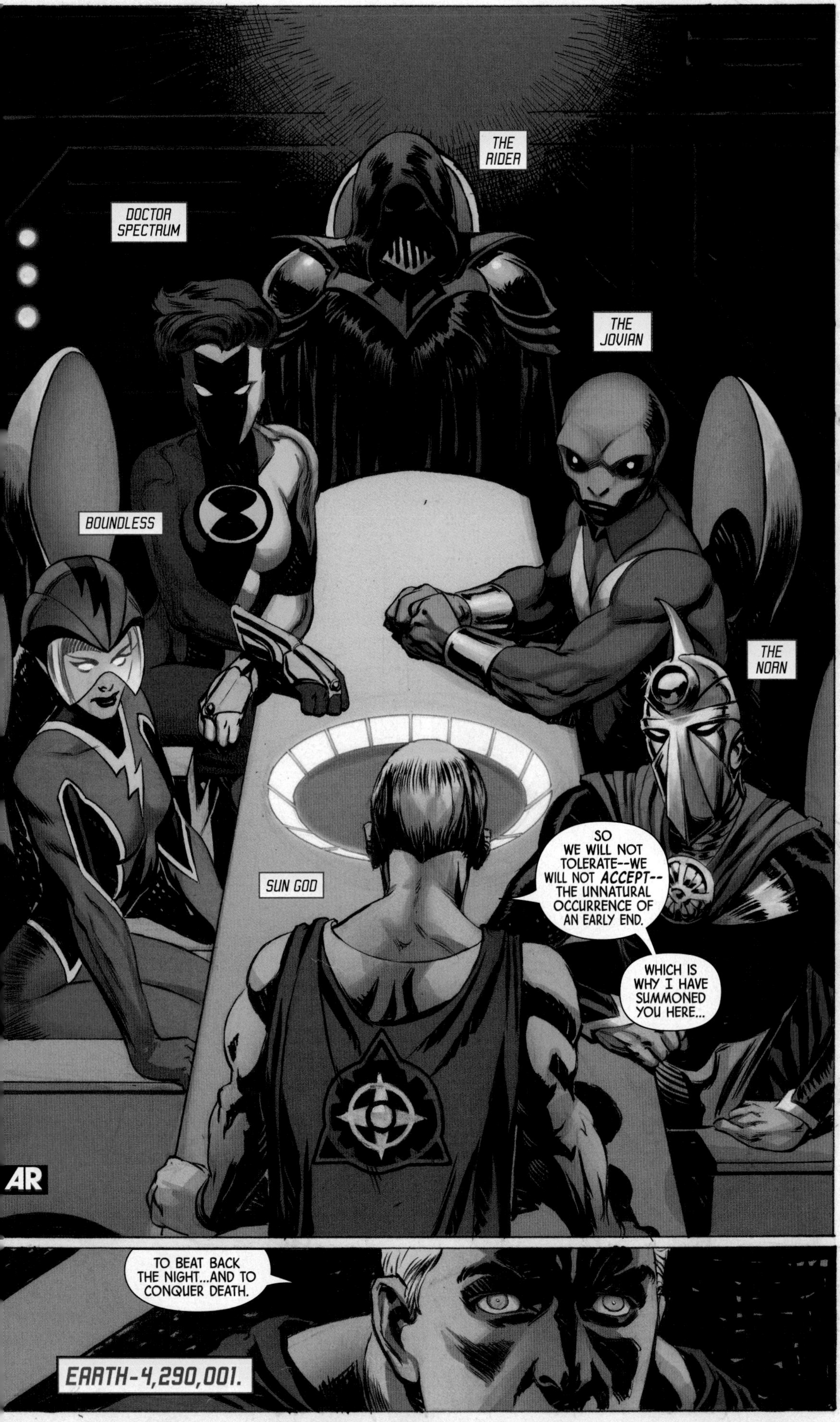
THE RIDER
DOCTOR SPECTRUM
THE JOVIAN
BOUNDLESS
THE NORN
SUN GOD
SO WE WILL NOT TOLERATE--WE WILL NOT ACCEPT-- THE UNNATURAL OCCURRENCE OF AN EARLY END.
WHICH IS WHY I HAVE SUMMONED YOU HERE...
AR
TO BEAT BACK THE NIGHT...AND TO CONQUER DEATH.
EARTH-4,290,001.

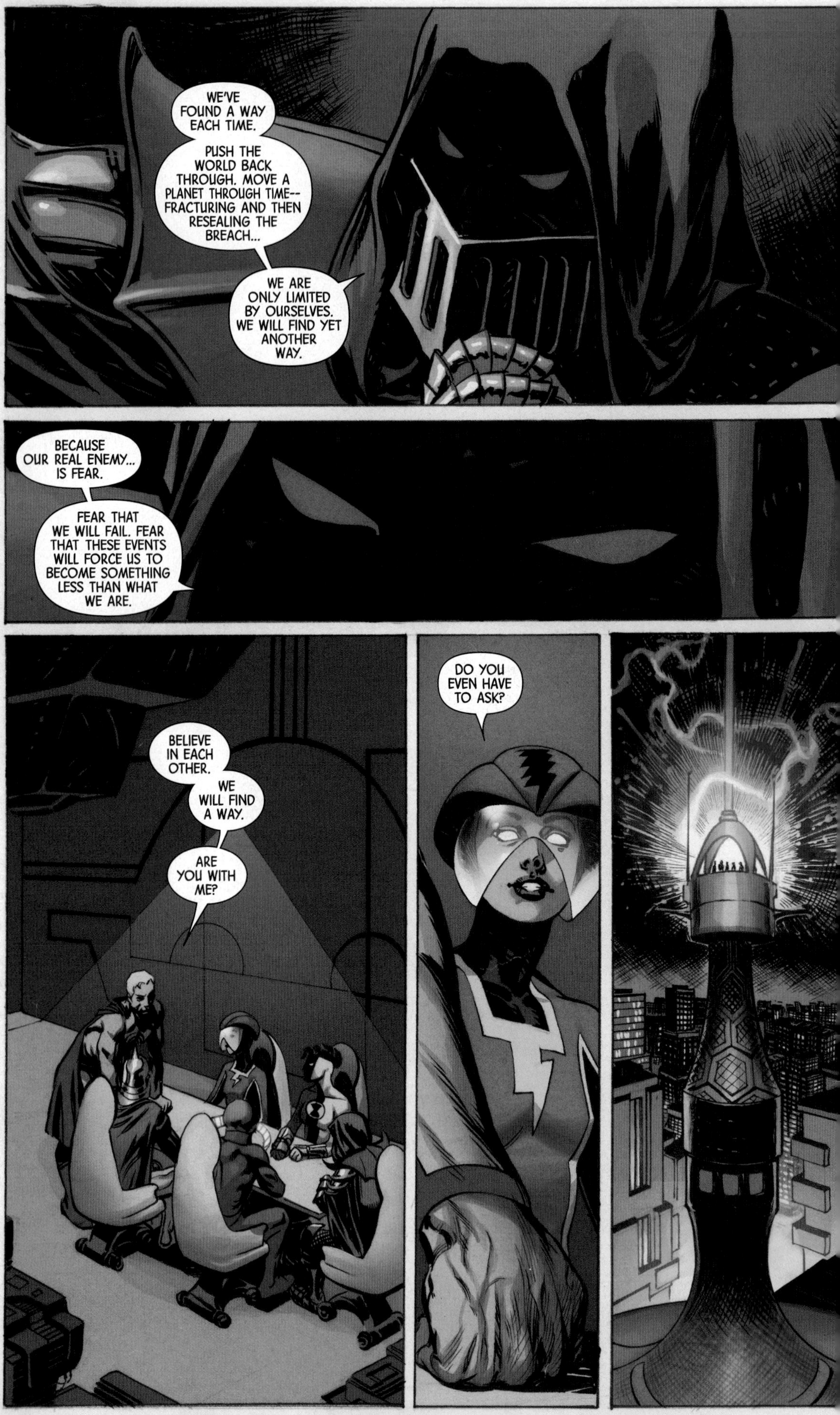
WE'VE FOUND A WAY EACH TIME.
PUSH THE WORLD BACK THROUGH. MOVE A PLANET THROUGH TIME-- FRACTURING AND THEN RESEALING THE BREACH...
WE ARE ONLY LIMITED BY OURSELVES. WE WILL FIND YET ANOTHER WAY.
BECAUSE OUR REAL ENEMY... IS FEAR.
FEAR THAT WE WILL FAIL. FEAR THAT THESE EVENTS WILL FORCE US TO BECOME SOMETHING LESS THAN WHAT WE ARE.
BELIEVE IN EACH OTHER.
WE WILL FIND A WAY.
ARE YOU WITH ME?
DO YOU EVEN HAVE TO ASK?

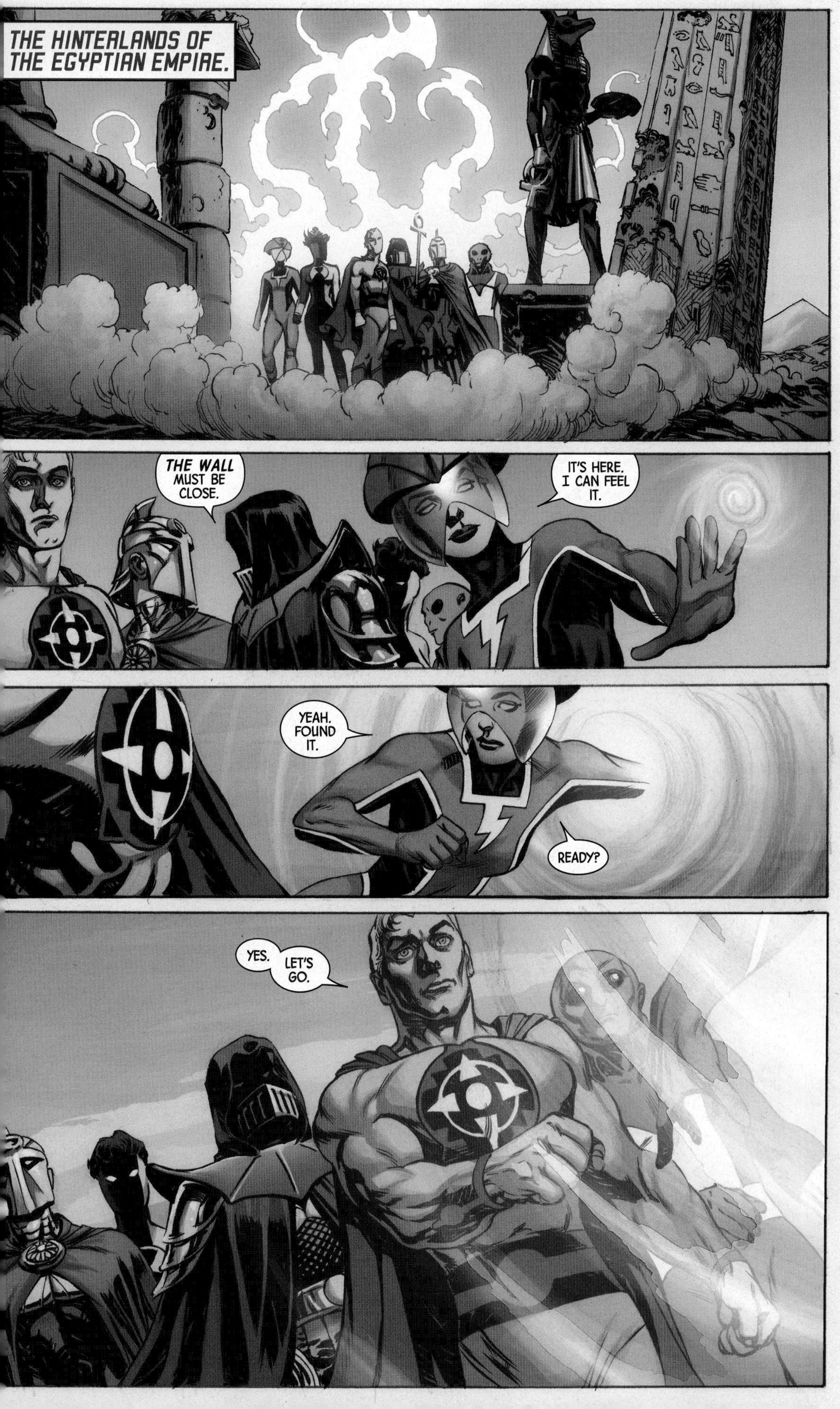
THE HINTERLANDS OF THE EGYPTIAN EMPIRE.
THE WALL MUST BE CLOSE.
IT'S HERE. I CAN FEEL IT.
YEAH. FOUND IT.
READY?
YES.
LET'S GO.

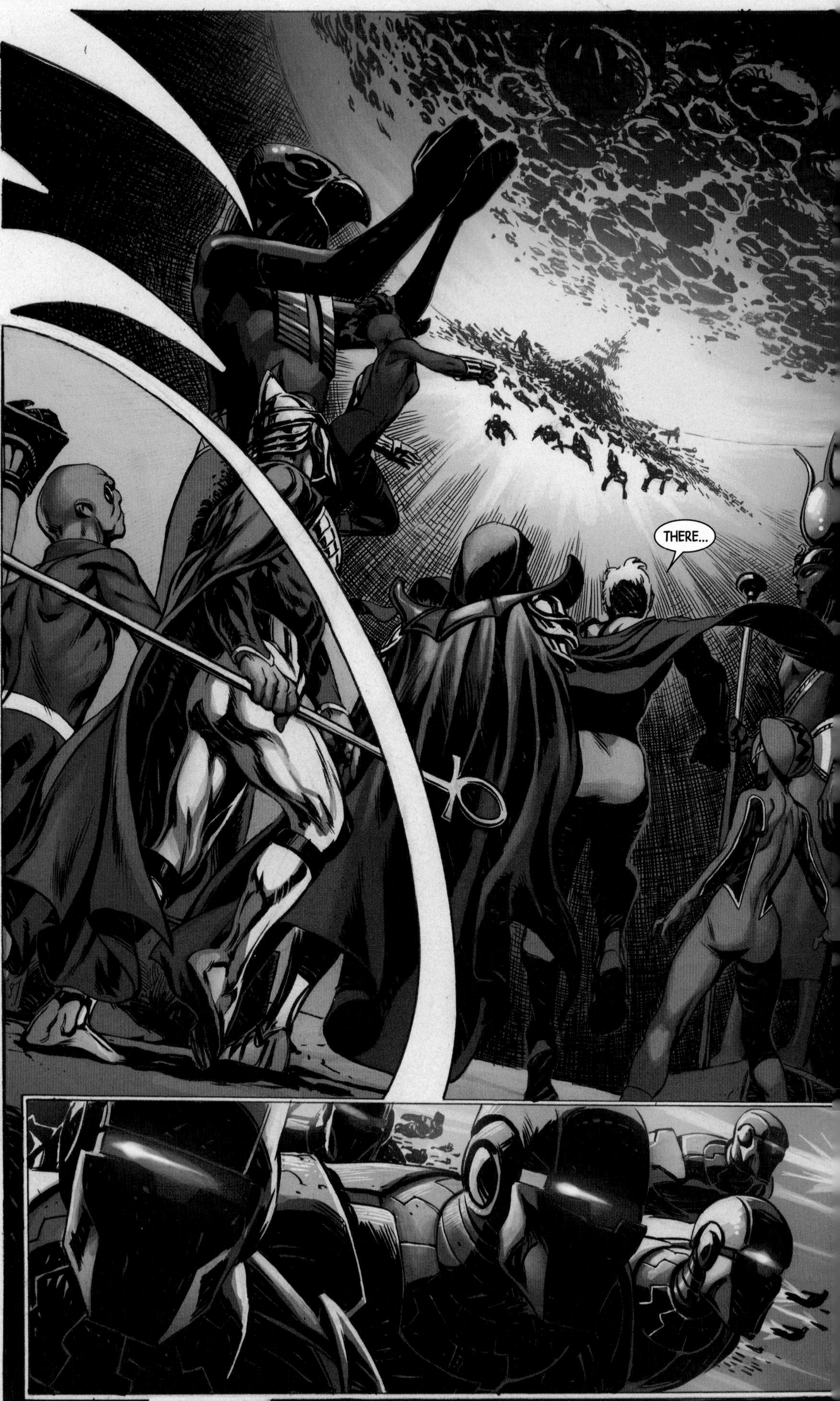
THERE...

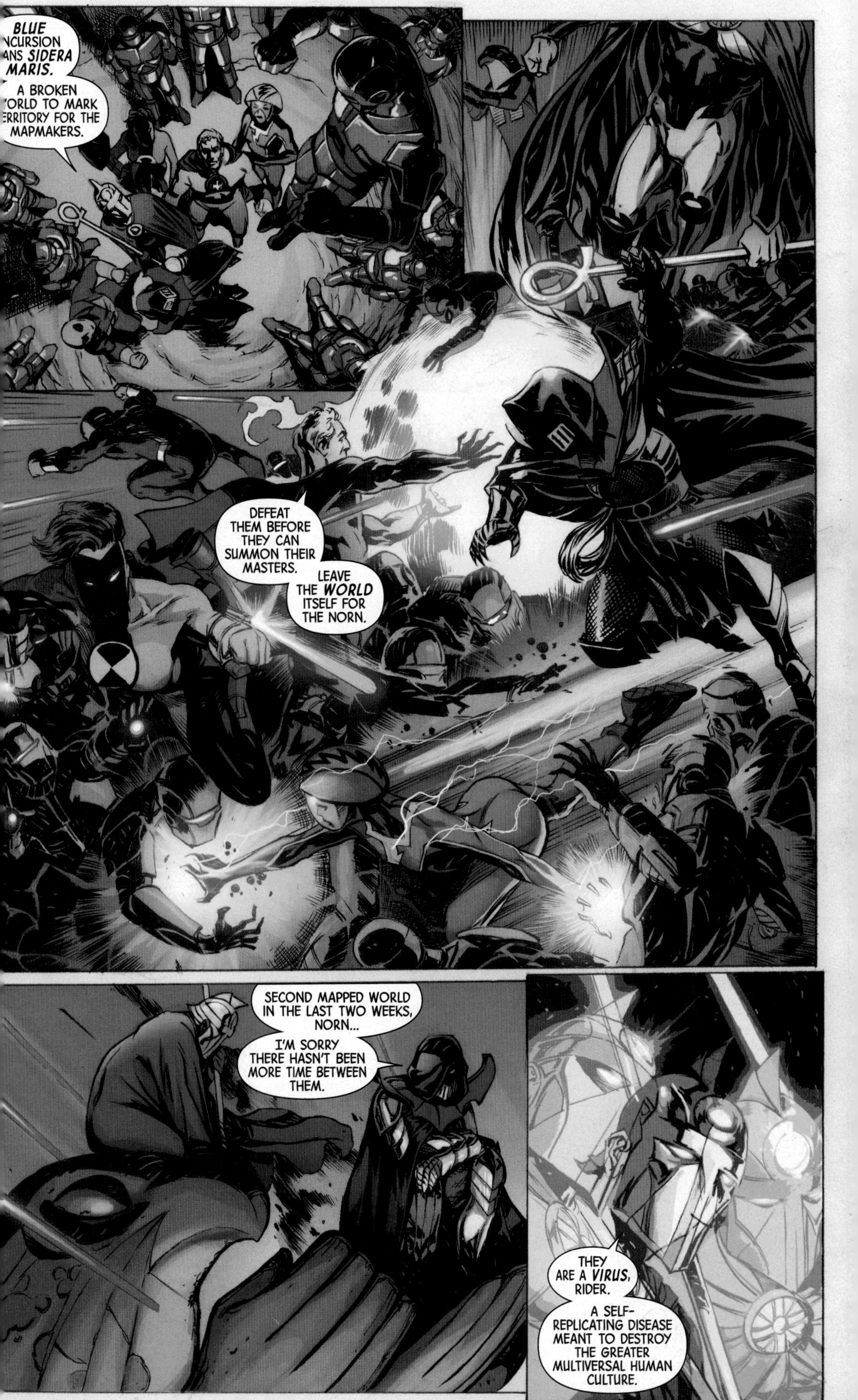
BLUE
NCURSION
ANS SIDERA
MARIS.
A BROKEN
ORLD TO MARK
ERRITORY FOR THE
MAPMAKERS.
DEFEAT THEM BEFORE THEY CAN SUMMON THEIR MASTERS.
LEAVE THE WORLD ITSELF FOR THE NORN.
SECOND MAPPED WORLD IN THE LAST TWO WEEKS, NORN...
I'M SORRY THERE HASN'T BEEN MORE TIME BETWEEN THEM.
THEY ARE A VIRUS, RIDER.
A SELF-REPLICATING DISEASE MEANT TO DESTROY THE GREATER MULTIVERSAL HUMAN CULTURE.

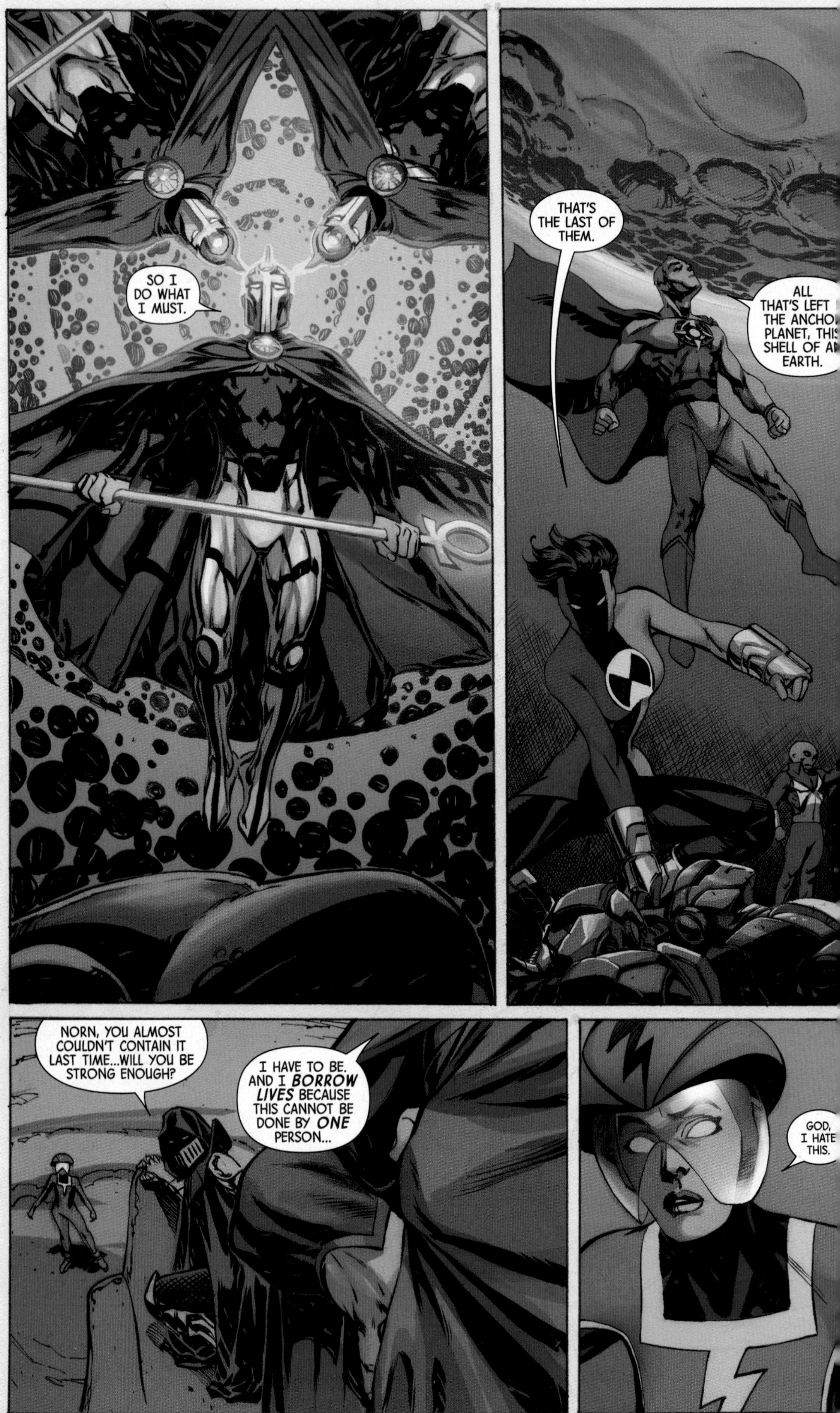

SO I DO WHAT I MUST.
THAT'S THE LAST OF THEM.
ALL THAT'S LEFT THE ANCHO PLANET, THIS SHELL OF A EARTH.
NORN, YOU ALMOST COULDN'T CONTAIN IT LAST TIME...WILL YOU BE STRONG ENOUGH?
I HAVE TO BE. AND I BORROW LIVES BECAUSE THIS CANNOT BE DONE BY ONE PERSON...
GOD, I HATE THIS.

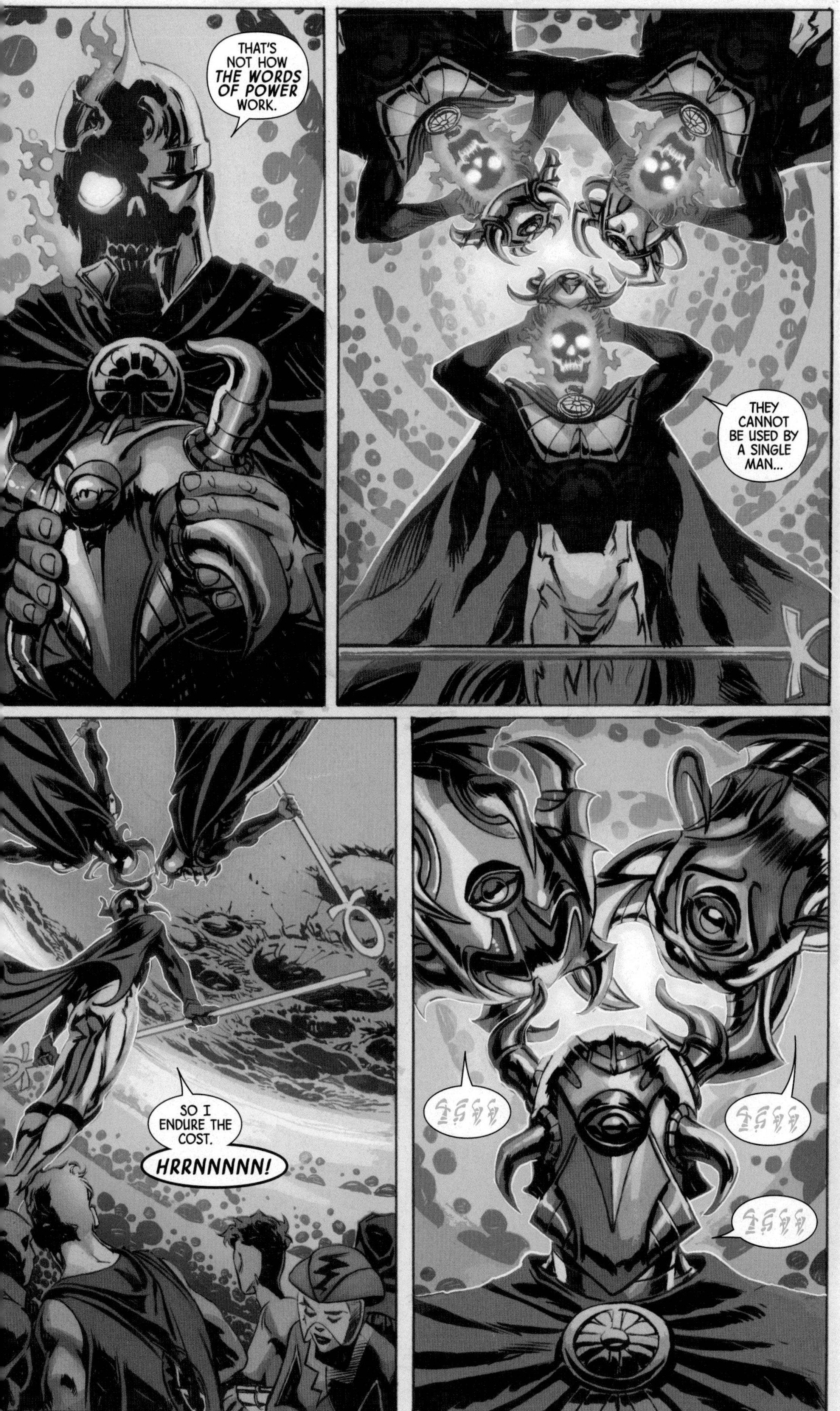
THAT'S NOT HOW *THE WORDS OF POWER* WORK.
THEY CANNOT BE USED BY A SINGLE MAN...
SO I ENDURE THE COST.
HRRNNNNN!

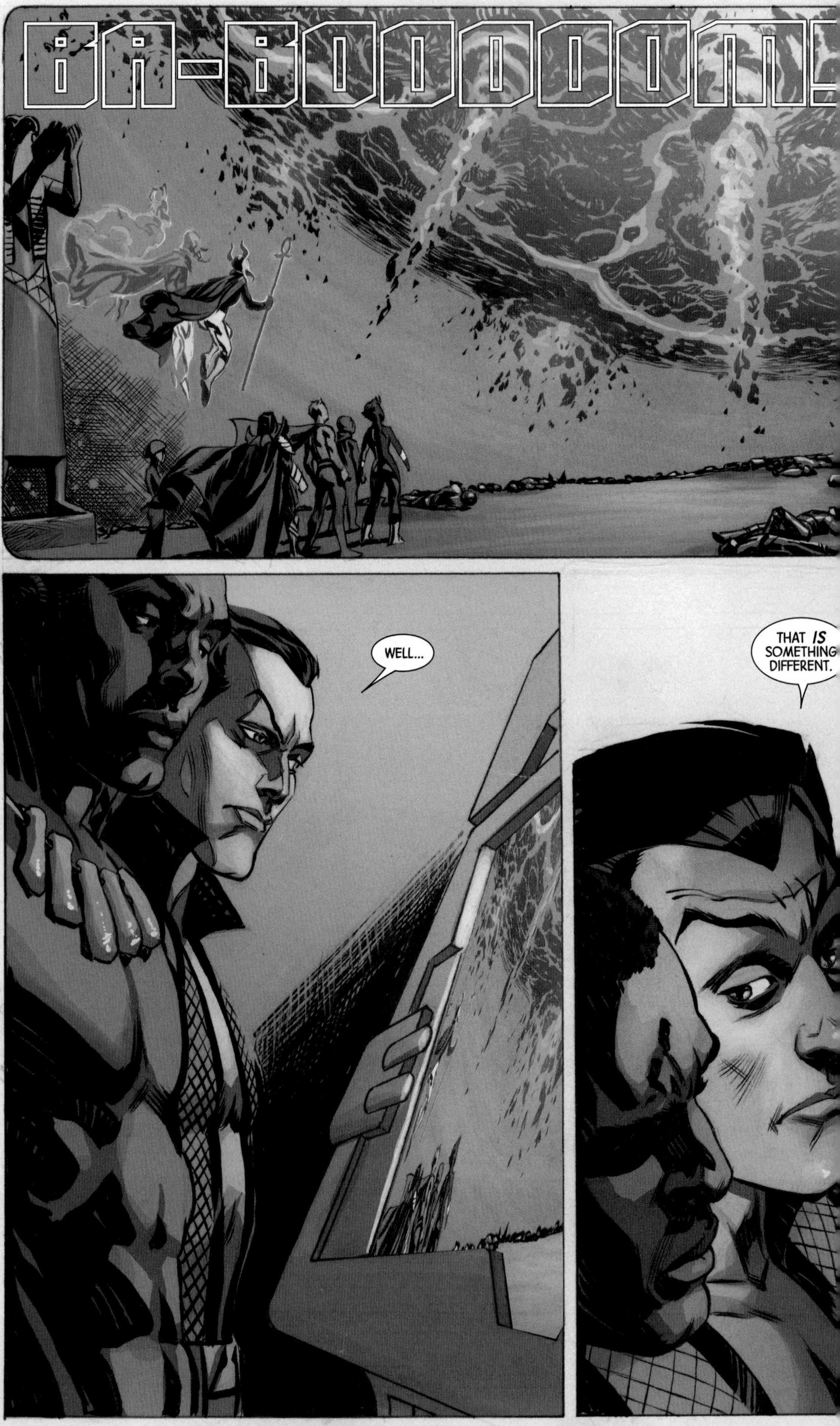
BA-BOOOOOM!
WELL...
THAT IS SOMETHING DIFFERENT.

"A PERFECT WORLD II"

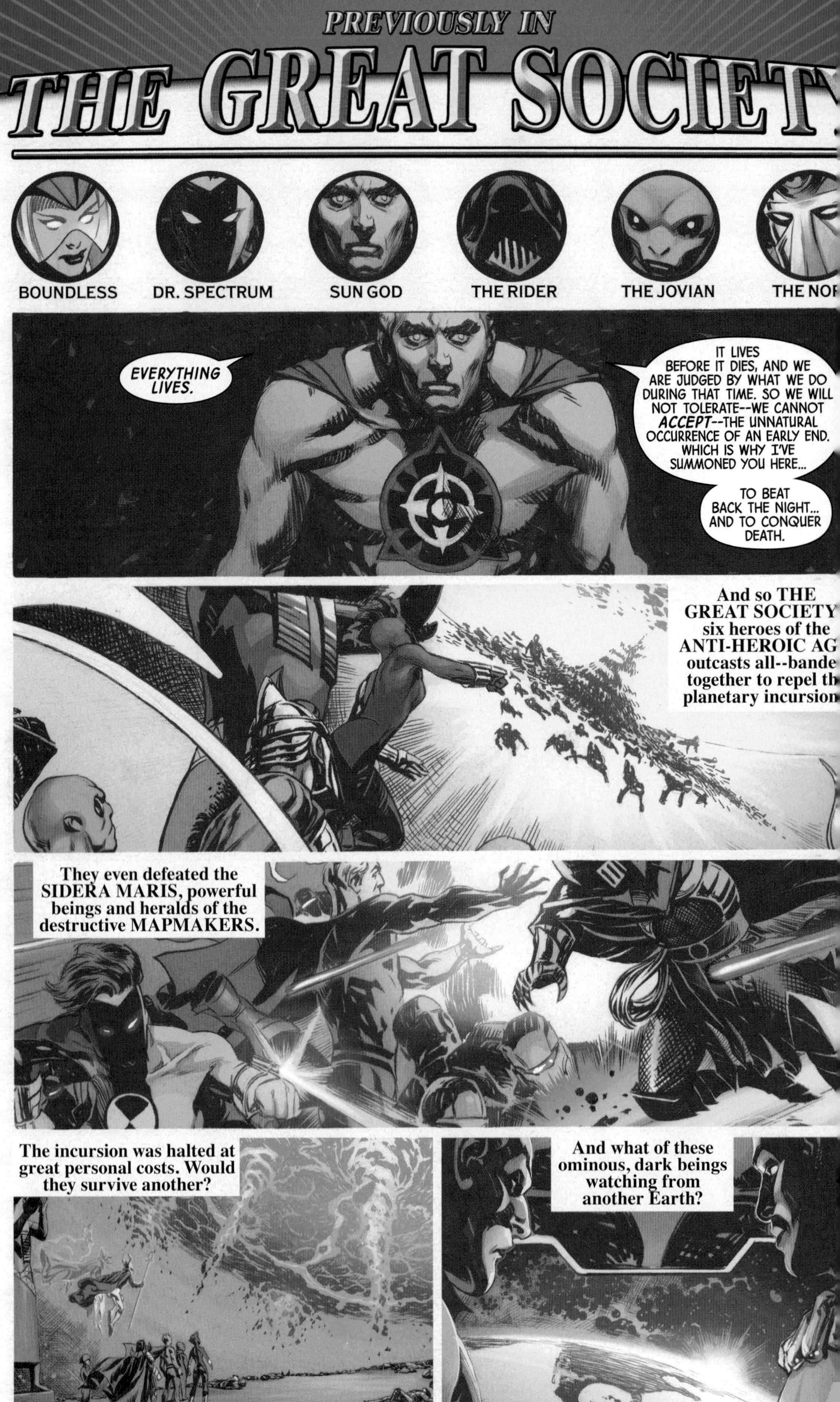
PREVIOUSLY IN
THE GREAT SOCIET
BOUNDLESS
DR. SPECTRUM
SUN GOD
THE RIDER
THE JOVIAN
THE NOR
EVERYTHING LIVES.
IT LIVES BEFORE IT DIES, AND WE ARE JUDGED BY WHAT WE DO DURING THAT TIME. SO WE WILL NOT TOLERATE--WE CANNOT ACCEPT--THE UNNATURAL OCCURRENCE OF AN EARLY END. WHICH IS WHY I'VE SUMMONED YOU HERE...
TO BEAT BACK THE NIGHT... AND TO CONQUER DEATH.
And so THE GREAT SOCIETY six heroes of the ANTI-HEROIC AG outcasts all--bande together to repel th planetary incursion
They even defeated the SIDERA MARIS, powerful beings and heralds of the destructive MAPMAKERS.
The incursion was halted at great personal costs. Would they survive another?
And what of these ominous, dark beings watching from another Earth?

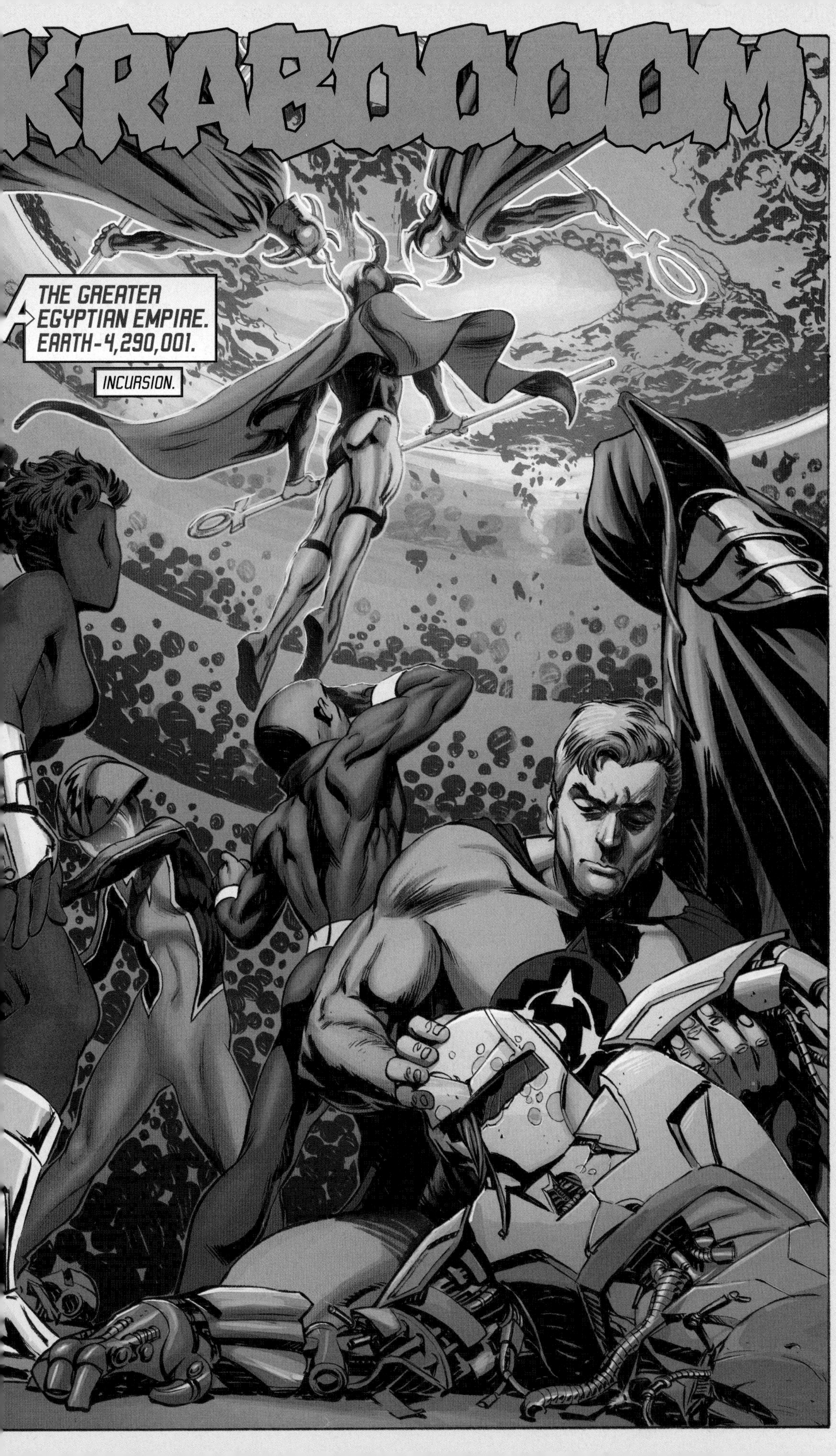
KRABOOOOM
THE GREATER EGYPTIAN EMPIRE. EARTH-4,290,001.
INCURSION.

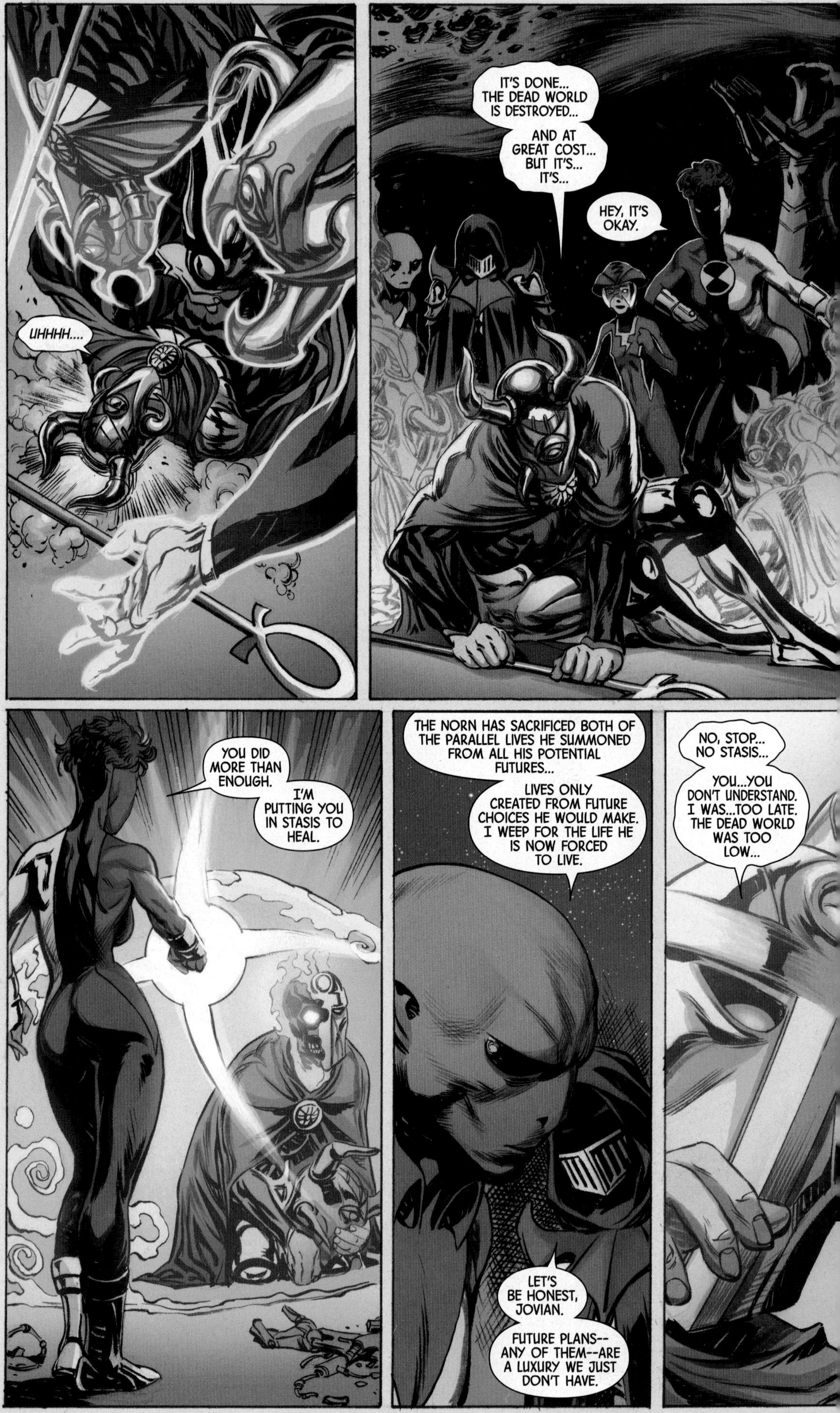
UHHHH....
IT'S DONE... THE DEAD WORLD IS DESTROYED...
AND AT GREAT COST... BUT IT'S... IT'S...
HEY, IT'S OKAY.
YOU DID MORE THAN ENOUGH.
I'M PUTTING YOU IN STASIS TO HEAL.
THE NORN HAS SACRIFICED BOTH OF THE PARALLEL LIVES HE SUMMONED FROM ALL HIS POTENTIAL FUTURES...
LIVES ONLY CREATED FROM FUTURE CHOICES HE WOULD MAKE. I WEEP FOR THE LIFE HE IS NOW FORCED TO LIVE.
LET'S BE HONEST, JOVIAN.
FUTURE PLANS--ANY OF THEM--ARE A LUXURY WE JUST DON'T HAVE.
NO, STOP... NO STASIS...
YOU...YOU DON'T UNDERSTAND. I WAS...TOO LATE. THE DEAD WORLD WAS TOO LOW...

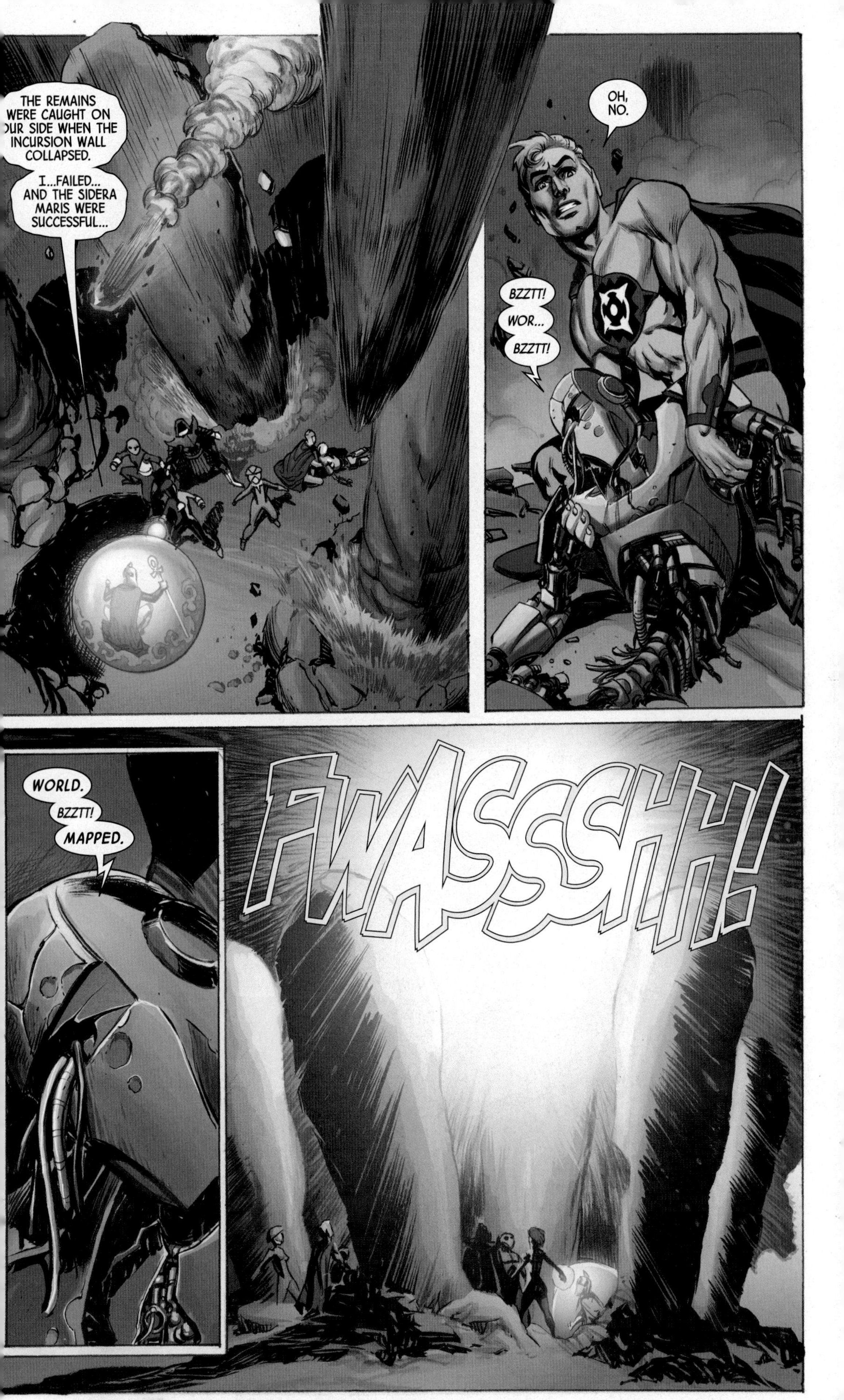
THE REMAINS WERE CAUGHT ON OUR SIDE WHEN THE INCURSION WALL COLLAPSED.
I...FAILED... AND THE SIDERA MARIS WERE SUCCESSFUL...
OH, NO.
BZZTT!
WOR...
BZZTT!
WORLD.
BZZTT!
MAPPED.
FWASSSHH!

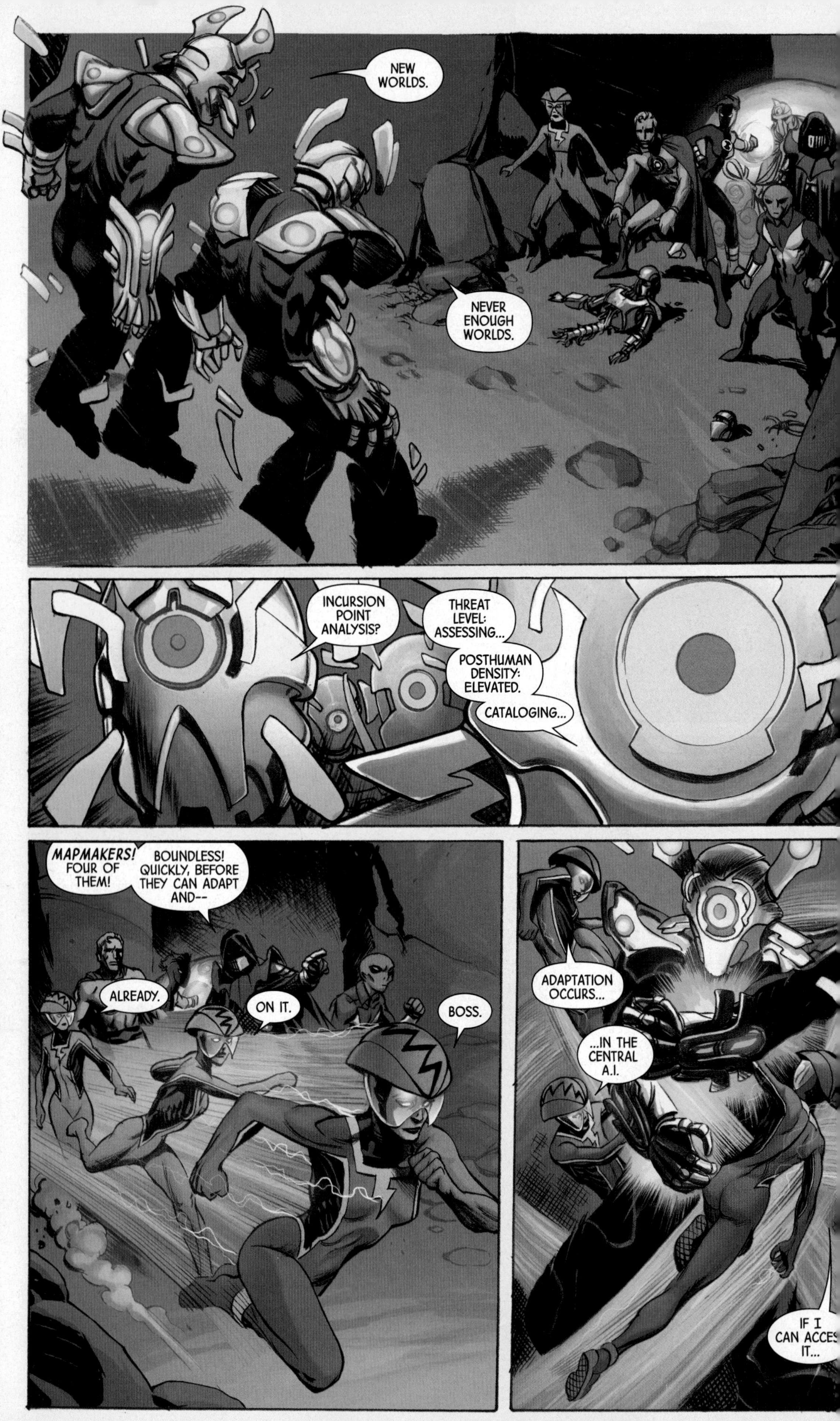
NEW WORLDS.
NEVER ENOUGH WORLDS.
INCURSION POINT ANALYSIS?
THREAT LEVEL: ASSESSING...
POSTHUMAN DENSITY: ELEVATED.
CATALOGING...
MAPMAKERS! FOUR OF THEM!
BOUNDLESS! QUICKLY, BEFORE THEY CAN ADAPT AND--
ALREADY.
ON IT.
BOSS.
ADAPTATION OCCURS...
...IN THE CENTRAL A.I.
IF I CAN ACCES IT...

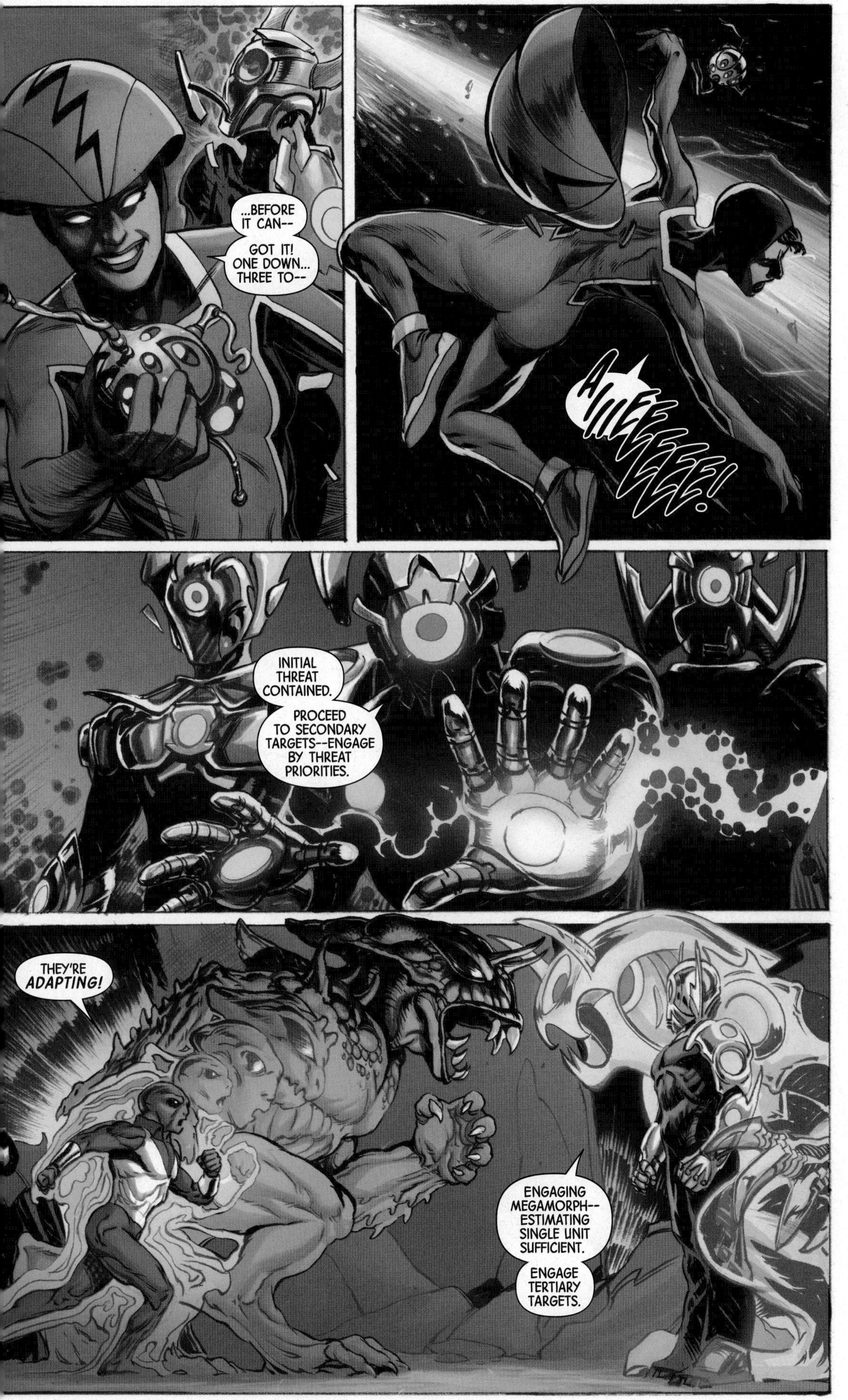
...BEFORE IT CAN--
GOT IT! ONE DOWN... THREE TO--
AIIIEEEEEEE!
INITIAL THREAT CONTAINED.
PROCEED TO SECONDARY TARGETS--ENGAGE BY THREAT PRIORITIES.
THEY'RE *ADAPTING!*
ENGAGING MEGAMORPH--ESTIMATING SINGLE UNIT SUFFICIENT.
ENGAGE TERTIARY TARGETS.

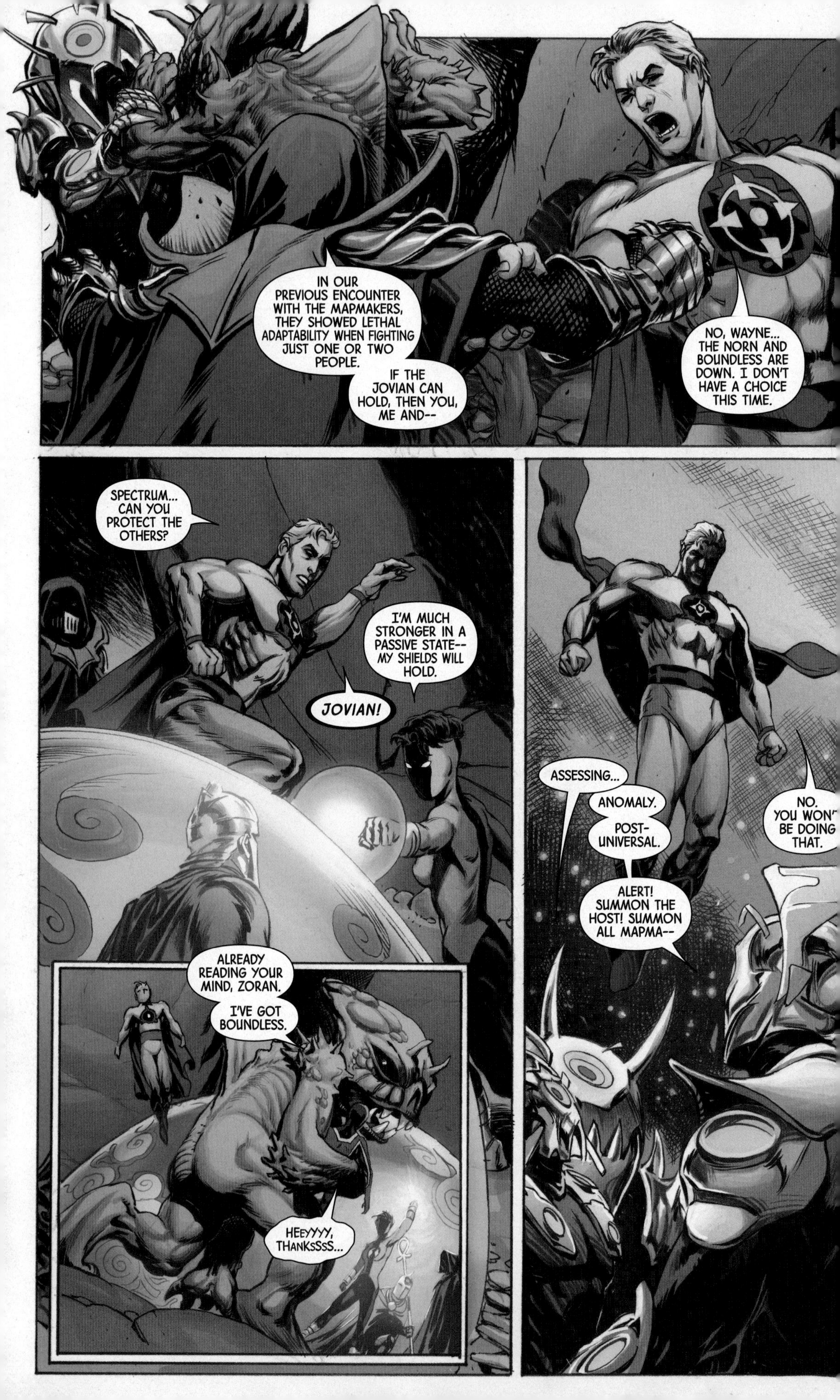
IN OUR PREVIOUS ENCOUNTER WITH THE MAPMAKERS, THEY SHOWED LETHAL ADAPTABILITY WHEN FIGHTING JUST ONE OR TWO PEOPLE.
IF THE JOVIAN CAN HOLD, THEN YOU, ME AND--
NO, WAYNE... THE NORN AND BOUNDLESS ARE DOWN. I DON'T HAVE A CHOICE THIS TIME.
SPECTRUM... CAN YOU PROTECT THE OTHERS?
I'M MUCH STRONGER IN A PASSIVE STATE-- MY SHIELDS WILL HOLD.
JOVIAN!
ALREADY READING YOUR MIND, ZORAN.
I'VE GOT BOUNDLESS.
HEEYYYY, THANKSSSS...
ASSESSING...
ANOMALY.
POST-UNIVERSAL.
ALERT! SUMMON THE HOST! SUMMON ALL MAPMA--
NO. YOU WON'T BE DOING THAT.

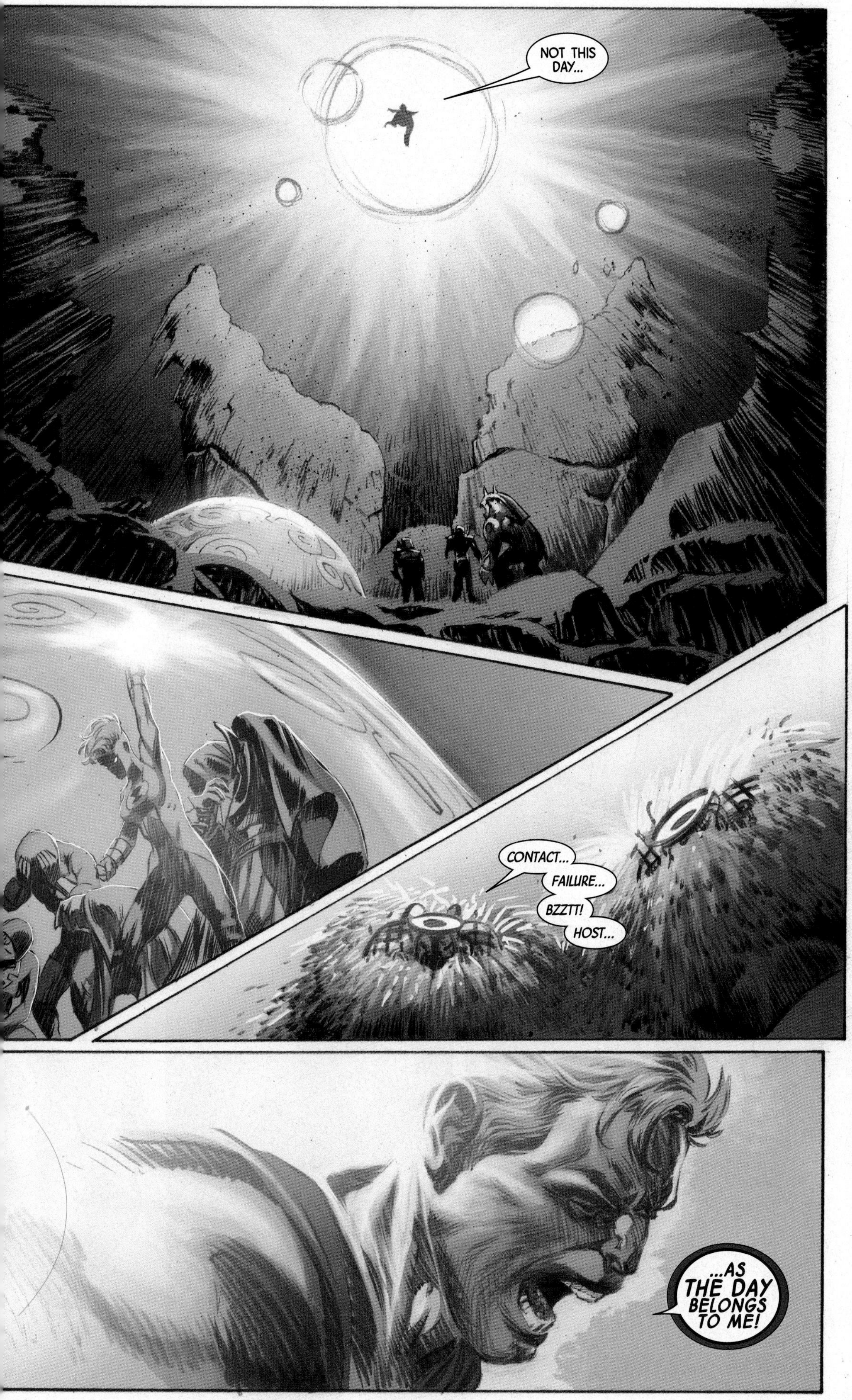
NOT THIS DAY...
CONTACT...
FAILURE...
BZZTT!
HOST...
...AS THE DAY BELONGS TO ME!

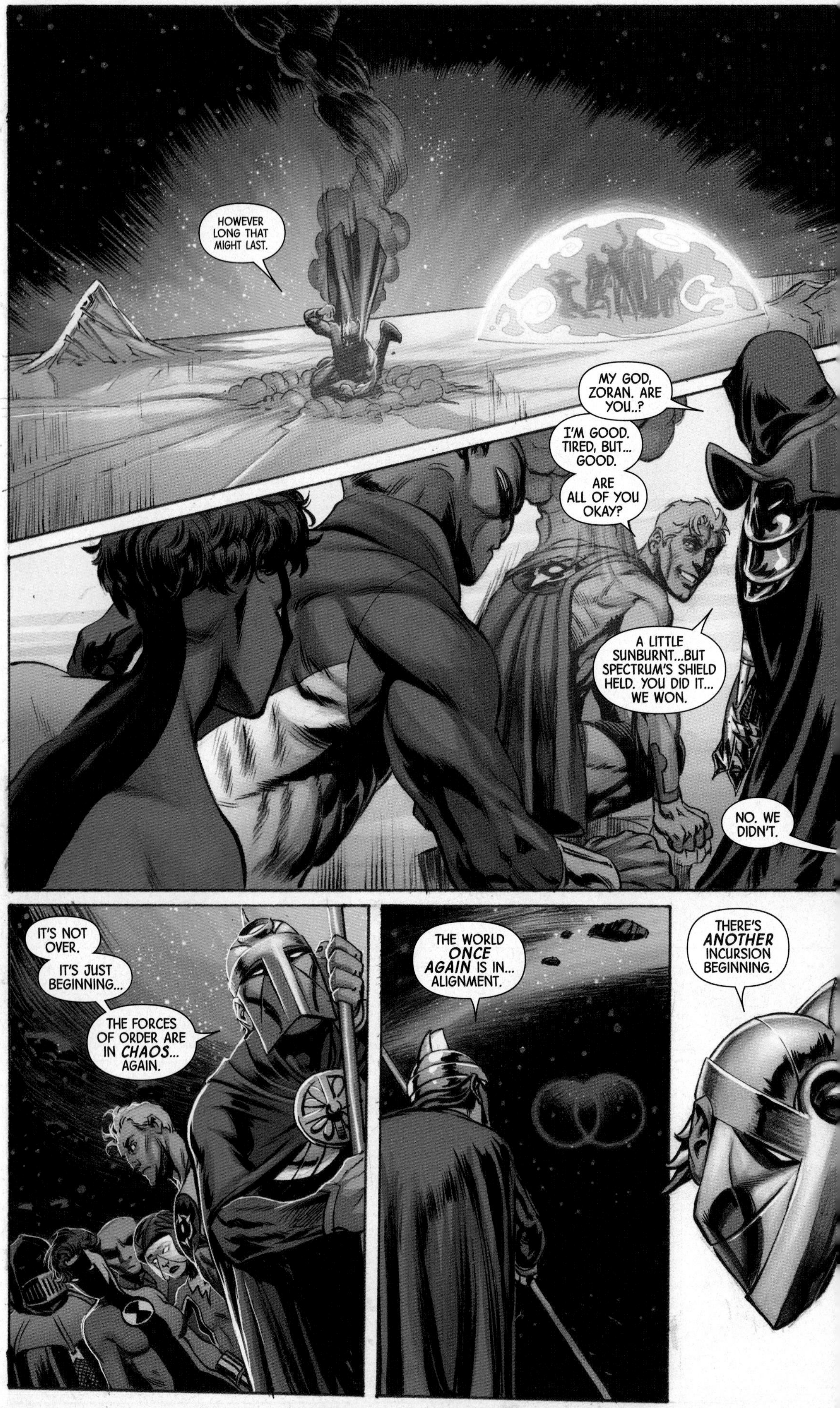
HOWEVER LONG THAT MIGHT LAST.
MY GOD, ZORAN. ARE YOU..?
I'M GOOD. TIRED, BUT... GOOD.
ARE ALL OF YOU OKAY?
A LITTLE SUNBURNT...BUT SPECTRUM'S SHIELD HELD. YOU DID IT... WE WON.
NO. WE DIDN'T.
IT'S NOT OVER.
IT'S JUST BEGINNING...
THE FORCES OF ORDER ARE IN *CHAOS*... AGAIN.
THE WORLD *ONCE AGAIN* IS IN... ALIGNMENT.
THERE'S *ANOTHER* INCURSION BEGINNING.

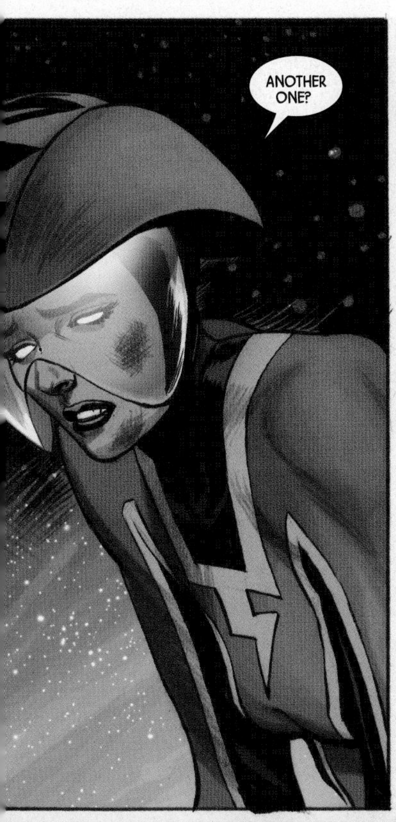
ANOTHER ONE?

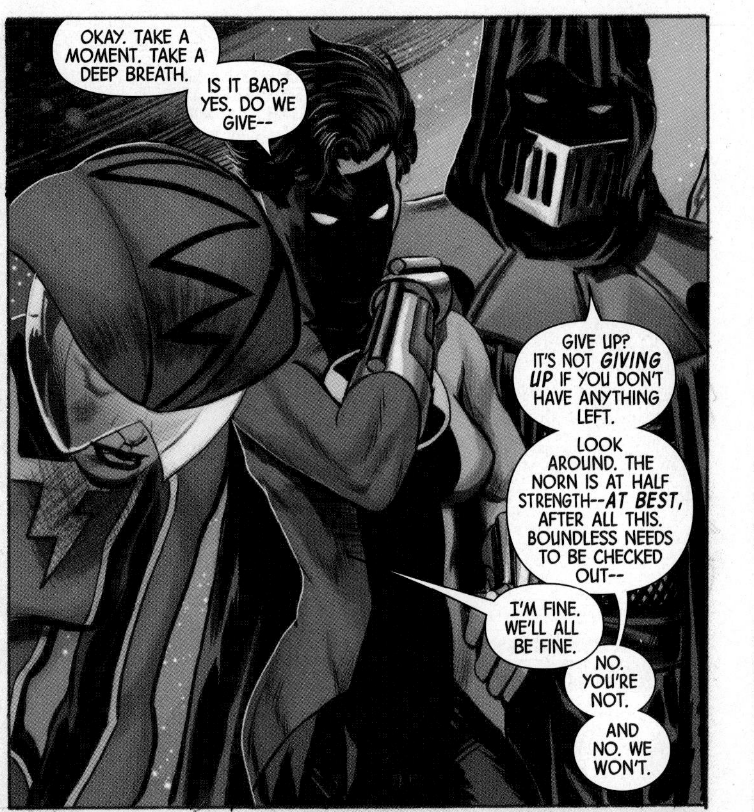
OKAY. TAKE A MOMENT. TAKE A DEEP BREATH.
IS IT BAD? YES. DO WE GIVE--
GIVE UP? IT'S NOT *GIVING UP* IF YOU DON'T HAVE ANYTHING LEFT.
LOOK AROUND. THE NORN IS AT HALF STRENGTH--*AT BEST,* AFTER ALL THIS. BOUNDLESS NEEDS TO BE CHECKED OUT--
I'M FINE. WE'LL ALL BE FINE.
NO. YOU'RE NOT.
AND NO. WE WON'T.

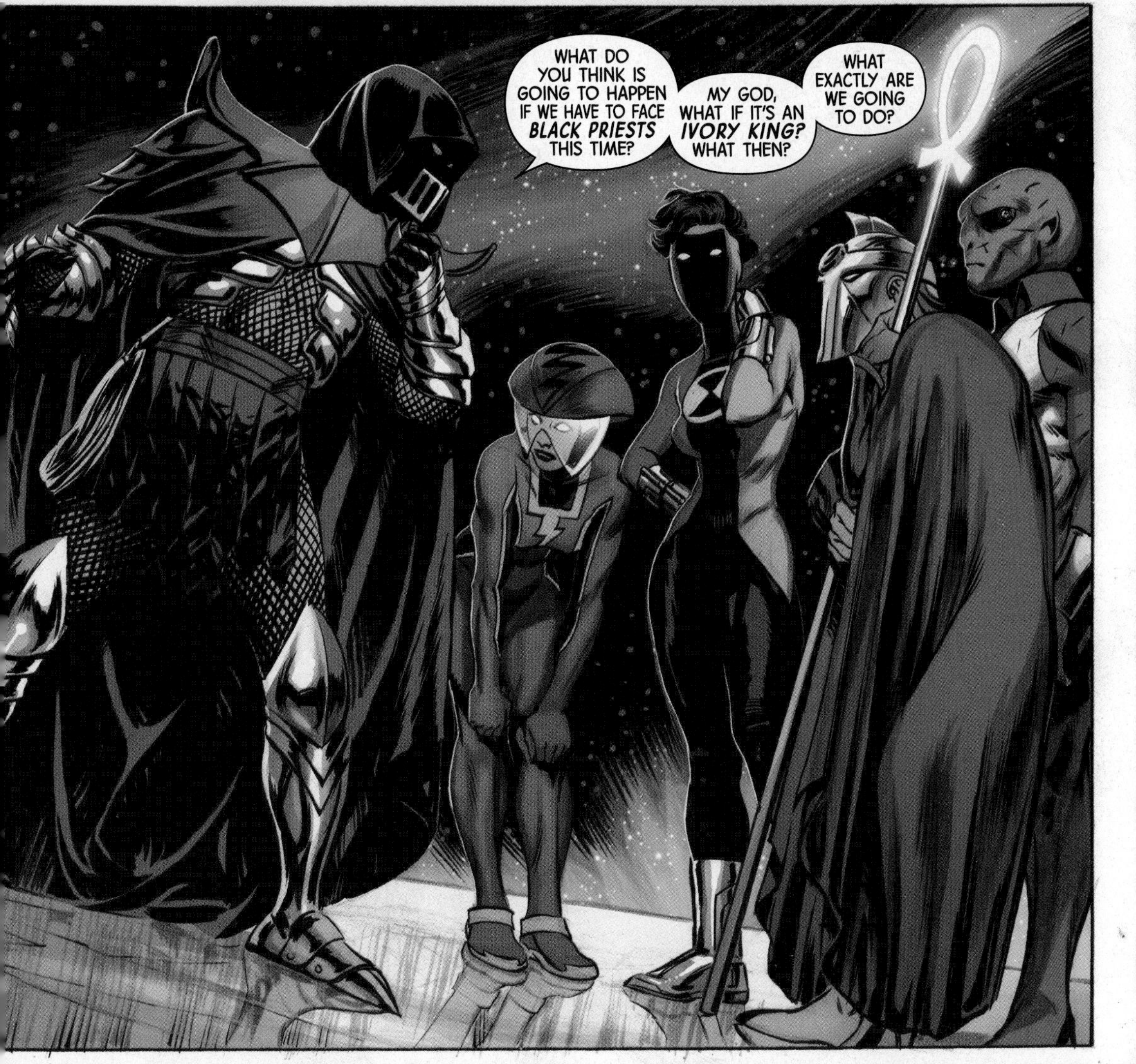
WHAT DO YOU THINK IS GOING TO HAPPEN IF WE HAVE TO FACE *BLACK PRIESTS* THIS TIME?
MY GOD, WHAT IF IT'S AN *IVORY KING?* WHAT THEN?
WHAT EXACTLY ARE WE GOING TO DO?

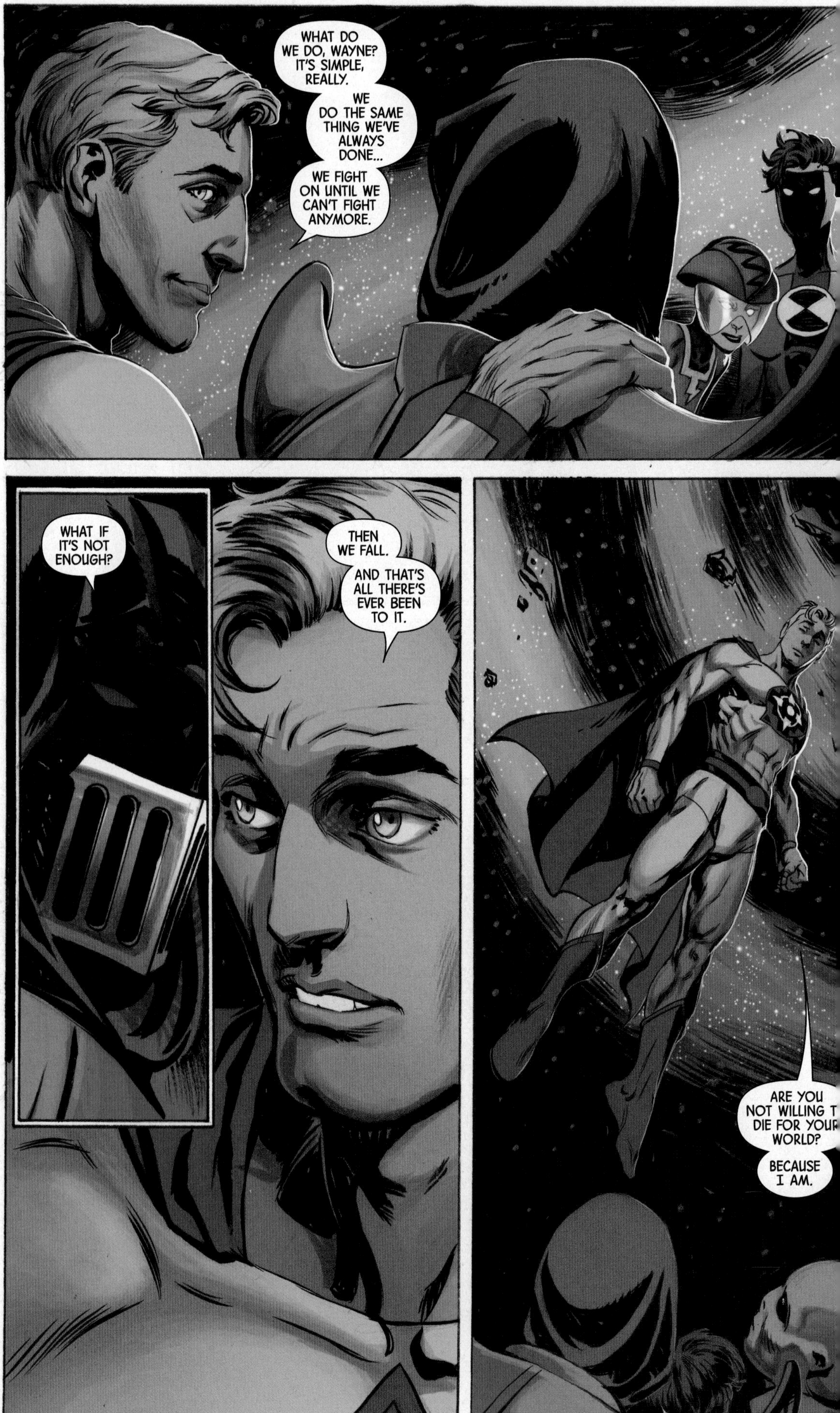
WHAT DO WE DO, WAYNE? IT'S SIMPLE, REALLY.
WE DO THE SAME THING WE'VE ALWAYS DONE...
WE FIGHT ON UNTIL WE CAN'T FIGHT ANYMORE.
WHAT IF IT'S NOT ENOUGH?
THEN WE FALL.
AND THAT'S ALL THERE'S EVER BEEN TO IT.
ARE YOU NOT WILLING T DIE FOR YOUR WORLD?
BECAUSE I AM.

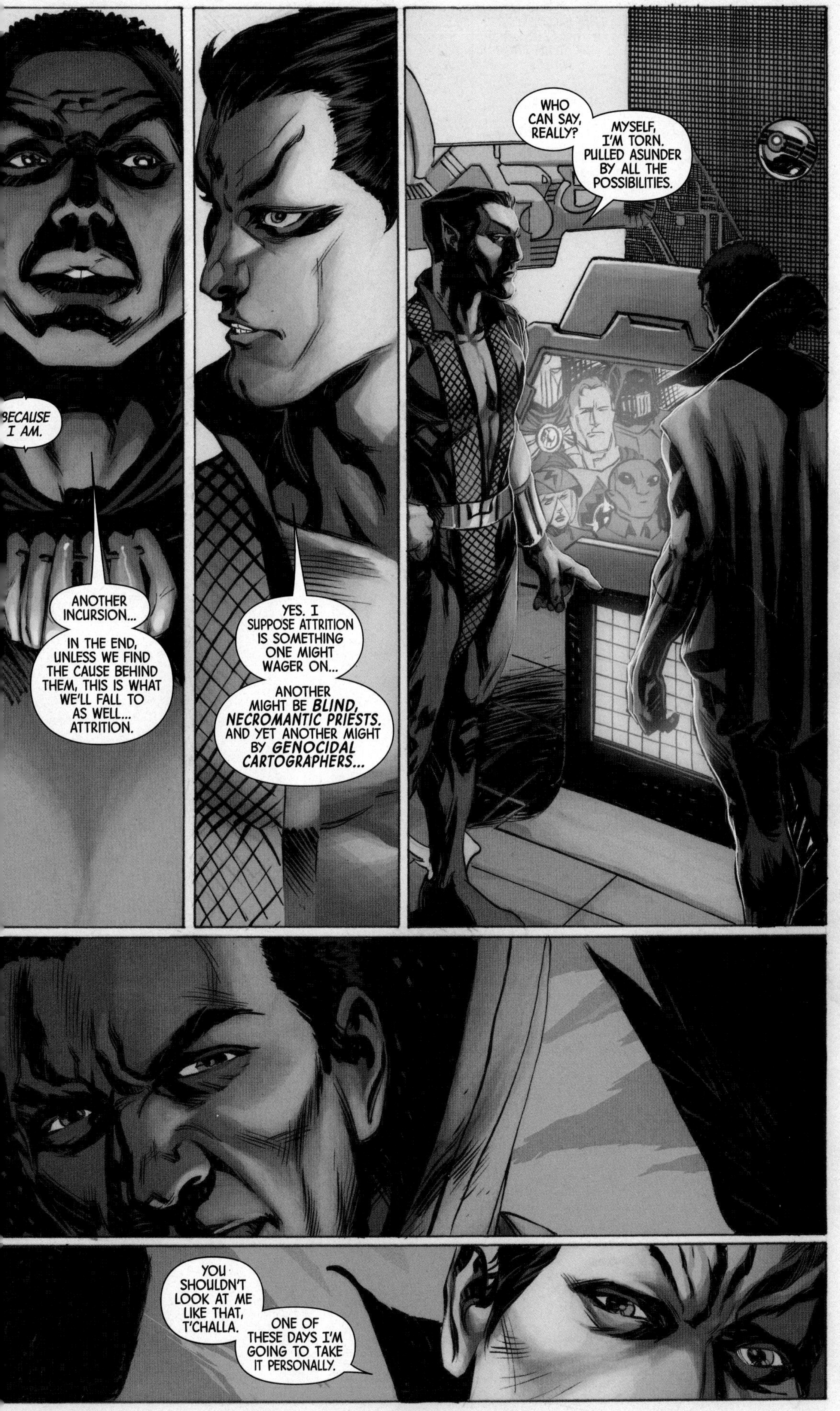

BECAUSE I AM.
ANOTHER INCURSION...
IN THE END, UNLESS WE FIND THE CAUSE BEHIND THEM, THIS IS WHAT WE'LL FALL TO AS WELL... ATTRITION.
YES. I SUPPOSE ATTRITION IS SOMETHING ONE MIGHT WAGER ON...
ANOTHER MIGHT BE BLIND, NECROMANTIC PRIESTS. AND YET ANOTHER MIGHT BY GENOCIDAL CARTOGRAPHERS...
WHO CAN SAY, REALLY?
MYSELF, I'M TORN. PULLED ASUNDER BY ALL THE POSSIBILITIES.
YOU SHOULDN'T LOOK AT ME LIKE THAT, T'CHALLA.
ONE OF THESE DAYS I'M GOING TO TAKE IT PERSONALLY.

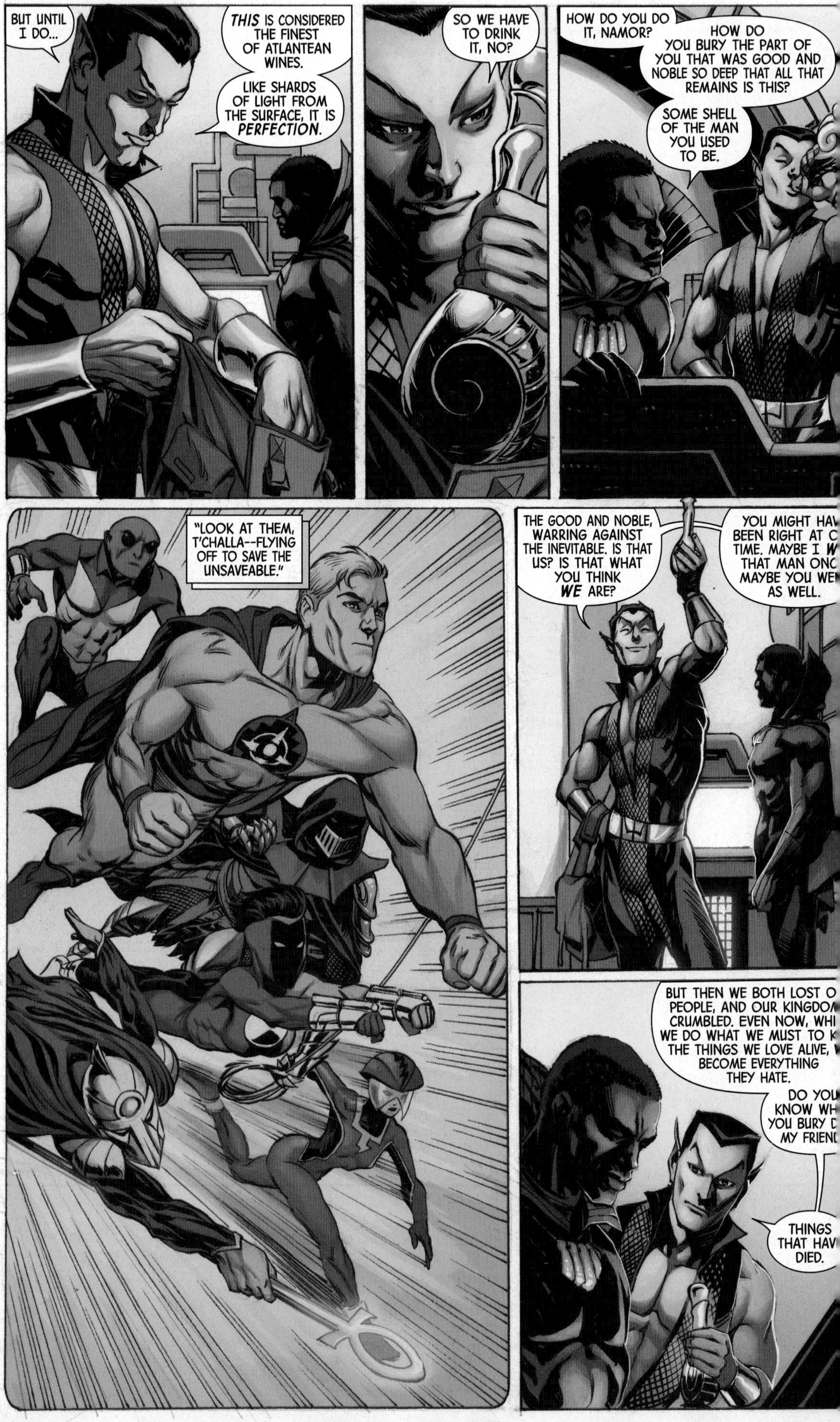
BUT UNTIL I DO...
THIS IS CONSIDERED THE FINEST OF ATLANTEAN WINES.
LIKE SHARDS OF LIGHT FROM THE SURFACE, IT IS PERFECTION.
SO WE HAVE TO DRINK IT, NO?
HOW DO YOU DO IT, NAMOR?
HOW DO YOU BURY THE PART OF YOU THAT WAS GOOD AND NOBLE SO DEEP THAT ALL THAT REMAINS IS THIS?
SOME SHELL OF THE MAN YOU USED TO BE.
"LOOK AT THEM, T'CHALLA--FLYING OFF TO SAVE THE UNSAVEABLE."
THE GOOD AND NOBLE, WARRING AGAINST THE INEVITABLE. IS THAT US? IS THAT WHAT YOU THINK WE ARE?
YOU MIGHT HAV
BEEN RIGHT AT O
TIME. MAYBE I W
THAT MAN ONC
MAYBE YOU WE
AS WELL.
BUT THEN WE BOTH LOST O
PEOPLE, AND OUR KINGDO
CRUMBLED. EVEN NOW, WHI
WE DO WHAT WE MUST TO K
THE THINGS WE LOVE ALIVE,
BECOME EVERYTHING
THEY HATE.
DO YOU
KNOW WH
YOU BURY
MY FRIEND
THINGS
THAT HAV
DIED.

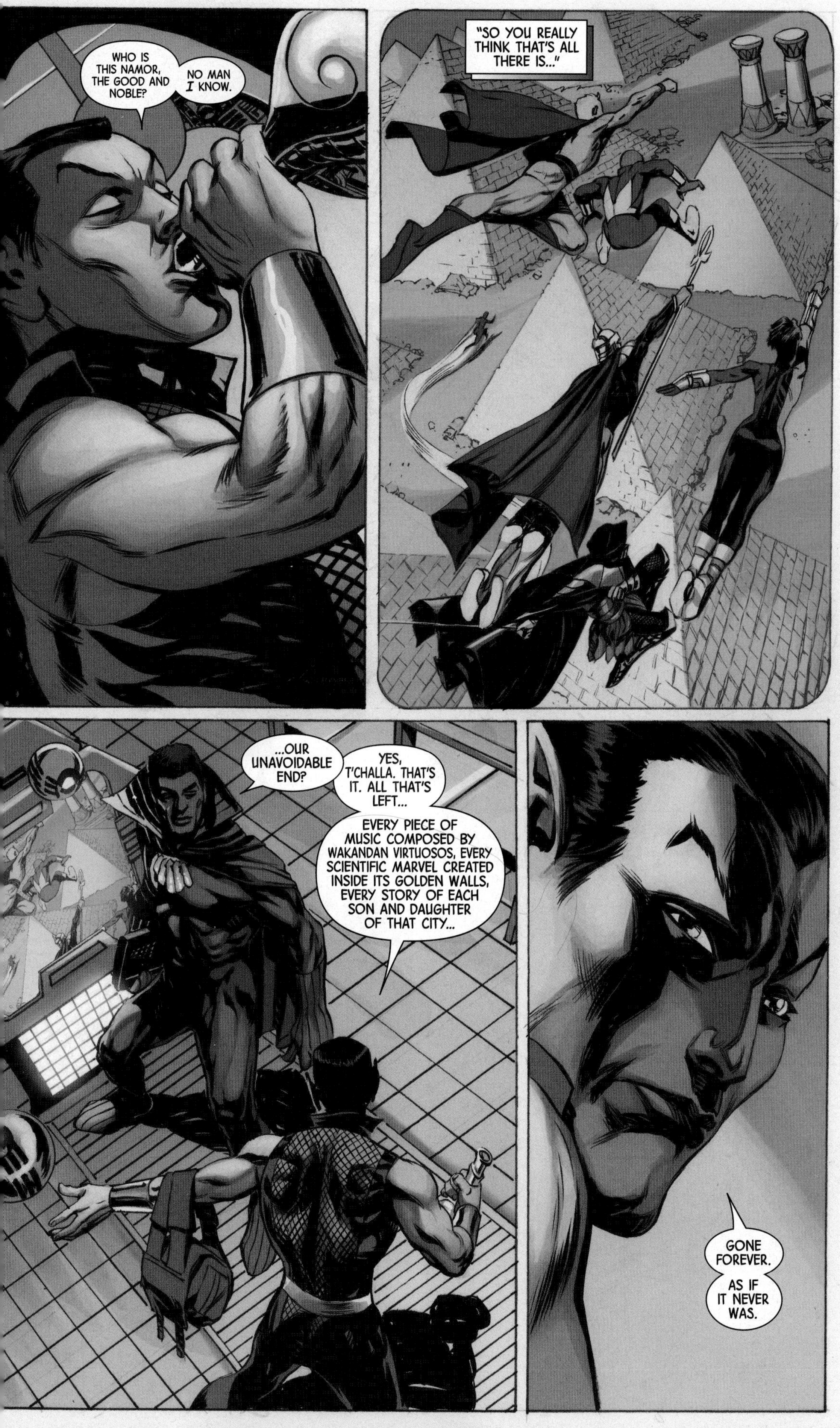
WHO IS THIS NAMOR, THE GOOD AND NOBLE?
NO MAN I KNOW.
"SO YOU REALLY THINK THAT'S ALL THERE IS..."
...OUR UNAVOIDABLE END?
YES, T'CHALLA. THAT'S IT. ALL THAT'S LEFT...
EVERY PIECE OF MUSIC COMPOSED BY WAKANDAN VIRTUOSOS, EVERY SCIENTIFIC MARVEL CREATED INSIDE ITS GOLDEN WALLS, EVERY STORY OF EACH SON AND DAUGHTER OF THAT CITY...
GONE FOREVER.
AS IF IT NEVER WAS.

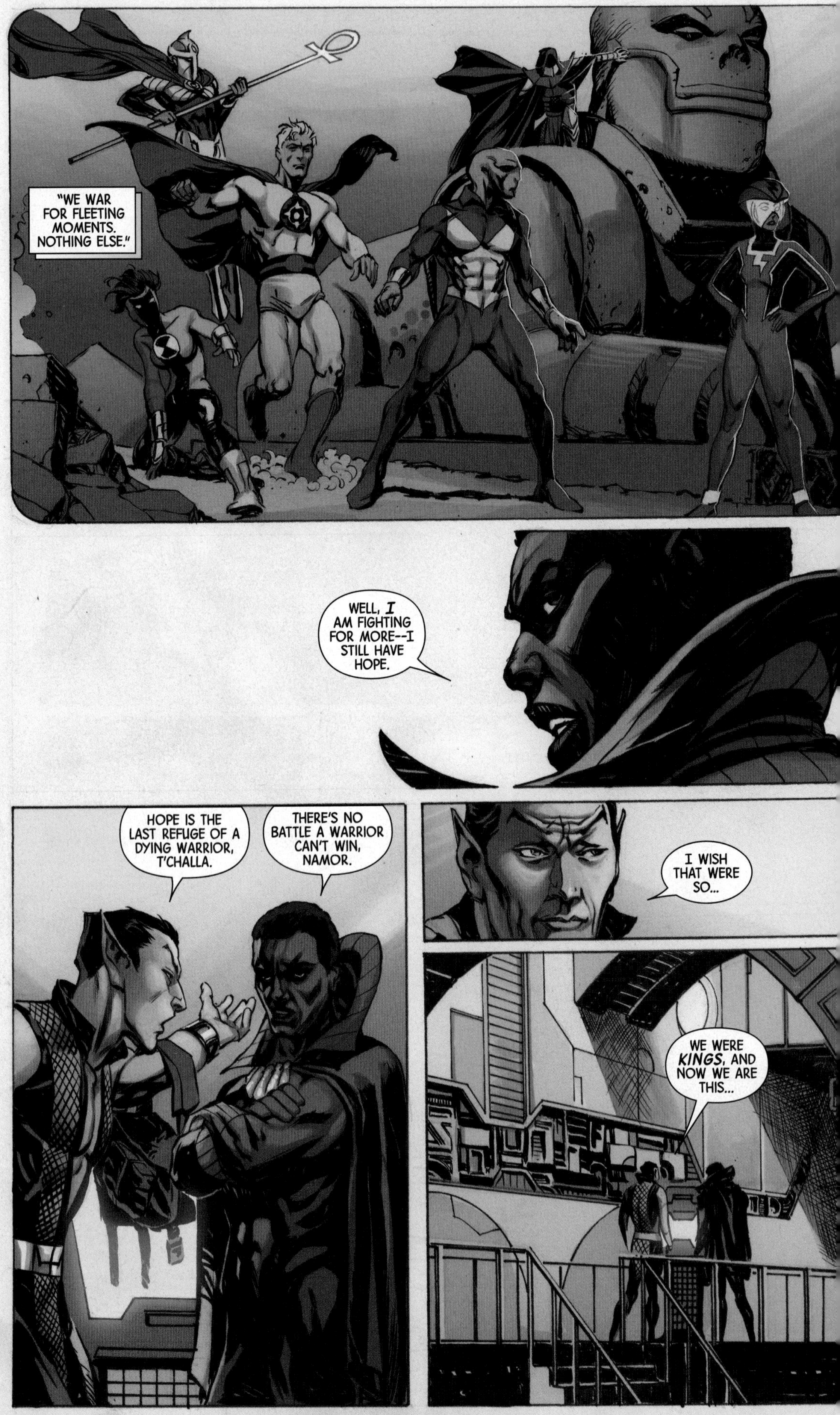
"WE WAR FOR FLEETING MOMENTS. NOTHING ELSE."
WELL, *I* AM FIGHTING FOR MORE--I STILL HAVE HOPE.
HOPE IS THE LAST REFUGE OF A DYING WARRIOR, T'CHALLA.
THERE'S NO BATTLE A WARRIOR CAN'T WIN, NAMOR.
I WISH THAT WERE SO...
WE WERE *KINGS*, AND NOW WE ARE THIS...

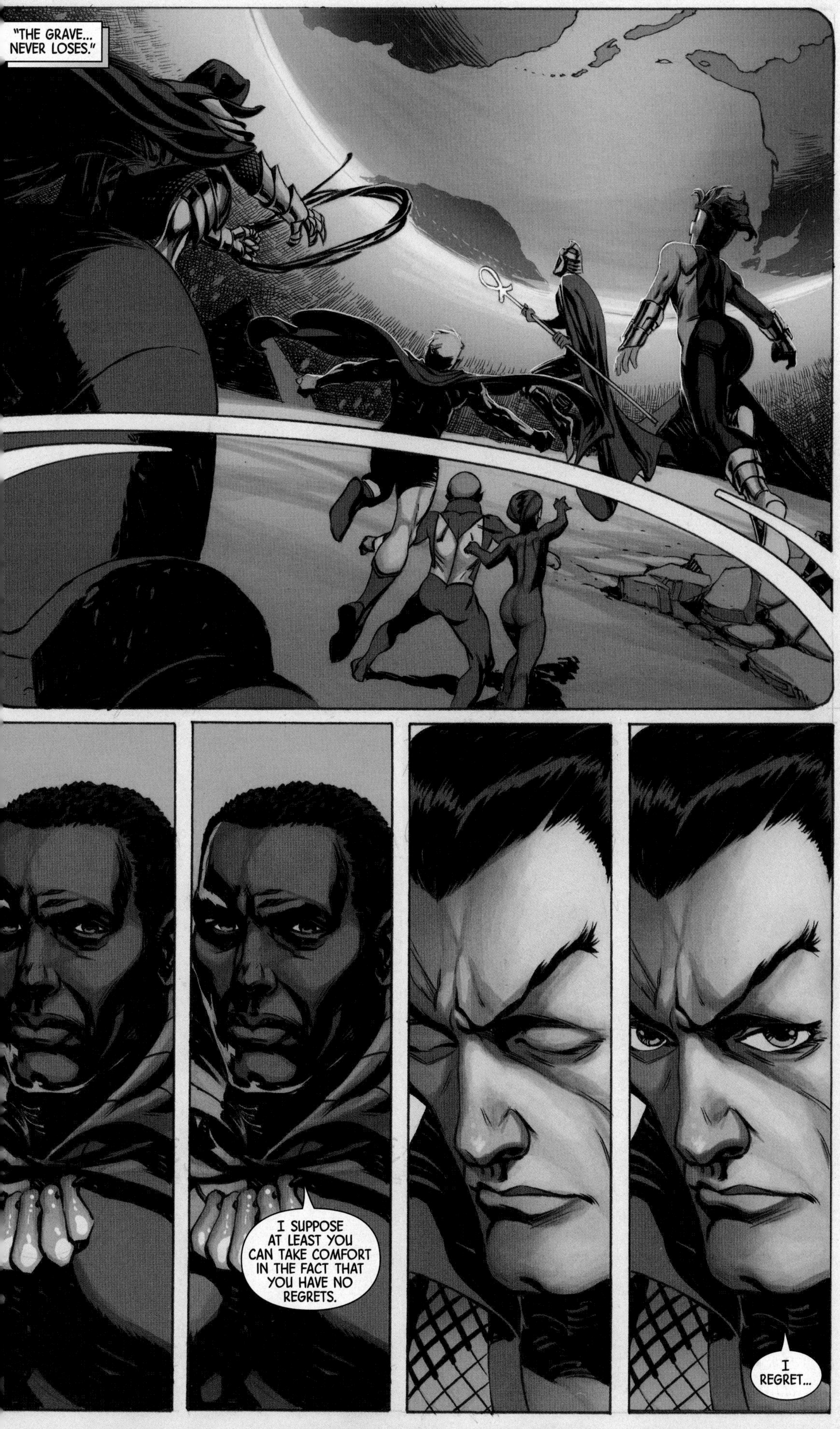
"THE GRAVE... NEVER LOSES."
I SUPPOSE AT LEAST YOU CAN TAKE COMFORT IN THE FACT THAT YOU HAVE NO REGRETS.
I REGRET...

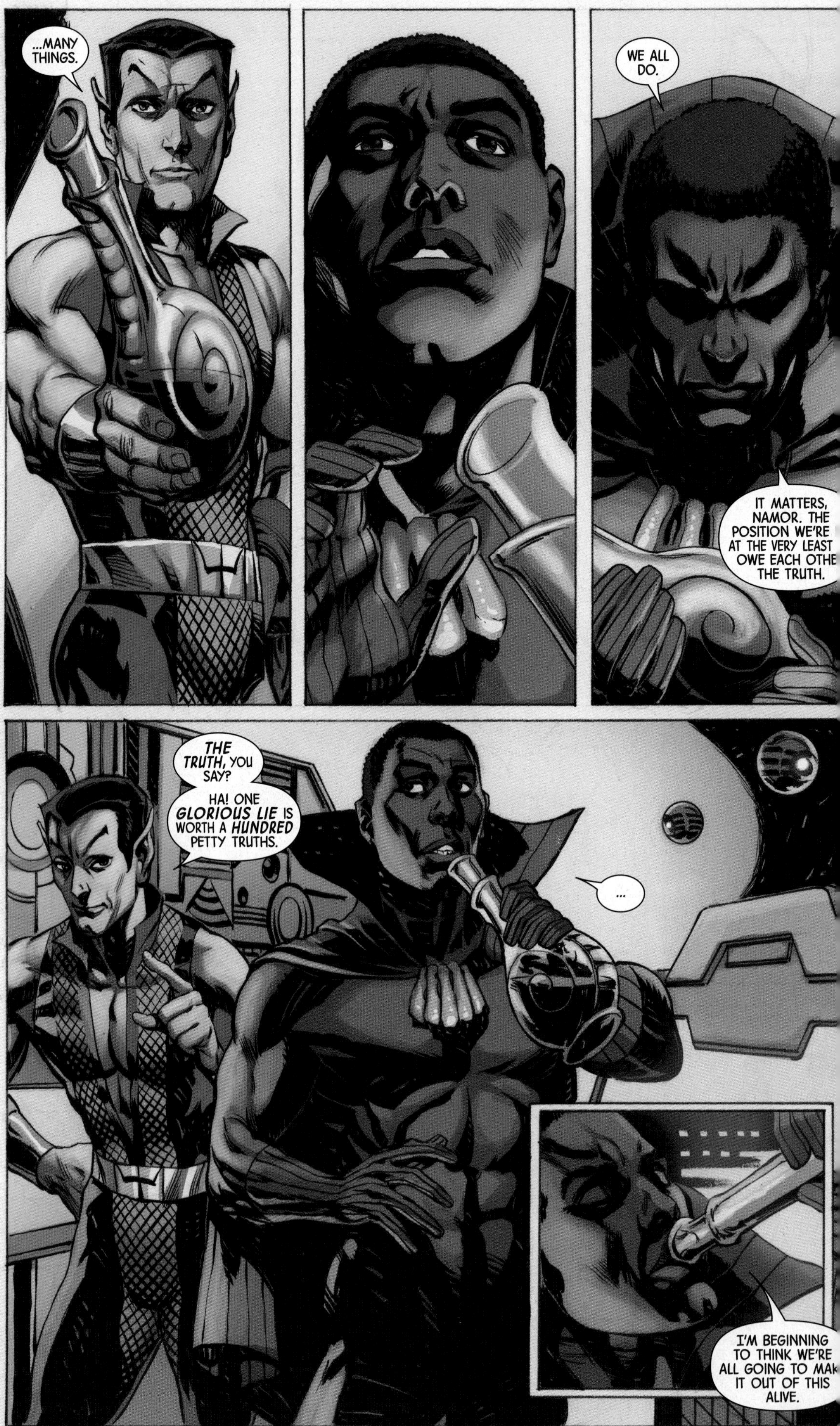
...MANY THINGS.
WE ALL DO.
IT MATTERS, NAMOR. THE POSITION WE'RE AT THE VERY LEAST OWE EACH OTHE THE TRUTH.
THE TRUTH, YOU SAY?
HA! ONE GLORIOUS LIE IS WORTH A HUNDRED PETTY TRUTHS.
...
I'M BEGINNING TO THINK WE'RE ALL GOING TO MAK IT OUT OF THIS ALIVE.

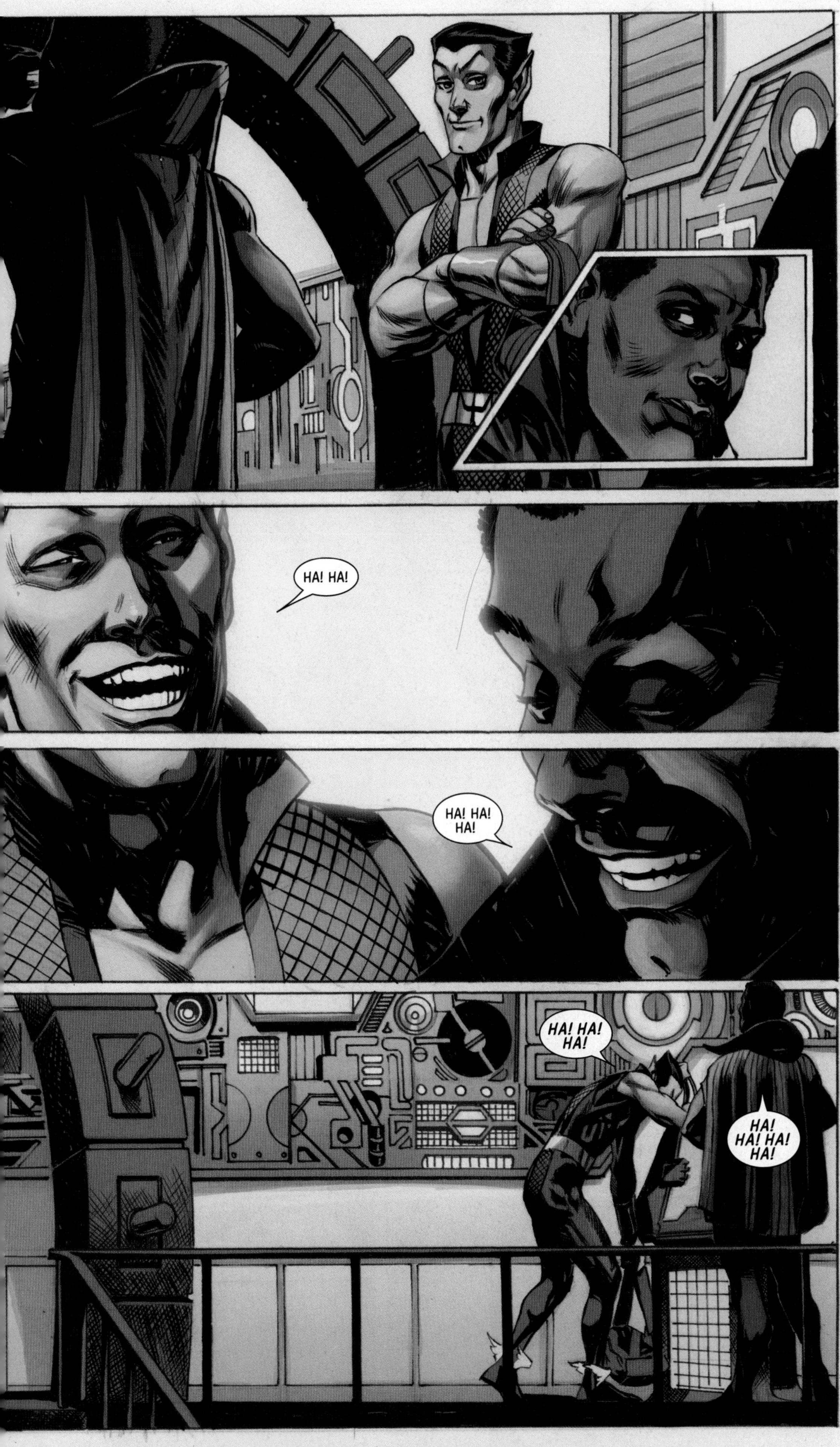
HA! HA!
HA! HA! HA!
HA! HA! HA!
HA! HA! HA! HA!

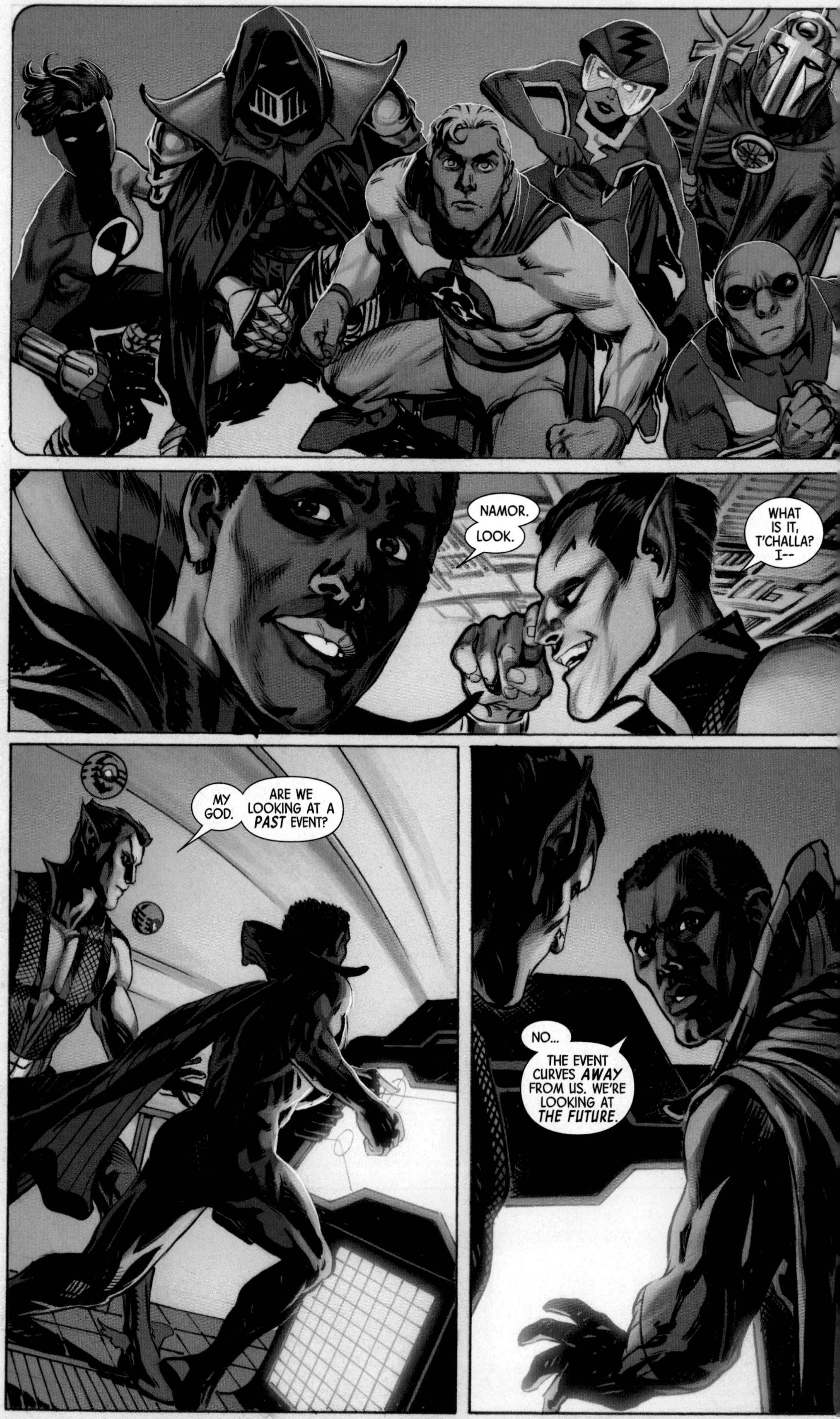
NAMOR.
LOOK.
WHAT IS IT, T'CHALLA? I--
MY GOD.
ARE WE LOOKING AT A *PAST* EVENT?
NO...
THE EVENT CURVES *AWAY* FROM US. WE'RE LOOKING AT *THE FUTURE*.

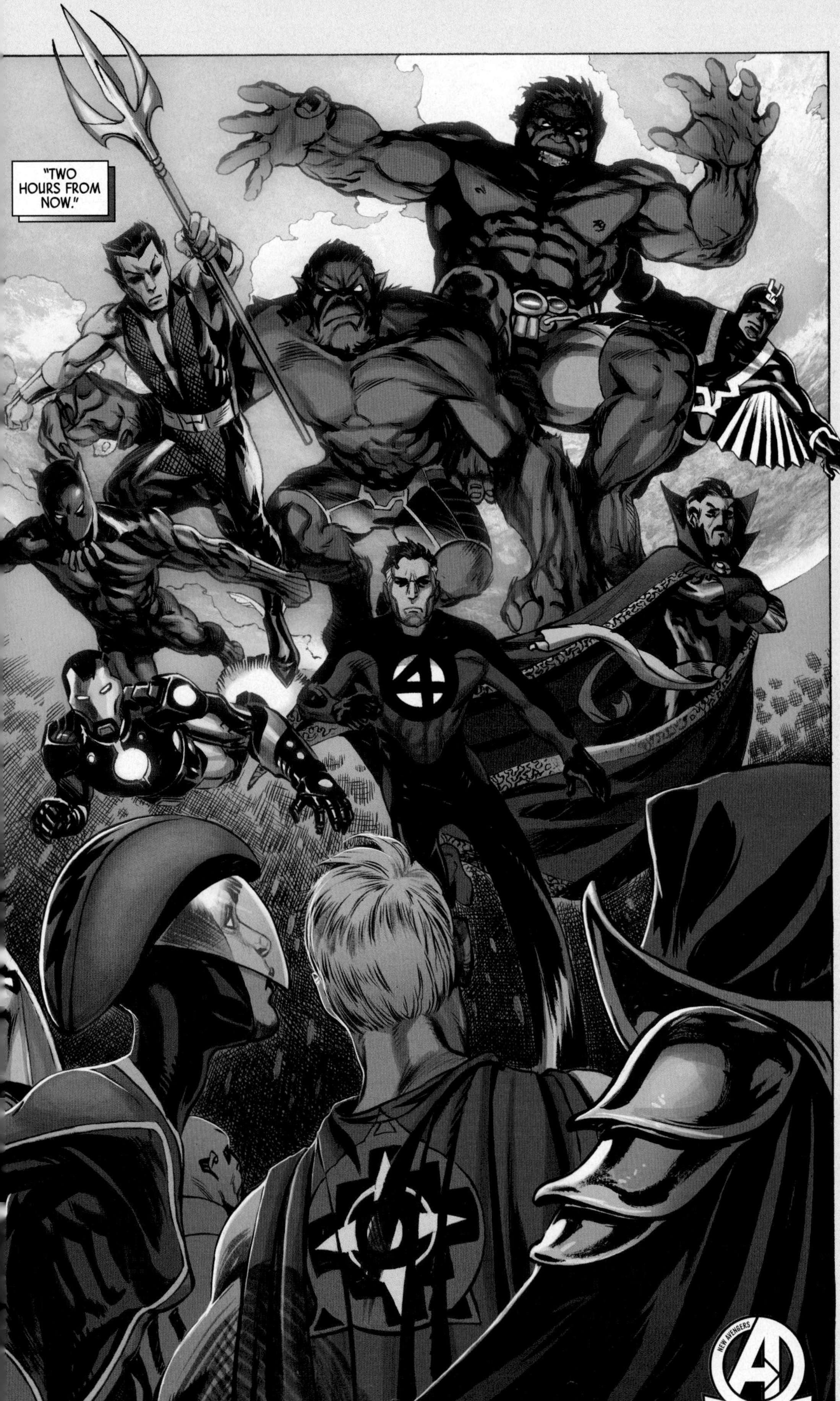
"TWO HOURS FROM NOW."
NEW AVENGERS

#13

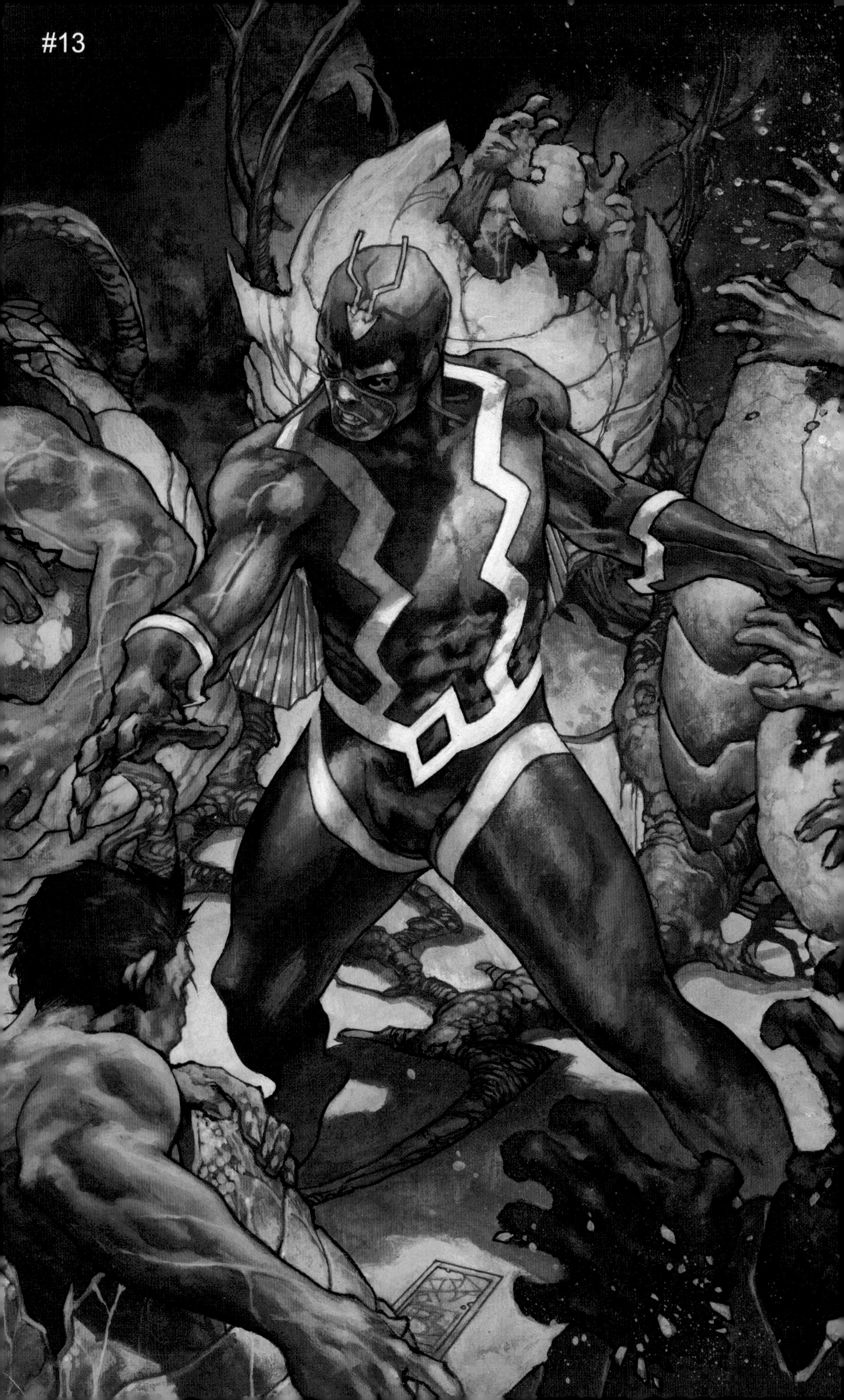

#14

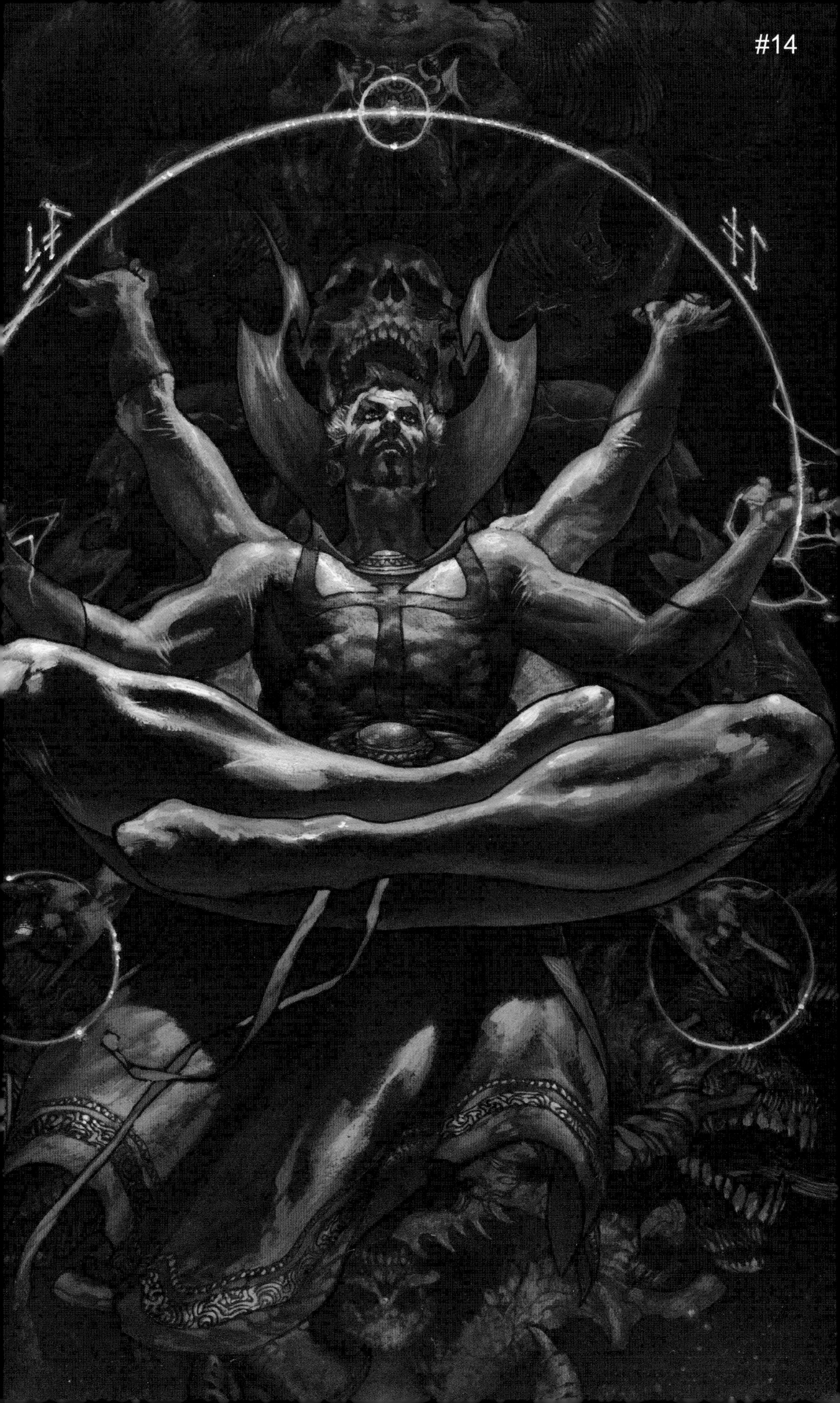

#15

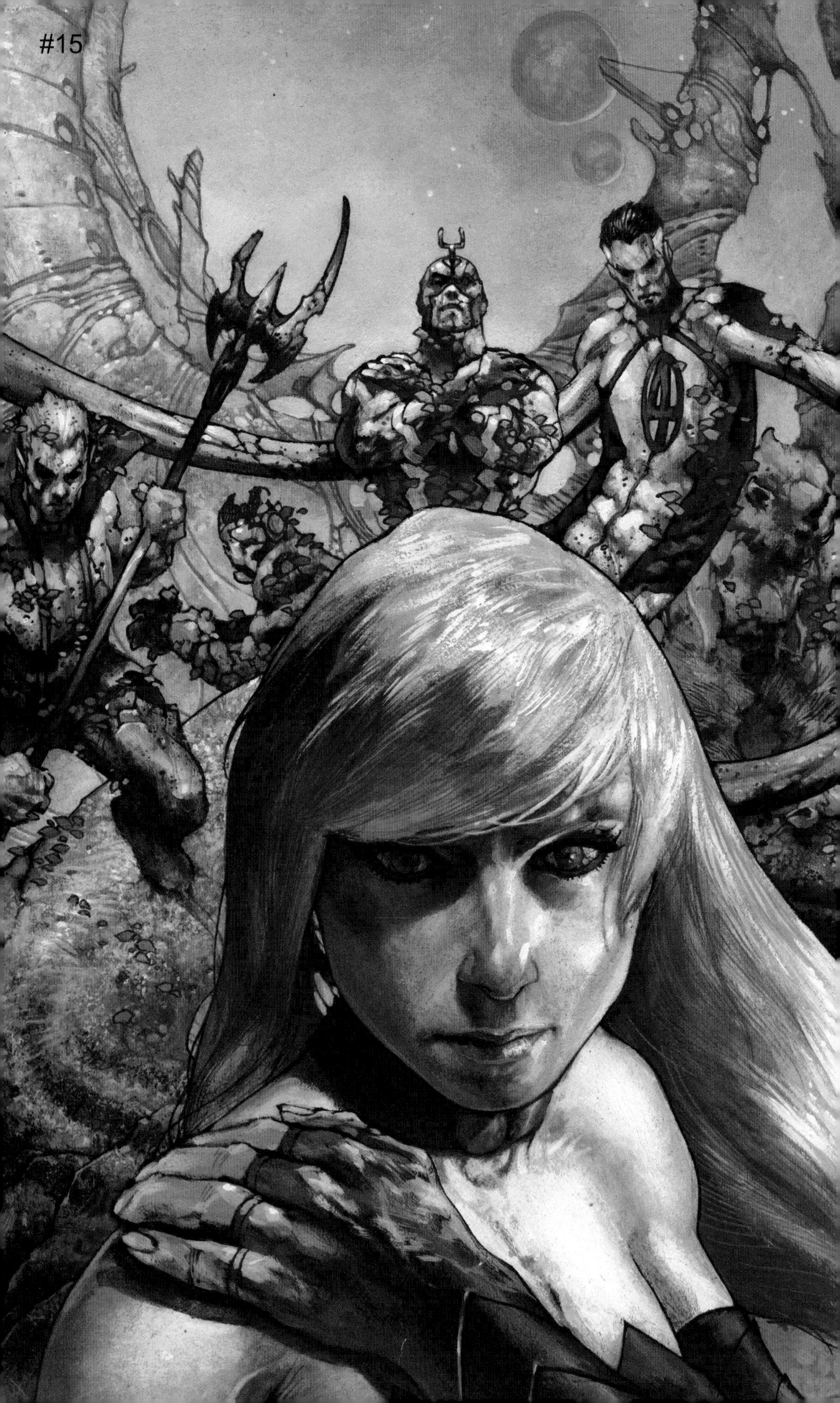

#16

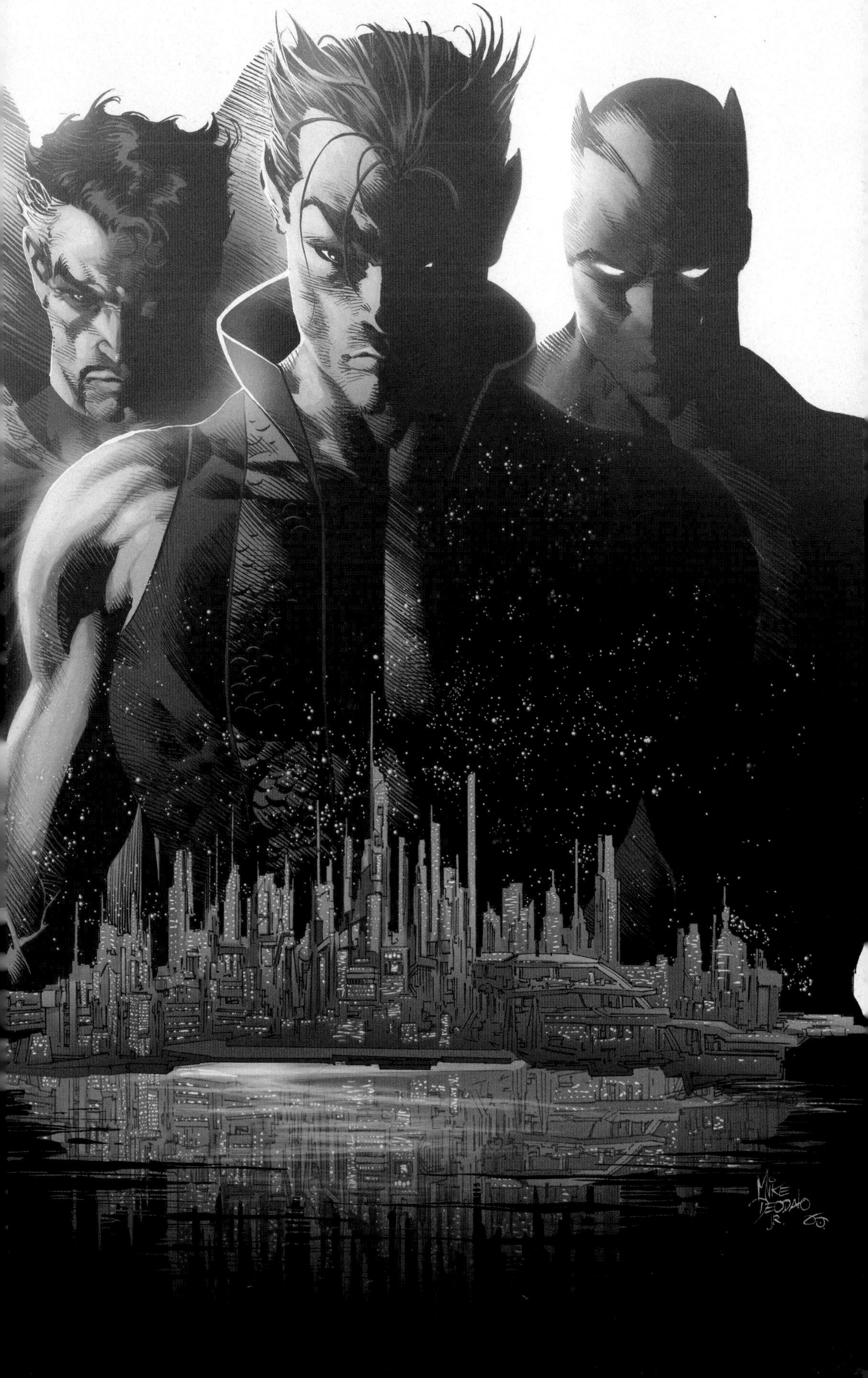

#17

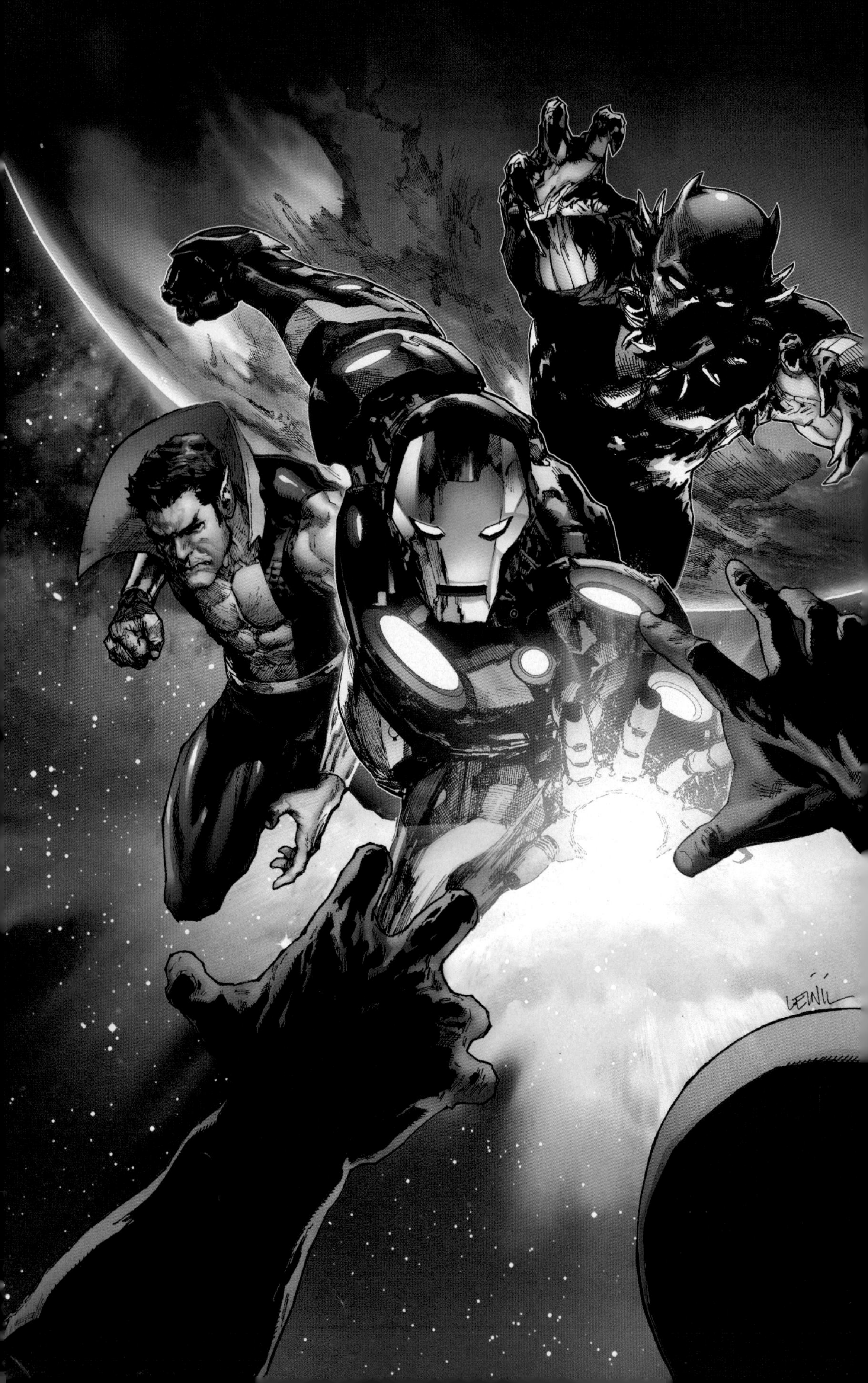

#13 VARIANT BY **MIKE DEODATO & RAIN BEREDO**

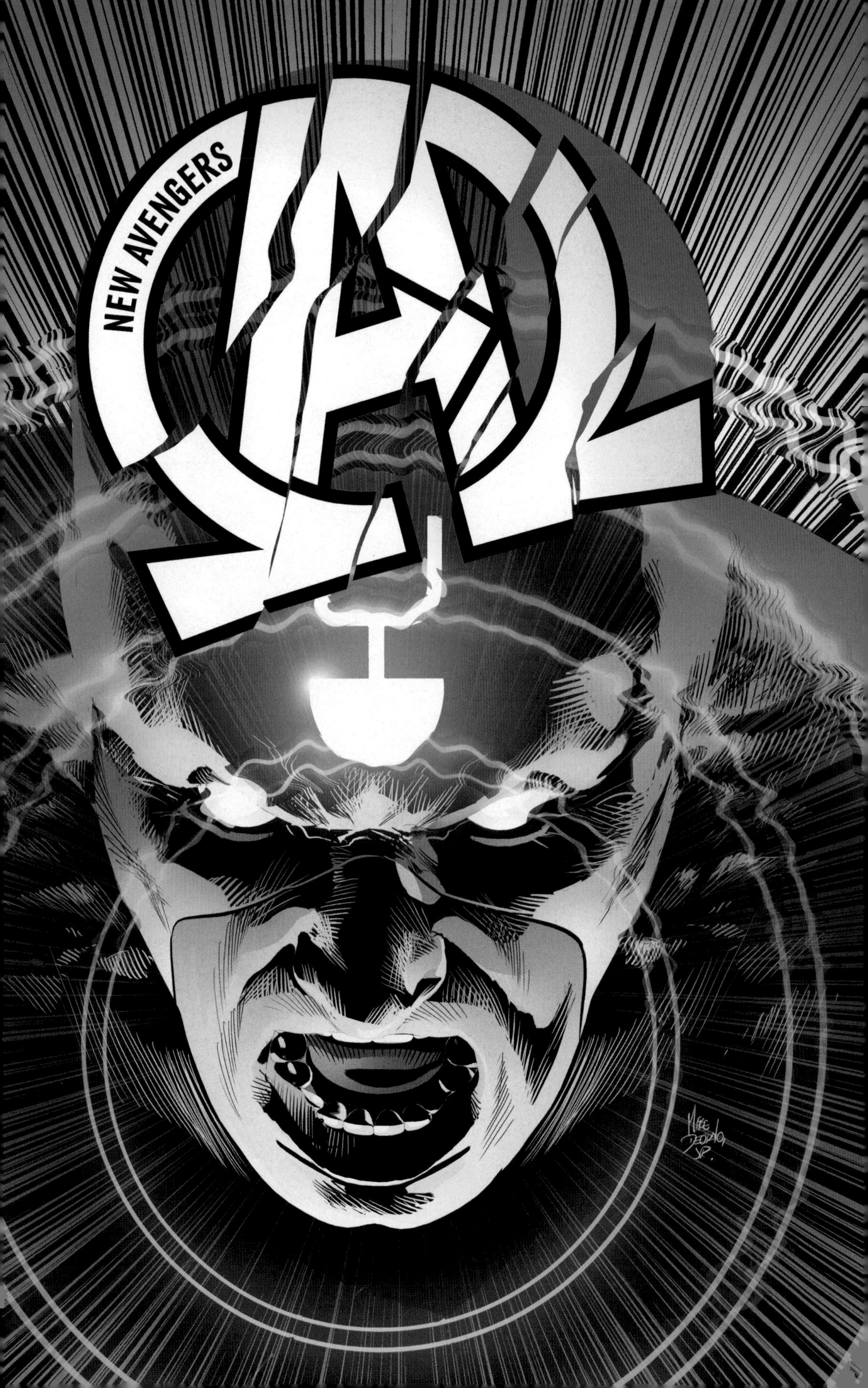
NEW AVENGERS

#16 VARIANT BY **RAGS MORALES & PAUL MOUNTS**

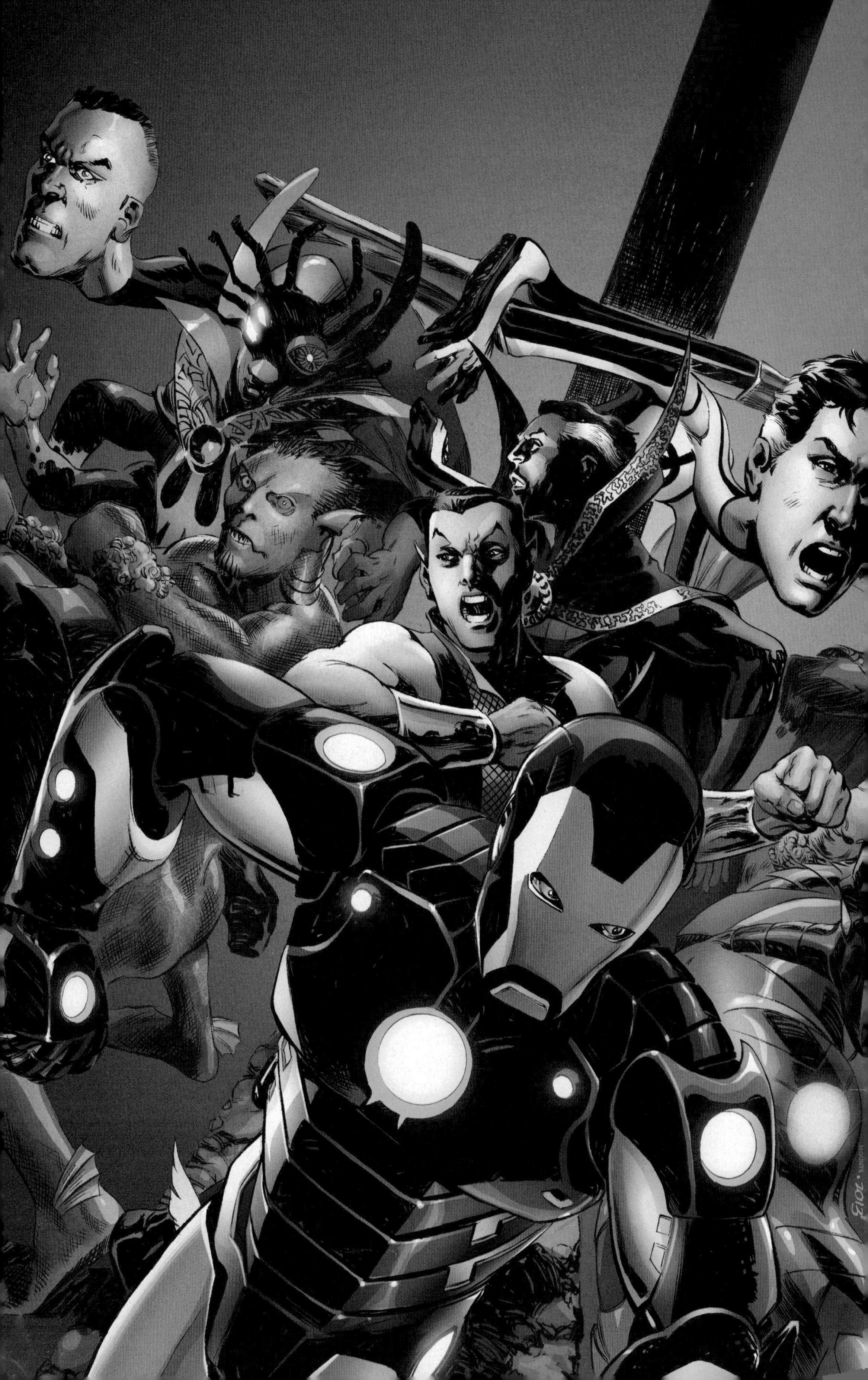

#17 CAPTAIN AMERICA TEAM-UP VARIANT BY **PAOLO RIVERA**

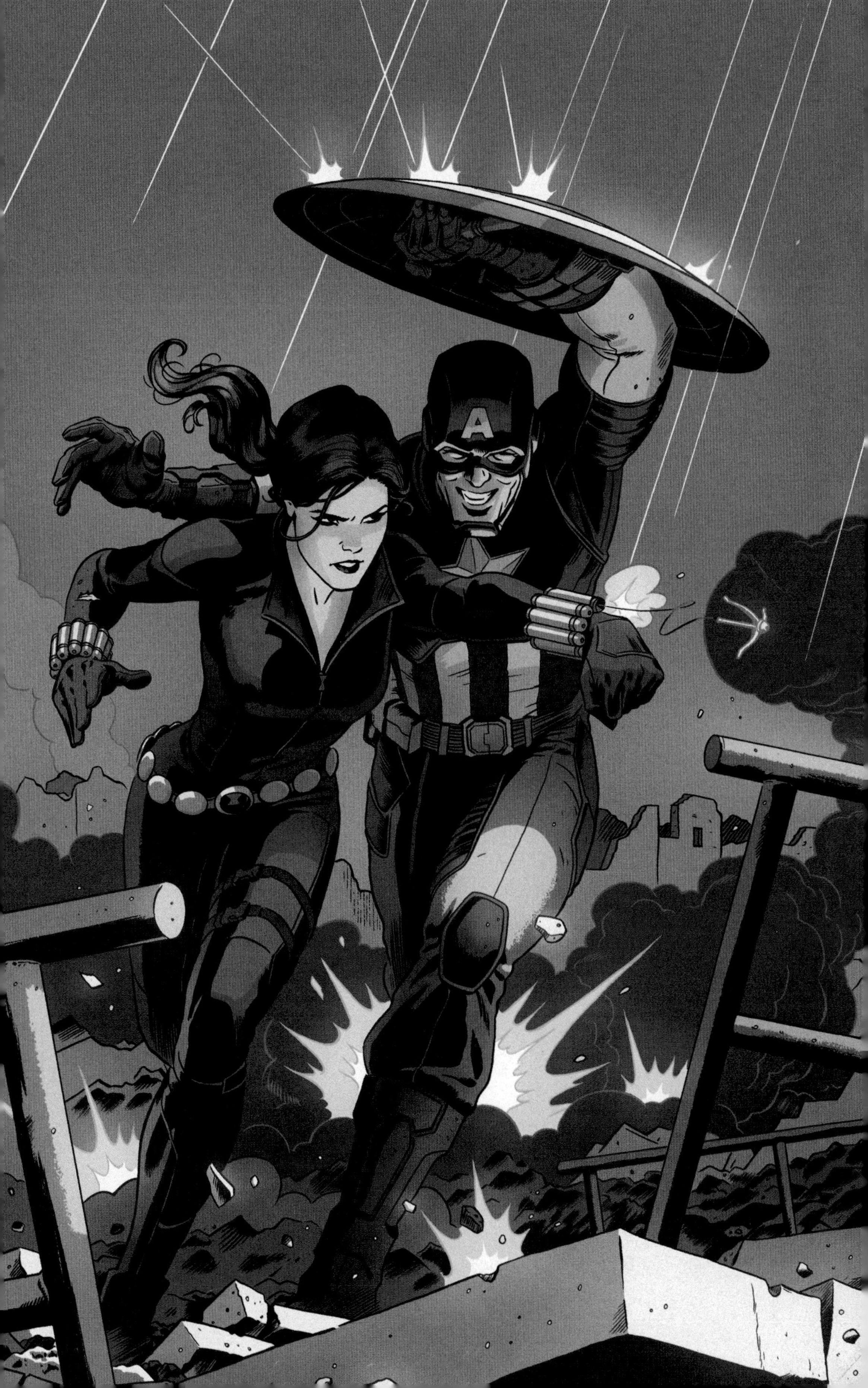

#17 VARIANT BY **PHIL JIMENEZ & RACHELLE ROSENBERG**

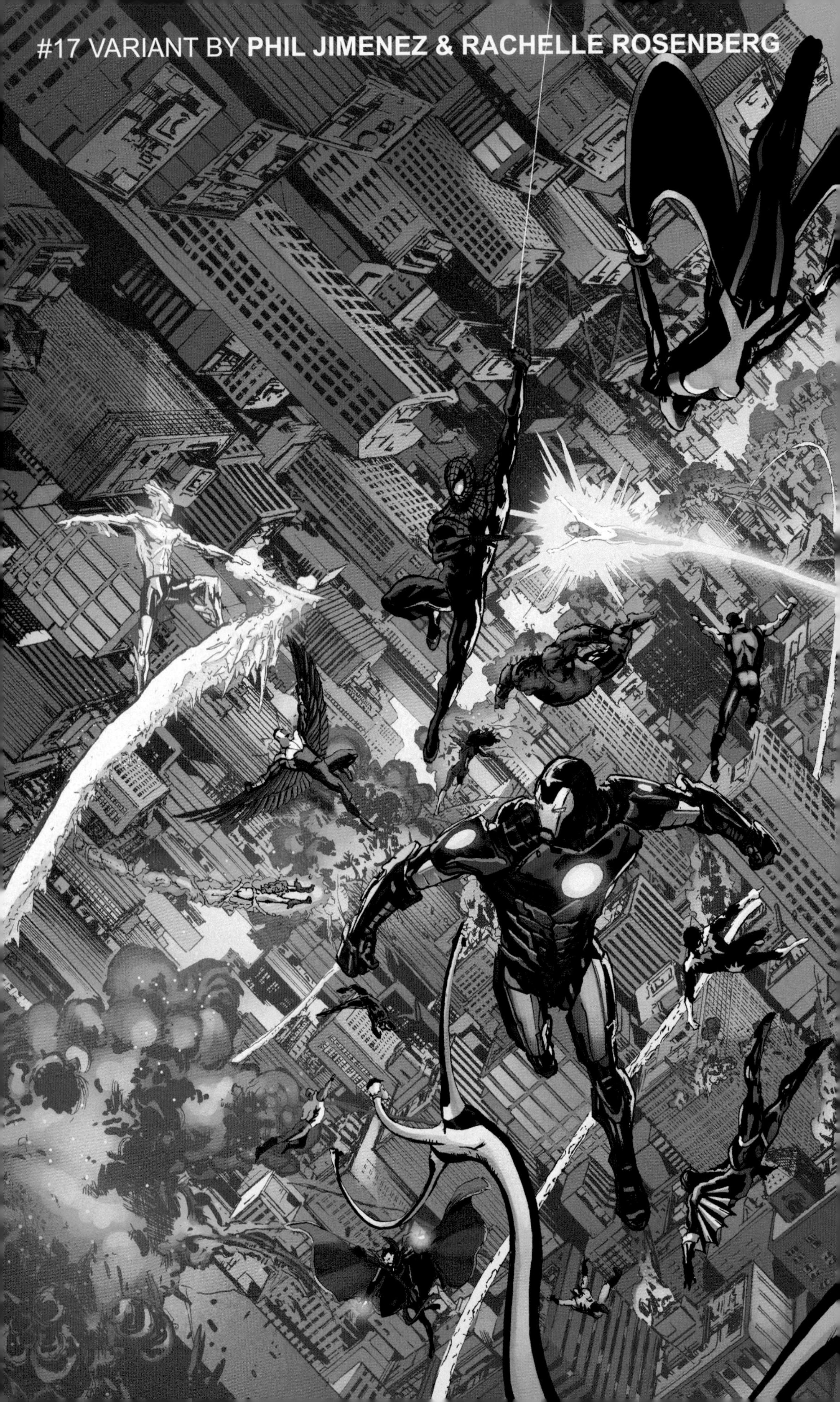

#13 COVER PROCESS BY **SIMONE BIANCHI**

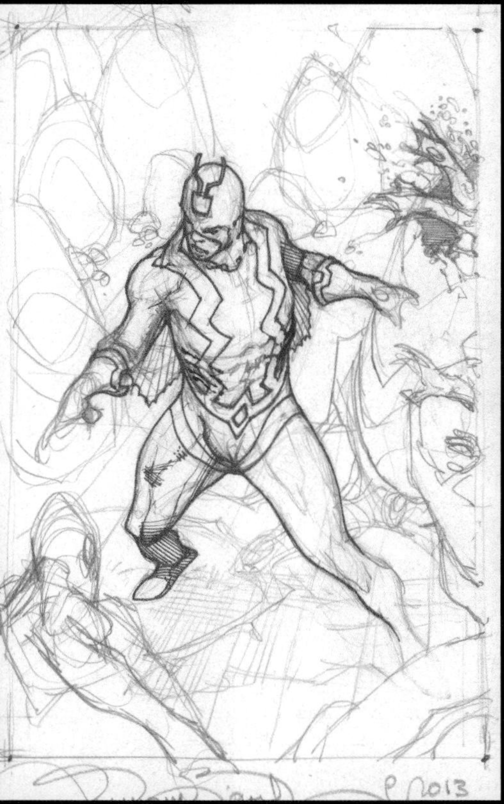

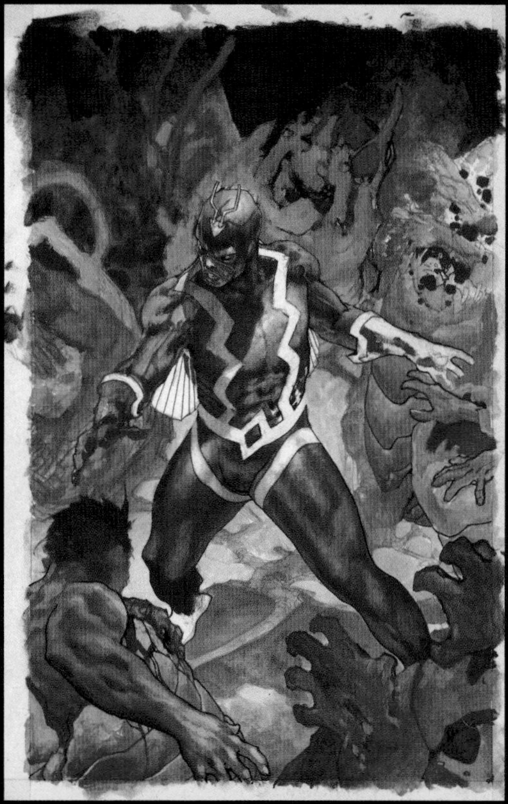

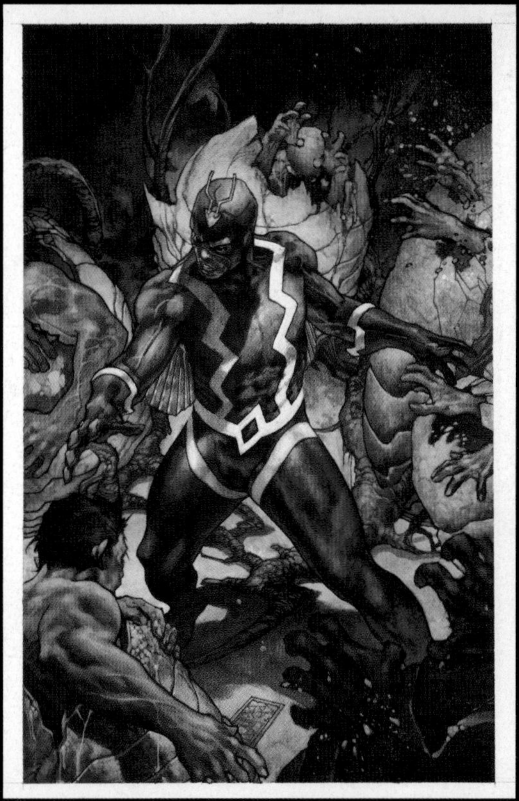

#14 & 15 COVER SKETCHES BY **SIMONE BIANCHI**

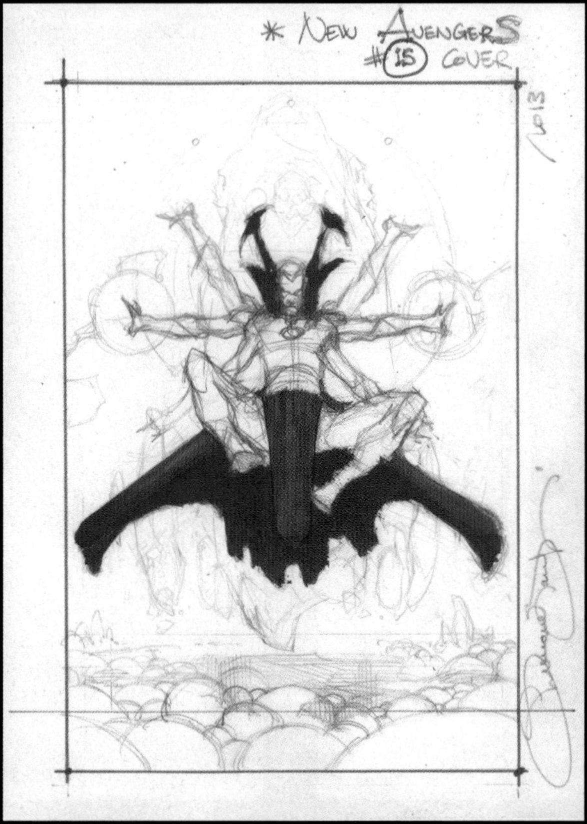
* NEW AVENGERS
#15 COVER
2013

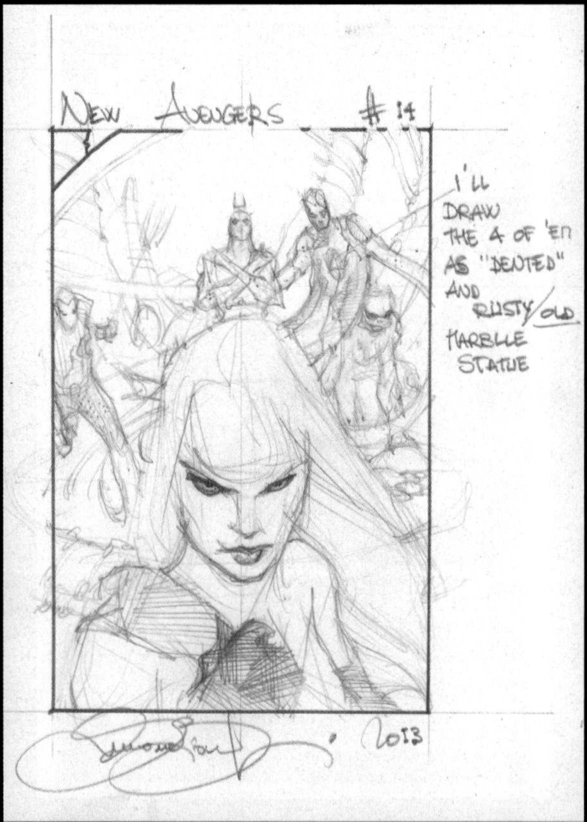
NEW AVENGERS #14
I'LL DRAW THE 4 OF 'EM AS "DENTED" AND RUSTY/OLD MARBLE STATUE
2013

#13 PAGES 10-11 PROCESS BY **SIMONE BIANCHI**

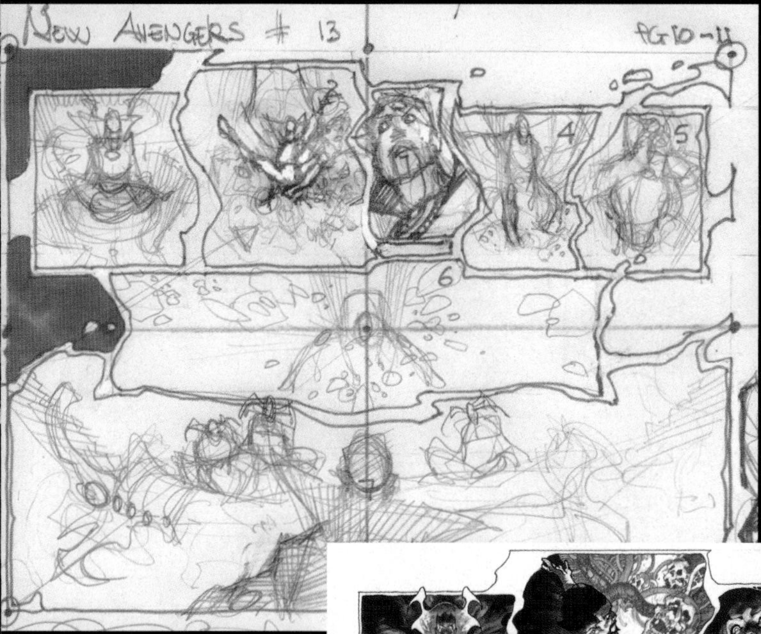
New Avengers # 13
PG 10-11

PENCILS

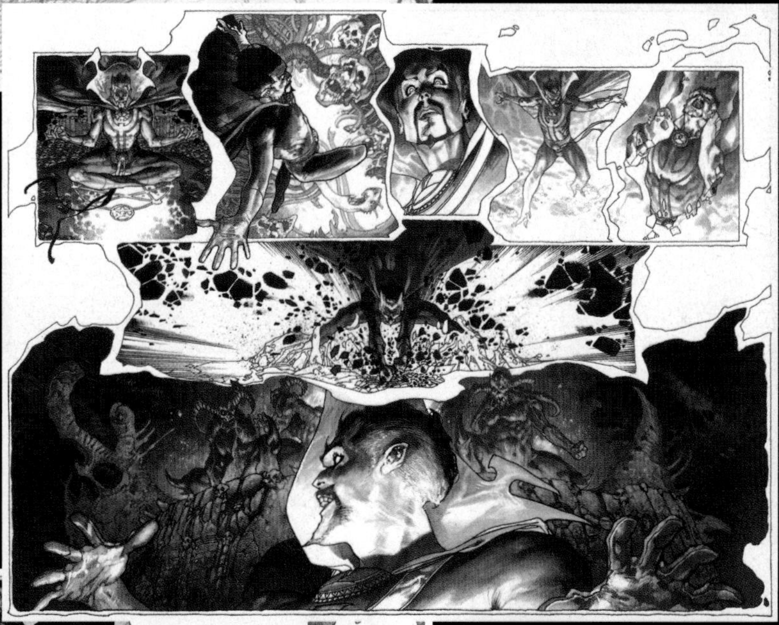

PARTIAL COLORS

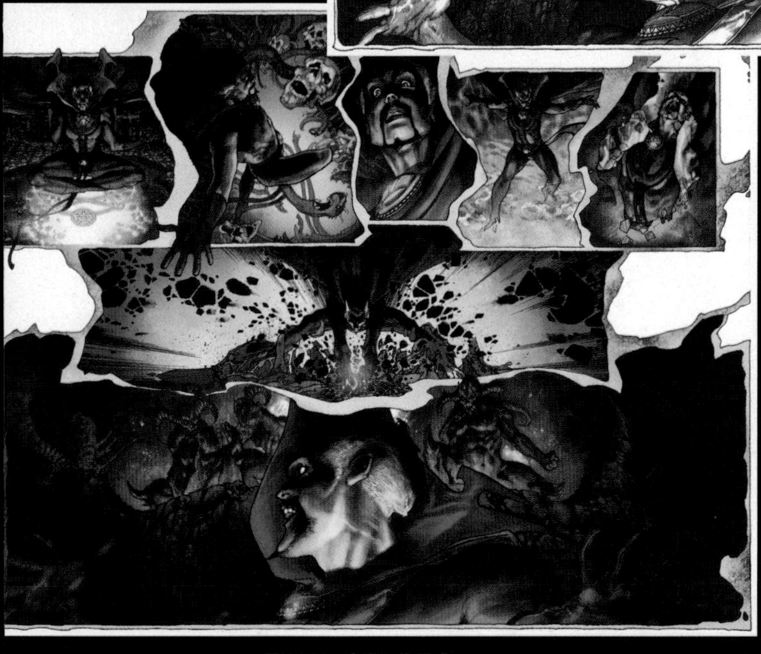

FINAL COLORS

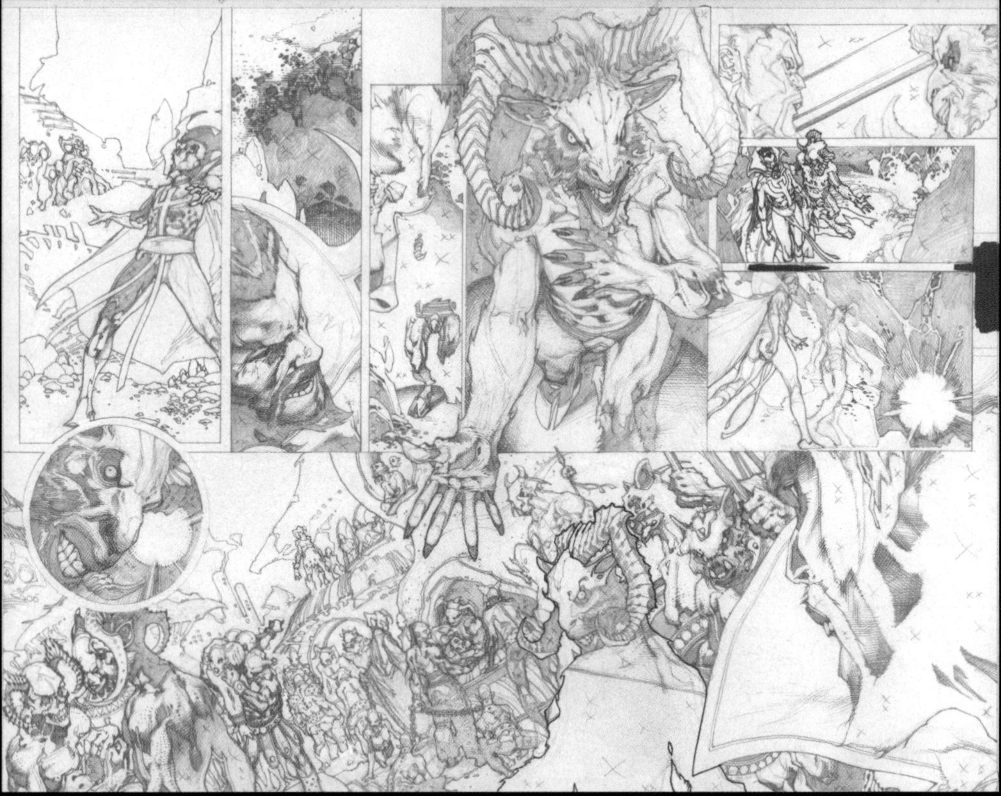

PAGES 6-7

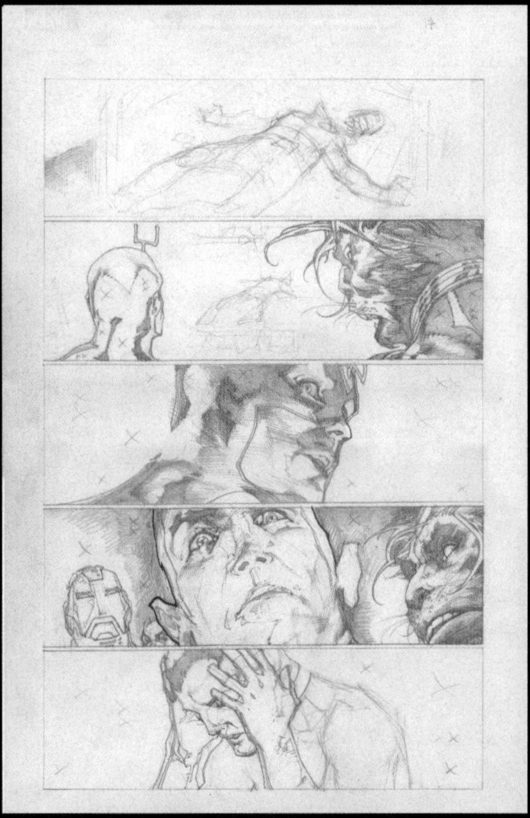

PAGE 16

#15 PENCILS BY **SIMONE BIANCHI**

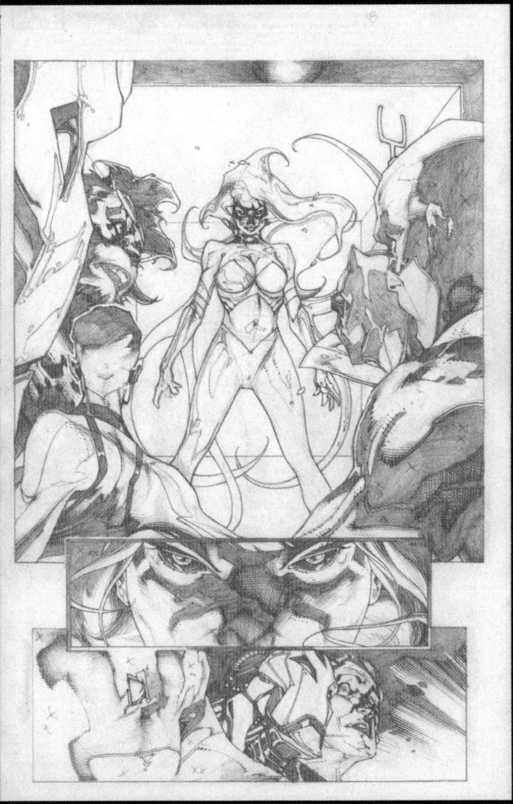

PAGE 18

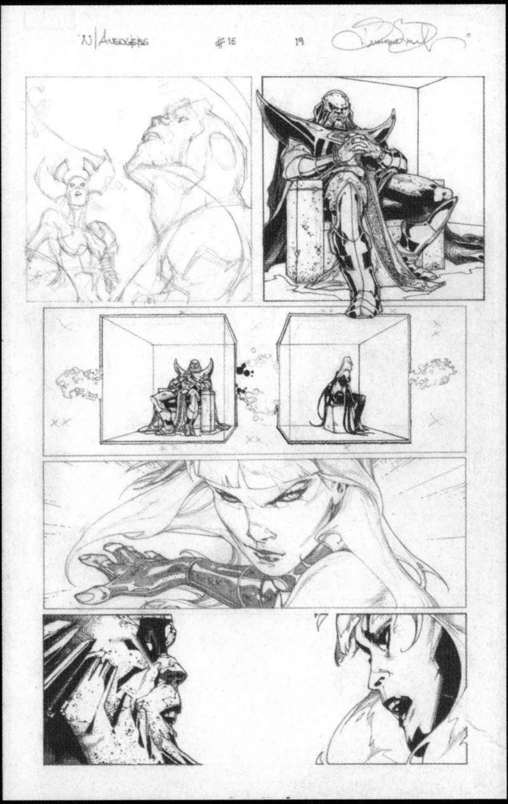
N|AVENGERS
#15
19

PAGE 19

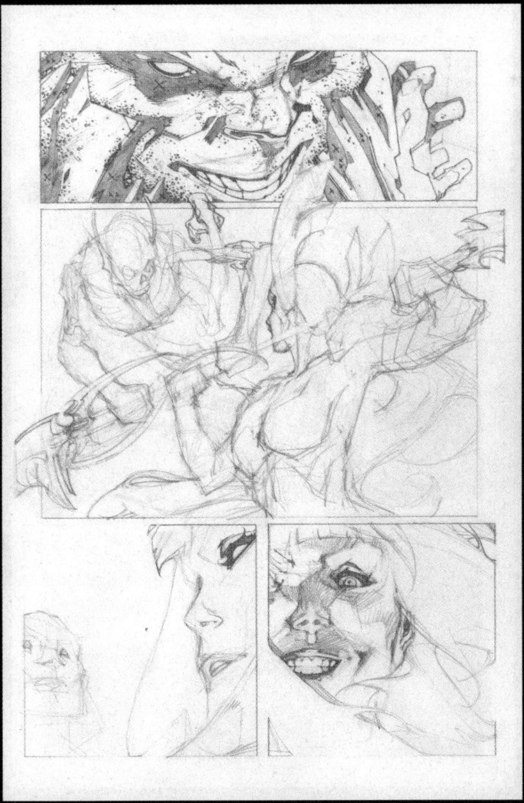

PAGE 20

#16 PAGE 6 PROCESS BY **RAGS MORALES**

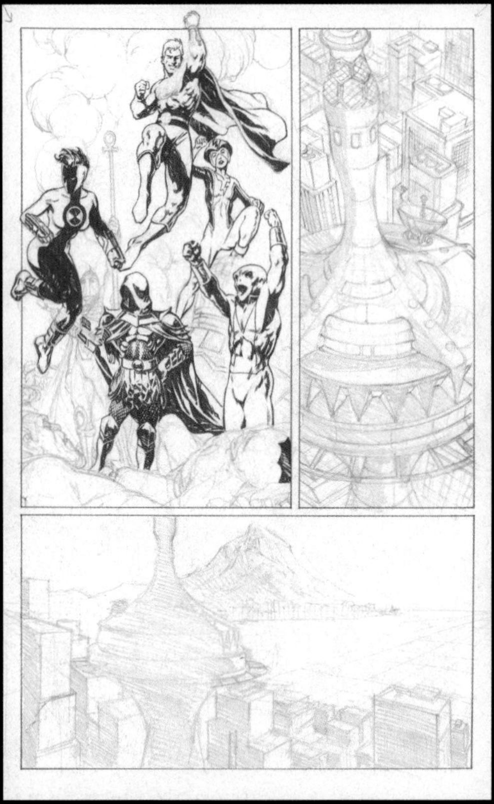
PENCILS

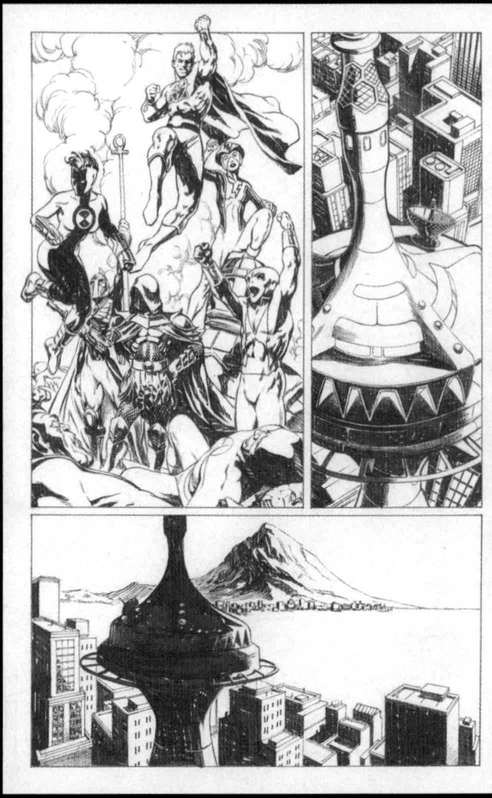
INKS

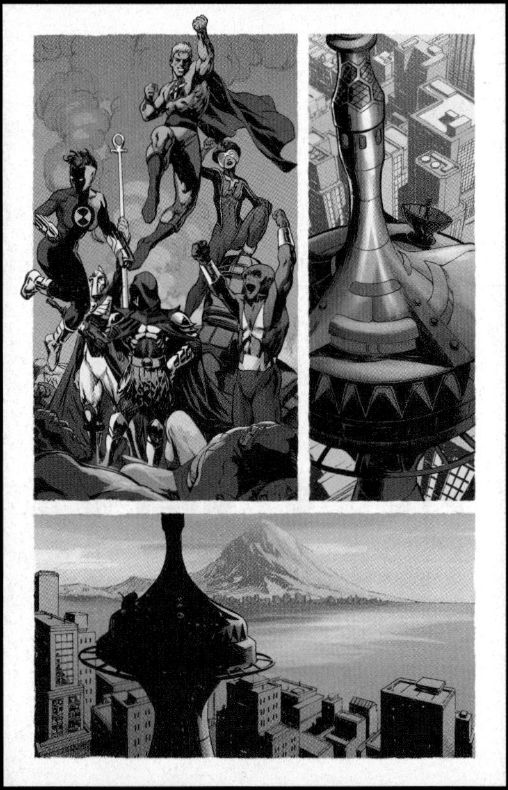
COLORS

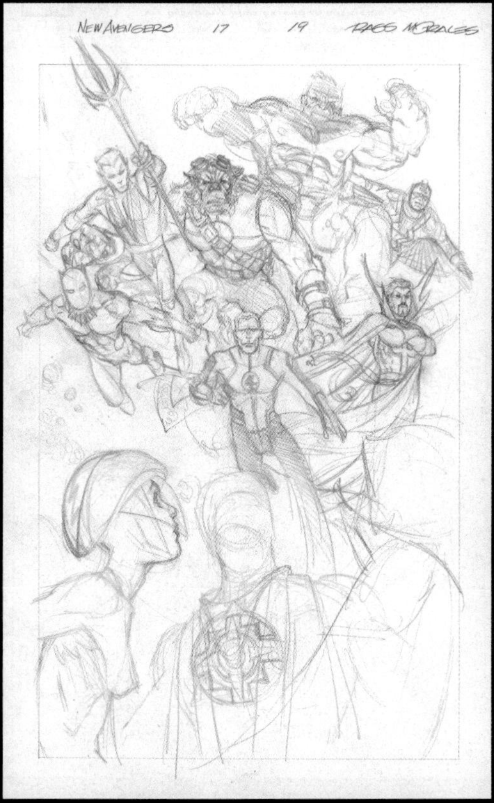
NEW AVENGERS 17 19 RAGS MORALES

PENCILS

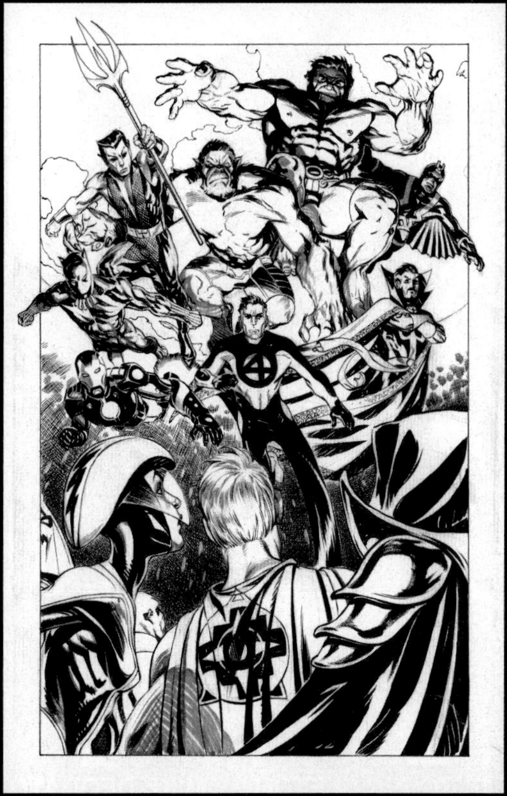

INKS

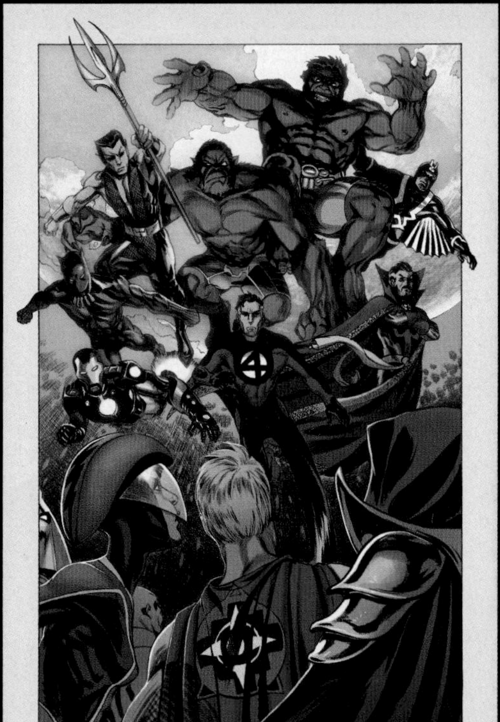

COLORS

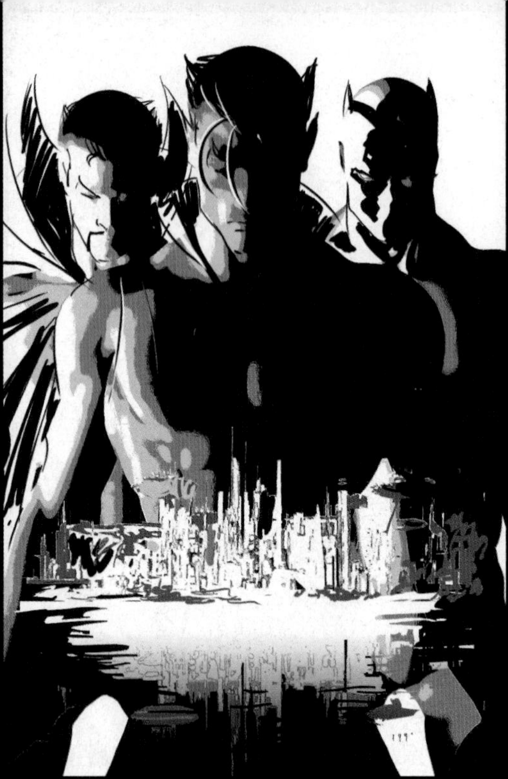

#16 COVER SKETCH BY **MIKE DEODATO**

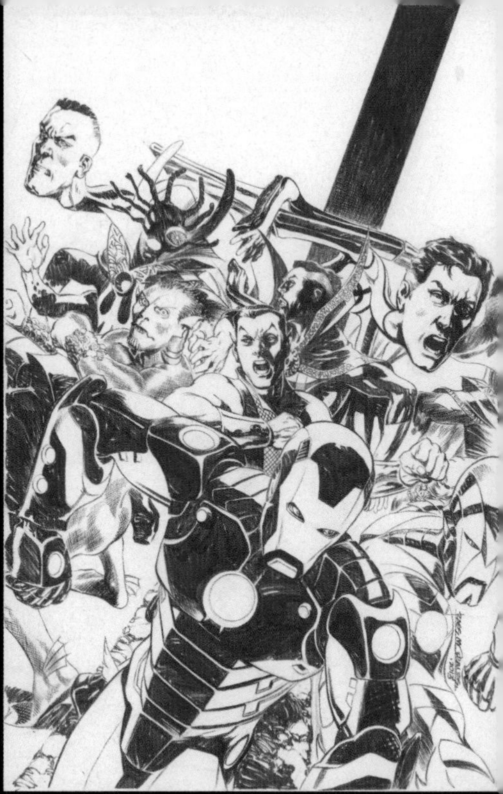

#16 VARIANT COVER INKS BY **RAGS MORALES**

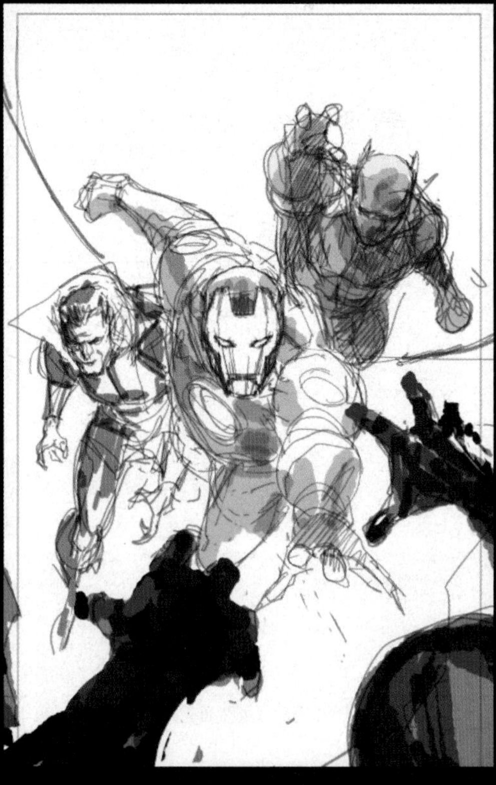

#17 COVER SKETCH BY **LEINIL YU**

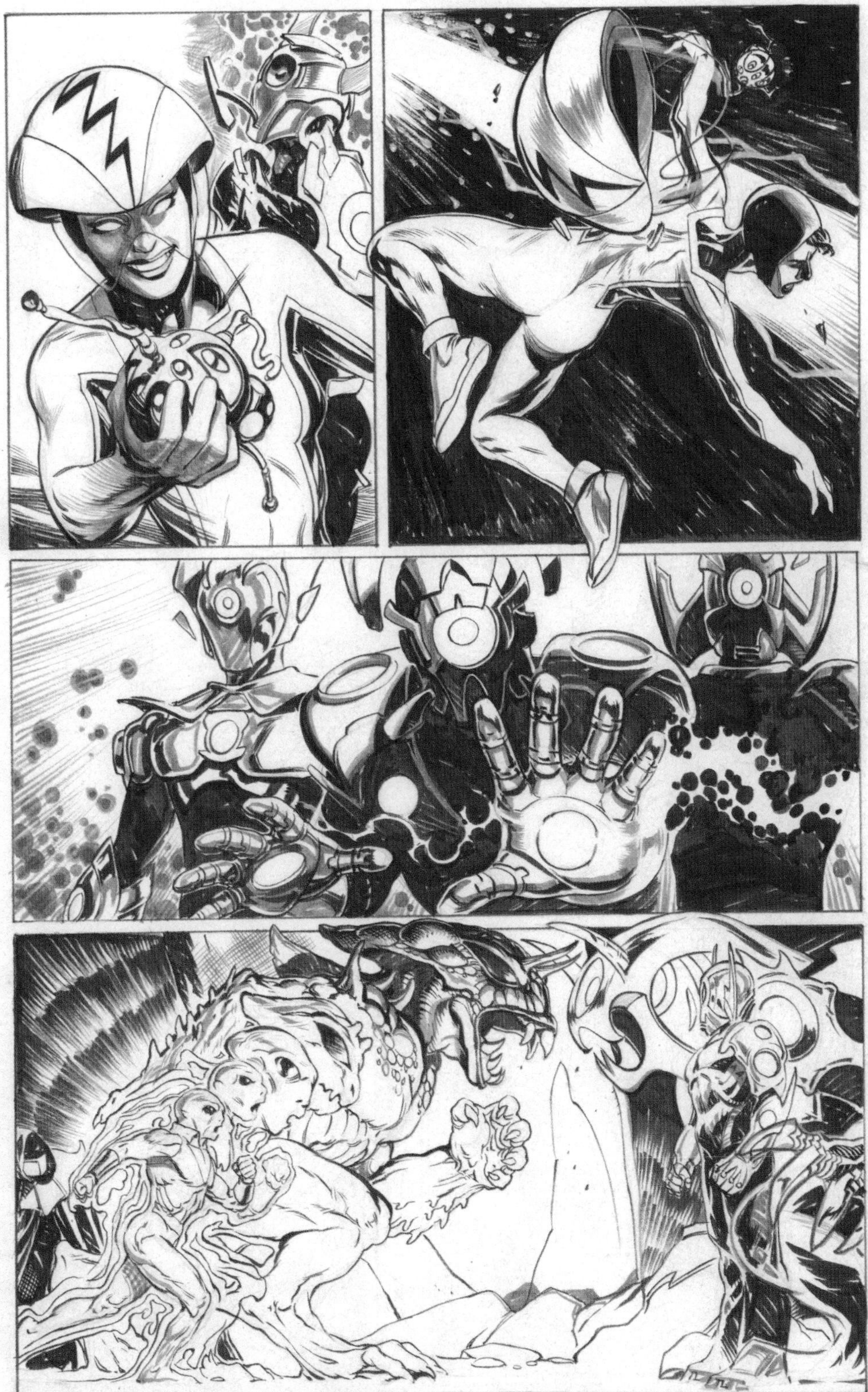

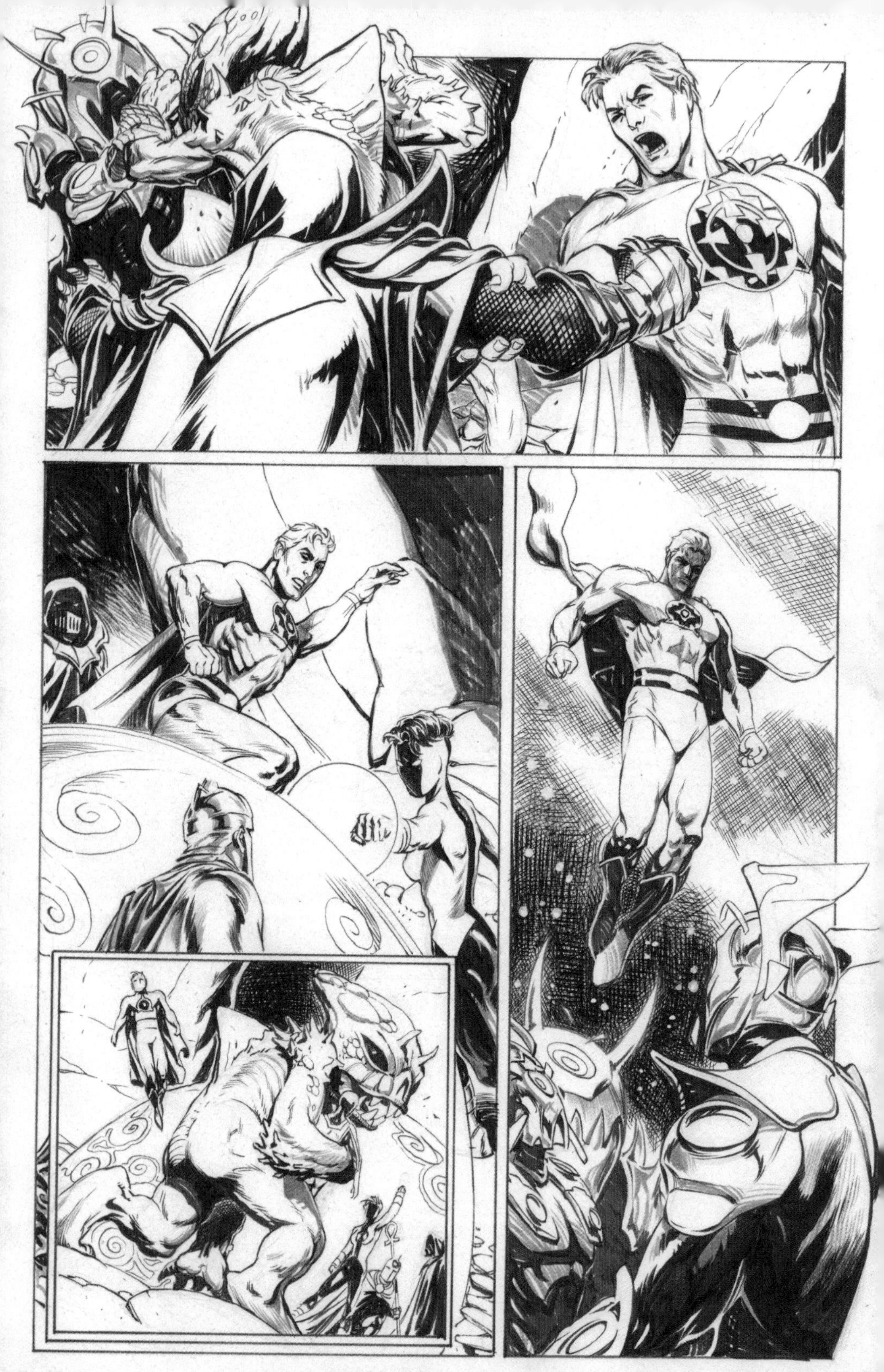

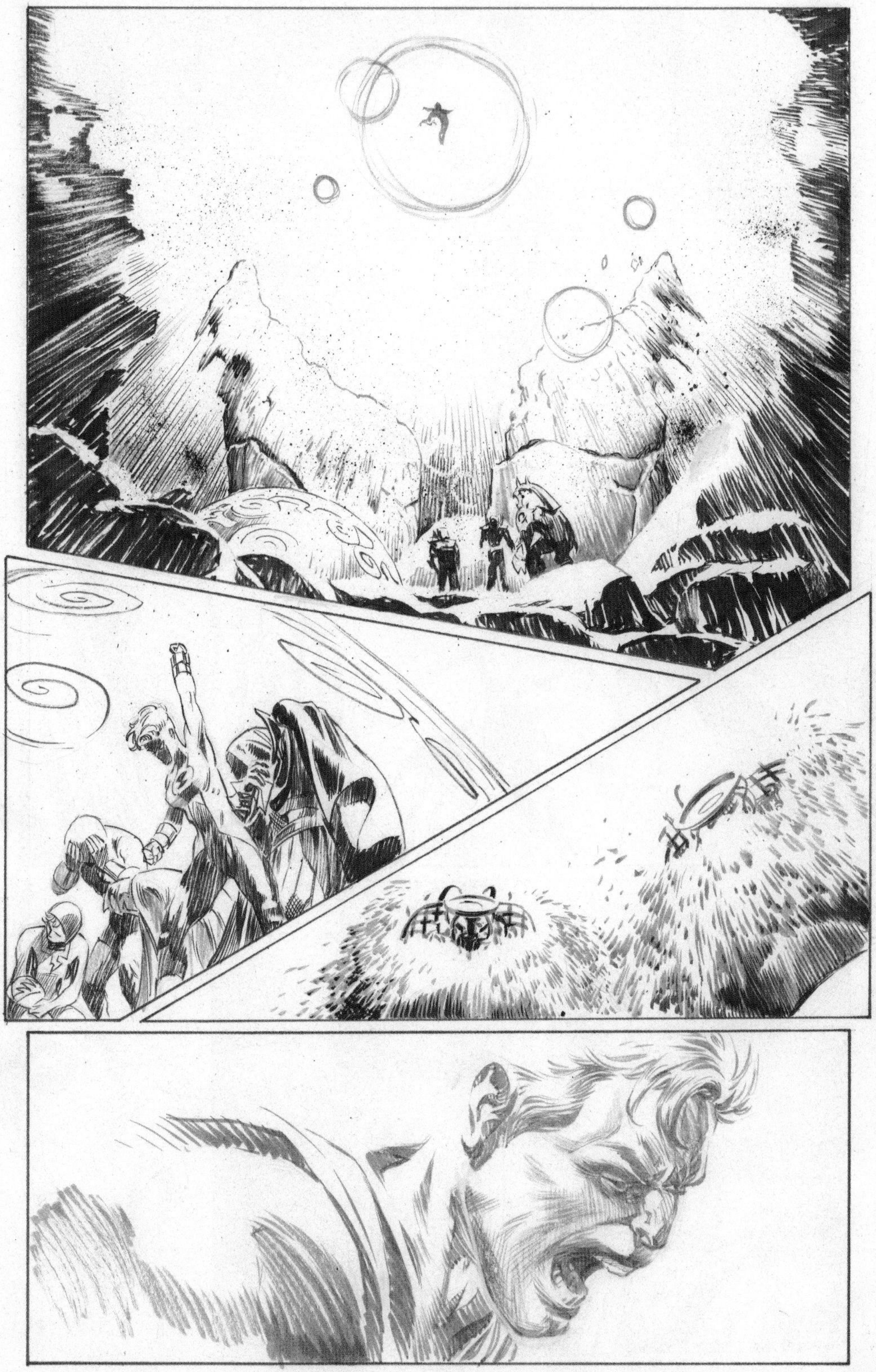

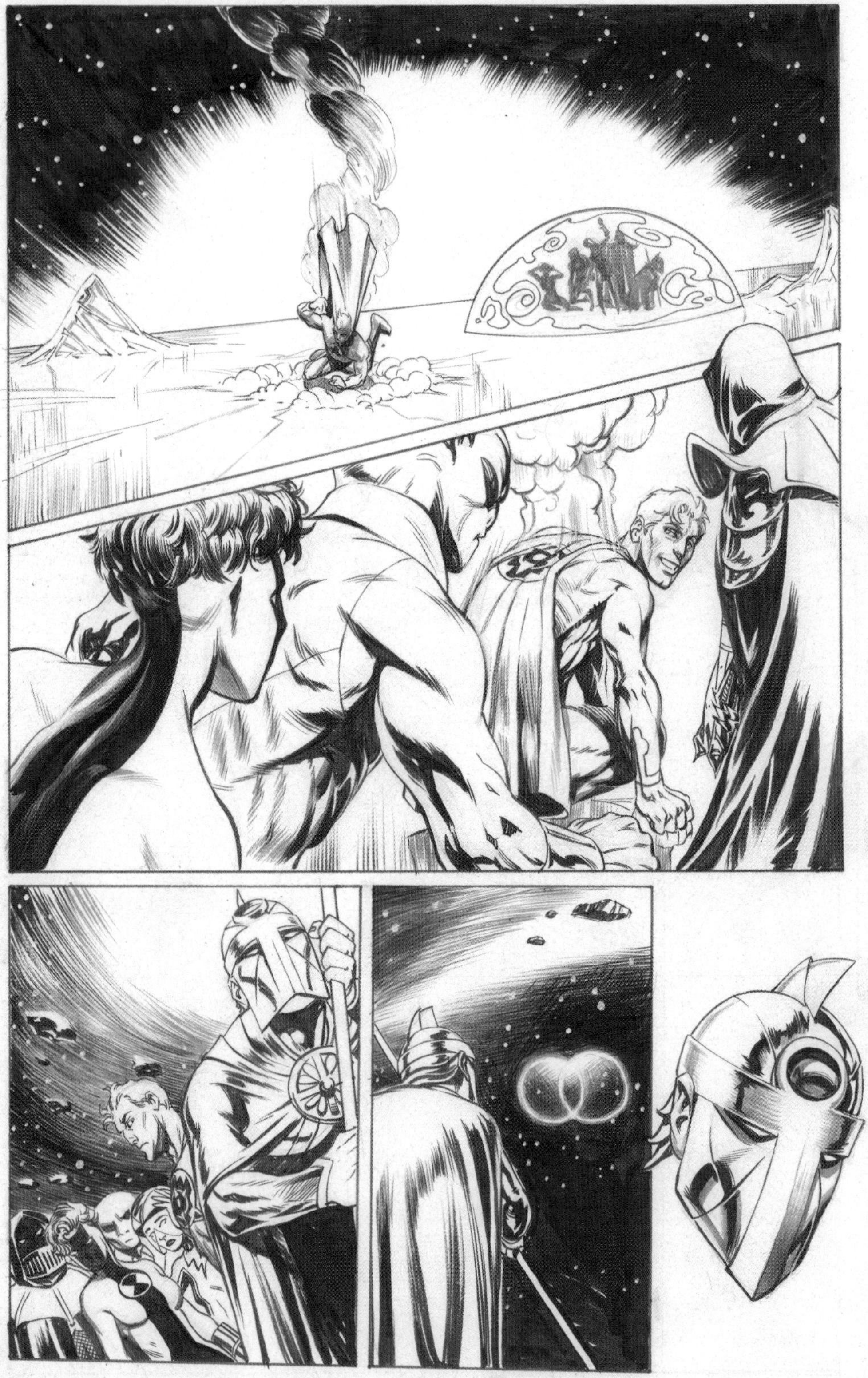

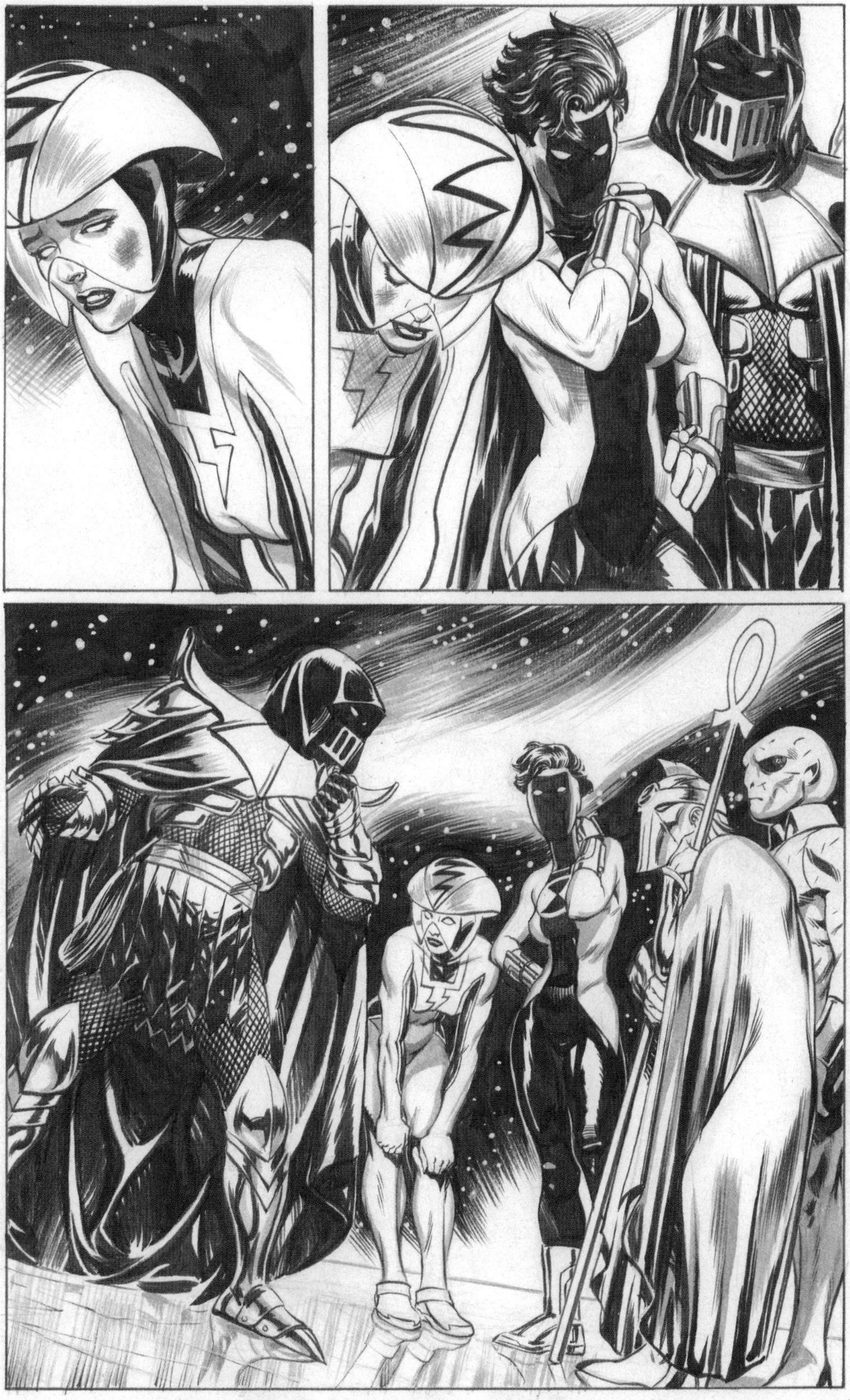

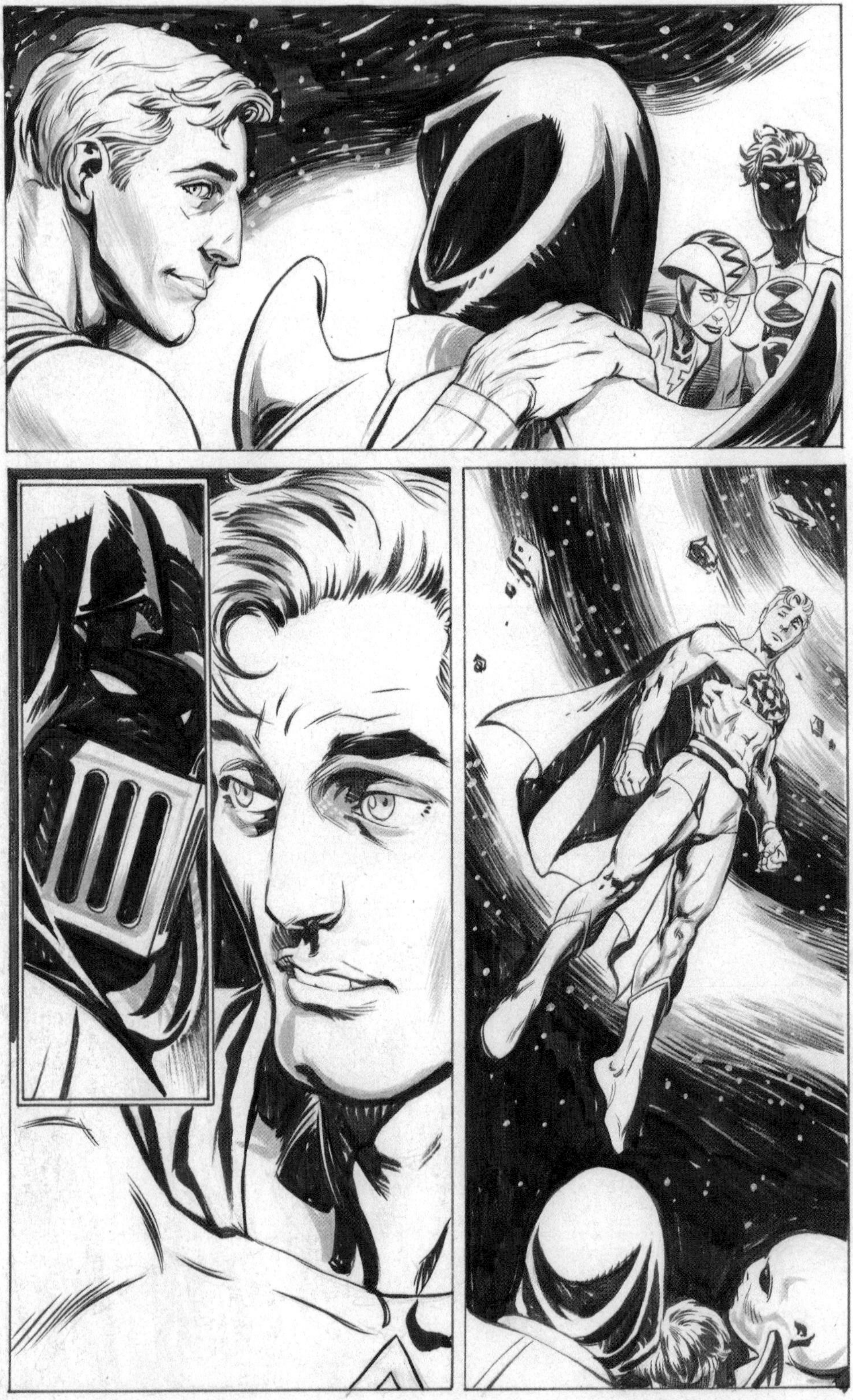

#17 PAGE 11 ART BY **RAGS MORALES**

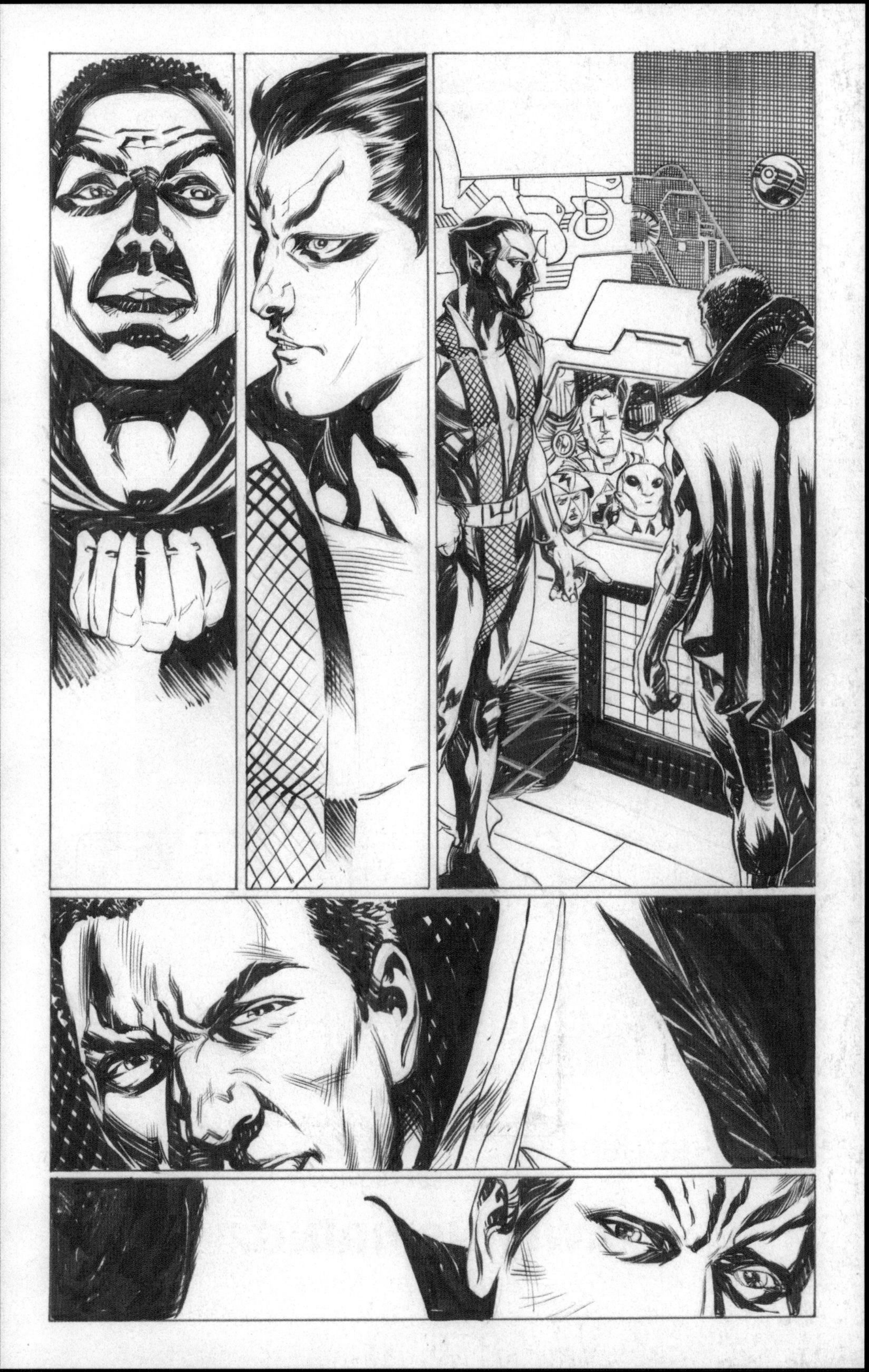